new day
new
you

new day new you

366 Devotions for Enjoying Everyday Life

JOYCE MEYER

Faith
Words

NEW YORK   BOSTON   NASHVILLE

Unless otherwise indicated, all Scripture quotations are taken from
The Amplified Bible (AMP). The Amplified Bible, Old Testament.
Copyright © 1965, 1987 by The Zondervan Corporation. The Amplified New
Testament, copyright © 1954, 1958, 1987 by The Lockman Foundation.
Used by permission.

Scriptures noted (THE MESSAGE) are taken from The Message: The Prophets by
Eugene Peterson. Copyright © 2000 by Eugene H. Peterson. NavPress Publishing
Group, P.O. Box 35001, Colorado Springs, CO 80935. Used by permission.

Scripture quotations marked "KJV" are taken from
the King James Version of the Bible.

Scripture quotations marked "NKJV" are taken from the New King James Version.
Copyright © 1982 by Thomas Nelson, Inc. Used by permission. All rights reserved.

Scripture quotations marked "NIV" are taken from The Holy Bible, New International
Version®. NIV®. Copyright © 1973, 1978, 1984 by International Bible Society.
Used by permission of Zondervan Publishing House. All rights reserved.

Scripture quotations marked "TLB" are taken from The Living Bible © 1971.
Used by permission of Tyndale House Publishers, Inc. All rights reserved.

Scripture quotations marked "GNT" are from the Good News Translation © 2001
by American Bible Society. Used by permission.

Scriptures noted (CEV) are taken from the Contemporary English Version,
copyright © 1995 by the American Bible Society. Used by permission.

FaithWords
Hachette Book Group
237 Park Avenue, New York, NY 10017
www.faithwords.com
Printed in the United States of America

First Edition: October 2007
10   9   8

FaithWords is a division of Hachette Book Group, Inc.

The FaithWords name and logo is a trademark of Hachette Book Group, Inc.

The publisher is not responsible for websites (or their content)
that are not owned by the publisher.

ISBN 978-0-446-58195-0

Introduction

> *Therefore if any person is [ingrafted] in Christ (the Messiah) he is a new creation (a new creature altogether); the old [previous moral and spiritual condition] has passed away. Behold, the fresh and new has come!*
>
> —2 CORINTHIANS 5:17

On so many occasions, a timely word from my heavenly Father has pulled me from the depths of discouragement or despair and brought me to a place of new hope and fresh vision. I have often found spending just a few minutes with Him in the morning has greatly helped me to enjoy my everyday life.

New Day, New You is one year's worth of these moments we have compiled from nineteen of my most popular books. Whether you are a new Christian or have been a believer for many years, I trust this book will be a great tool to help you gain wisdom and inspiration from God's Word.

I encourage you to commit the next year to your heavenly Father . . . to devote each day to Him with quiet and focused moments in His Word. As you do, expect the God of the universe to descend into your everyday life and fill it with joy beyond measure. Just as He makes each day new, He will make a *new you,* a person full of His Spirit and confident in His purpose for your life.

Joyce Meyer

Joyce Meyer

new day
new
y✿u

Be Christlike

God said, Let Us [Father, Son, and Holy Spirit]
make mankind in Our image, after Our likeness.

—GENESIS 1:26

When God said, "Let Us make man in Our image," this image refers to character likeness. He meant that we were going to take on His nature, His character, as reflected in His Son Jesus. In Colossians 1:15, Paul tells us that Jesus is "the exact likeness of the unseen God [the visible representation of the invisible]; He is the Firstborn of all creation." As believers, we are to be transformed into His image and likeness.

The greatest goal of every believer, and certainly those of us who want to be used by God in positions of leadership, should be Christlikeness. We should want to handle situations and treat people the way Jesus would. That should be our goal. Jesus is to be our example.

In John 13:15 He said to His disciples, after washing their feet like a servant, "For I have given you this as an example, so that you should do [in your turn] what I have done to you." And Peter tells us in 1 Peter 2:21, "For even to this were you called [it is inseparable from your vocation]. For Christ also suffered for you, leaving you [His personal] example, so that you should follow in His footsteps." The vocation, the high calling of every believer, is to be transformed into the image of Jesus Christ.

God is going to keep working with each of us until we get to the place where we act the way Jesus would act in every situation of life, until we manifest the same kind of fruit of the Spirit that He manifested.

Give God Your Best, Part 1

I trusted in, relied on, and was confident in You, O Lord;
I said, You are my God. My times are in Your hands.

—PSALM 31:14-15

I've trained myself now to start each day by giving God the first fruits of my time. I've realized that I'm not going to get through the day peacefully if I don't spend time with God. So, each morning, I get coffee, and usually while still in my pajamas, I just spend as much time with God as I need to in order to feel I can behave properly and walk in the fruit of the Spirit throughout the day.

I learned to use the best part of my day to give God the best part of my heart. Giving God the first moments of the morning helps keep my priorities straight for the rest of the day. Don't use this gift of time with God to meditate on your problems. During this time with God, set your heart as the psalmist did, who wrote, "But I trusted in, relied on, and was confident in You, O Lord; I said, You are my God. **My times are in Your hands.**" (PSALM 31:14-15, EMPHASIS MINE)

The Bible says to "lean on, trust in, and be confident in the Lord with all your heart and mind and do not rely on your own insight or understanding. In all your ways know, recognize, and acknowledge Him, and He will direct and make straight and plain your paths. Be not wise in your own eyes." (PROVERBS 3:5-7)

God wants to hear us say, "Lord, I don't know how You're going to do this. I don't care how You do it. I know it's going to be right. I trust all my circumstances to You. *My times are in Your hands.* Trusting You is my first priority in life."

Give God Your Best, Part 2

*For on My holy mountain, on the mountain height of Israel, says
the Lord God, . . . There will I require your offerings and the firstfruits
and the choicest of your contributions, with all your sacred things.*

—EZEKIEL 20:40

Ezekiel 20:40 says that we should bring the Lord our first fruits, the choicest selections of all our offerings. To stay in perfect peace, we should give God the best of our time and our goods. We must be honest with ourselves about what our priorities really are and start making changes to keep God in first place. Don't give God your leftovers; don't give Him the part of your day when you're worn out and you can't think straight or hardly keep your eyes open. Give God the first fruits of your attention. Give Him the best part of your day. That's where your real priorities will be found.

God needs to be your priority in *everything* you do. From getting dressed to setting your schedule, you can ask God for wisdom to make choices that will glorify Him. You can intermingle your time with God into everything you do to such a degree that you can pray without ceasing (pray your way through the day). As you become aware of His presence, it will not be possible to compartmentalize God or separate secular activities from sacred ones. Even ordinary events will become sacred because He is involved in them.

Talk to God as you go about your day, asking Him to direct you in the choices you are making and to empower you for the jobs you need to get done. As you acknowledge that God is always with you, you will keep Him first in everything you set out to do, and He will show you a direct path that will lead you to peace. Following the moment-by-moment leading of the Holy Spirit will cause you to enjoy every day of your life.

Heart Attitudes

Amaziah was twenty-five years old when he began to reign, and he reigned twenty-nine years in Jerusalem . . . He did right in the Lord's sight, but not with a perfect or blameless heart.

—2 CHRONICLES 25:1-2

When God asks for our heart, He is asking for our entire life, which includes our personality, character, body, mind, emotions. The heart is the real person, not the person everybody sees. The church and the world are looking for someone who is real. In 2 Chronicles 25:1-2 we read about a king who had a negative condition of the heart. In this passage King Amaziah did all the right things, but his heart was not right. Therefore, God was not pleased with him.

That's a scary thing. We can do the right thing, and still not be acceptable to God because we do it with a wrong heart. Let's take giving, for example. In 2 Corinthians 9:7 we are told that God loves a cheerful giver, one who does not give out of compulsion or with a bad attitude but out of a willing heart. In fact, it says that God loves a cheerful giver so much that He is absolutely unwilling to do without one. He will take our gift even if we are stingy and unwilling. He may take our money, and He may use it for His kingdom, but that is not the heart attitude He wants us to have when we give. There is a physical heart and a spiritual heart, and the two are parallel.

Physically speaking, the heart is the most important bodily organ. Spiritually speaking, I believe the heart is the most important aspect of the spiritual body. And it is the most important thing the believer or the leader can give to God. That is why the condition of our heart is so important. It is not lack of ability or potential that prevents most people from making progress and enjoying fulfillment in life; I believe it is wrong heart attitudes.

The Master Builder

For [of course] every house is built and furnished by someone, but the Builder of all things and the Furnisher [of the entire equipment of all things] is God.

—HEBREWS 3:4

God is the Master Builder. Jesus is the Chief Cornerstone. God is the one who has to build us and equip us for the work of the Lord Jesus Christ. In Philippians 1:6 the apostle Paul writes to assure us, "He Who began a good work in you will continue until the day of Jesus Christ [right up to the time of His return], developing [that good work] and perfecting and bringing it to full completion in you." What he was saying to us is simply this: "It was God who started this work in you, and it is God who will finish it!" That means we should leave God alone to do His work. We need to stay out of His business and mind our own.

There are certain things only God can do. We are to do our part and let Him do His. We are to handle our responsibility but cast our care on Him. We are to confess our sins and failures to the Lord, confident that He will forgive us of those sins and failures and cleanse us from all unrighteousness, as He has promised in His Word (SEE 1 JOHN 1:9). We are to trust to Him the job of perfecting us for the work He has for us to do in this life. That takes the pressure off of us, which relieves us of the worry and anxiety we feel so often as we try to perfect ourselves.

Start with What You Have

Do not say to your neighbor, Go, and come again; and tomorrow I will give it.

—PROVERBS 3:28

We can have good intentions and still be disobedient. Procrastination is very deceptive. We don't see it as disobedience because we intend to obey God; it is just that we are going to do it *when*—when we have more money, when we are not so busy, as soon as Christmas is over, after we get the kids in school this year, as soon as vacation is over, etc.

There is no point in praying for God to give you more money so you can be a blessing to others if you are not being a blessing with what you already have. Don't believe Satan's lies that you have nothing to give. Even if it is only a pack of gum or a ballpoint pen, start using what you have to bless others.

Change the Course of Your Day

I am the Vine; you are the branches. Whoever lives in Me
and I in him bears much (abundant) fruit. However, apart from Me [cut off
from vital union with Me] you can do nothing.

—JOHN 15:5

If you get up in the morning in a terrible mood, the best thing you can do is find a place and spend some time with the Lord. Being in His presence transforms us. We can change the course of a day that Satan has negative plans for by learning to seek God quickly when we sense any attitude or behavior that is not Christlike. Apart from Him, we can do nothing (JOHN 15:5), but with and through Him, we can do all things (PHILIPPIANS 4:13). I have learned that I will always have feelings, but I don't have to let them rule me. I can't override them on my own; but if I seek God for help, He will strengthen me to walk in His Spirit, not in my emotions.

What if someone offends us or hurts our feelings? The Bible says we are not to be easily offended or touchy. We are all commanded to quickly forgive those who hurt us. We may want to do what is right but find the doing of it difficult. That is when we need to take time to pray, spend some time with God, go to His Word and let our hearts meditate on a few scriptures that deal with what we are going through. As a result, you and I will find strength to do the right thing. Remember, we are in a war; we are soldiers in God's army, and we must be ready at any time to use our weapons. Some of those weapons are prayer, worship, praise, and the Word of God.

Our Desires, His Desires

> *It is God Who is all the while effectually at work in you*
> *[energizing and creating in you the power and desire], both to will*
> *and to work for His good pleasure and satisfaction and delight.*
>
> —PHILIPPIANS 2:13

The Bible says that God puts in us the desire both to will and to work for His good pleasure. We should pray for sanctified, holy desires. God puts desires in us to lead us in the way He wants us to go. If we desire to read the Word, then God is *inviting* us to read the Word. If we desire to pray when we are watching television, then God is speaking to us about the *need* to pray.

John 15 tells us that if we abide in Christ, if we continue our relationship with the Lord and dwell with Him over a period of time, His Word will abide in us. Then we can ask whatever we desire, and He has promised to give it to us. To abide with Him is to "hang out" with Him, to live with Him, to become like Him, and to nurture the desires He puts in our hearts, because that is His will for us. He puts desires in our hearts so we will pray and ask for those things He wants us to have.

Without prayer, God has no vehicle through which to work. If you sense that God has put certain desires in your heart, then it's important to pray and ask for those things you desire. If you're not sure whether your desires are from Him, then say, "Lord, I believe You have put this desire in my heart, so I am asking You for it. But I can be happy without it, because I am happy with You. Now it is up to You to do whatever You want to do."

Above all, remember that we are to be led by peace. No matter how much we may desire something, if we don't have peace deep in our hearts about it, then it is not right for us.

Walking Wholeheartedly

And he [Abram] believed in (trusted in, relied on, remained steadfast to) the
Lord, and He counted it to him as righteousness (right standing with God).

—GENESIS 15:6

We are to seek the Lord wholeheartedly. Many Christians only have a halfhearted interest in the pursuit of God. They want God to take care of them, but they don't really want to make the sacrifice of time and devotion it takes to grow in knowledge of Him and His Word—and they don't want to commit time to pray.

God told Abram, "I will make a covenant with you. I will make your name famous. I will make you rich. I will do things for you that nobody else could do. I will give you a child in your old age. But here's your part; you must walk *wholeheartedly* before me" (SEE GENESIS 12-15). Abram fell on his face before God. He knew he was standing in the presence of an awesome God who meant business. Abram understood that God had a plan for his life. God wanted Abram and his heirs to prosper. God wanted good things to happen to Abram.

That promise was passed on to all who would accept Jesus as their Lord. God wants us so happy that people will look at us and say, "That man serves a mighty God who cares for him; nobody else could make those things happen in that man's life but God." God's glory is a wonderful exchange for our wholehearted devotion.

Hunger and Thirst for Peace

> *Live in peace, and [then] the God of love [Who is the Source*
> *of affection, goodwill, love, and benevolence toward men]*
> *and the Author and Promoter of peace will be with you.*
>
> —2 CORINTHIANS 13:11

When Jesus sent out the disciples two by two to preach and heal, He told them to go into each city, find in it a suitable house in which to stay, and to say to the people, "Peace be unto you." He went on to say that if they were accepted, they should stay there and minister. But if they were not accepted, they were to leave, shaking the very dust of that place off their feet (SEE MATTHEW 10:11-15).

I used to wonder why Jesus said that. Then the Lord revealed to me that if the disciples remained in a house or city that was in strife, they could not do any real work there. Do you know why? Because strife grieves the Holy Spirit. When peace leaves, the Holy Spirit leaves, and He is the one who does the real work.

When you picture Jesus going about ministering to others, how do you see Him? Certainly not with the hurry-up attitude we often have. Don't you instead get an image of Him ministering in quiet, tranquil peace? That is a trait you and I need to develop. As ambassadors for Christ, we need to be more like our Master. If we want to do anything for our Lord and Savior, we need to learn to hunger and thirst for peace.

Which Way Will You Choose?

*Enter through the narrow gate; for wide is the gate and spacious and broad is the
way that leads away to destruction, and many are those who are entering through
it. But the gate is narrow (contracted by pressure) and the way is straitened
and compressed that leads away to life, and few are those who find it.*

—MATTHEW 7:13-14

Here in this passage, Jesus speaks of two different ways: the broad way
that leads to destruction and the narrow way that leads to life. As I was
meditating on this passage, the Lord spoke to my heart and said, "Joyce,
on the broad way there is room for all kinds of fleshly things like bitterness
and unforgiveness and resentment and vindictiveness. But on the narrow
way there is only room for the Spirit."

In the flesh it is easy to take the broad path, but the end result is
destruction. Emotions move us to take the easy way, to do what feels
good for the moment. Wisdom moves us to take the hard way that leads
to life. The question is: *Which will we choose?*

No matter what has happened to you in your lifetime, even if you have
been abandoned by your spouse or abused by your parents or hurt by
your children or others, if you'll stay on that narrow path and leave all
your excess baggage behind, sooner or later you will find the peace, joy,
and fulfillment you seek.

Jesus is the Way, and He has shown us the way in which we are to walk.
The Lord has sent upon us His Holy Spirit to lead and guide us in the way
we are to go, the narrow way that leads to life and not the broad way that
leads to destruction. We must keep walking in the ways of the Lord: "And
let us not lose heart and grow weary and faint in acting nobly and doing
right, for in due time and at the appointed season we shall reap, if we do
not loosen and relax our courage and faint." (GALATIANS 6:9)

Finding Your Destiny

Now you [collectively] are Christ's body and [individually] you are members of it, each part severally and distinct [each with his own place and function].

—I CORINTHIANS 12:27

We wonder, *What am I to do with my life? What is my purpose here? Does God have a calling on my life?* God answers these questions through our natural gifts and abilities. He leads us to our purpose through the natural skills and unique talents He bestows upon us. God-given gifts are the skills a person easily performs without formal training. We derive great pleasure from doing what we are naturally good at doing.

If you aren't sure of your purpose, just do what you do well, and then watch God confirm you by blessing your endeavors. Don't spend your life trying to do what you are not gifted to do. I tried to grow a garden and can tomatoes and sew my husband's clothes. I wasn't at all good at any of these things, and I even despised trying! It was obvious that God wasn't calling me to grow and preserve vegetables or to sew. But what if no one enjoyed gardening or canning or making clothes? God keeps our world in balance by giving each of us natural talent and pleasure in doing what needs to be done for the good of everyone around us.

We know we are operating in our gifts and calling when what we do ministers life to others. If what we do makes us miserable and fills us with a sense of dread, it's possible we are not in God's perfect will. God gives us peace and joy to let us know we are fulfilling His perfect plan.

I encourage you to look at what you enjoy, what you're good at, what God is giving you grace to do—and then let God be God in your life. He wants to flow through you in many different ways, but it may not be the same way He flows through others. Trust His ability in and through you, and don't be afraid to be unique.

Willpower: The Fair-weather Friend

But I say, walk and live [habitually] in the [Holy] Spirit [responsive to and controlled and guided by the Spirit]; then you will certainly not gratify the cravings and desires of the flesh (of human nature without God).

—GALATIANS 5:16

Willpower sure sounds like a great thing. We are led to believe that we have enough of it to fight off every temptation that comes our way. And sometimes it works. But let me tell you a little secret about willpower. Willpower is your best friend when things go well, but it's the first friend to check out when you get weary. I have found that if I really don't want to do something, my mind gives me plenty of reasons why I don't have to. My emotions even join in, saying, "I agree because I don't feel like doing it anyway."

Our souls (mind, will, emotions) would love to run our lives, but the Bible says we are to be led by God's Spirit. We are never instructed to be willpower-led, we are told to be Spirit-led. Willpower and discipline are important and vitally necessary to a successful life, but willpower alone won't be enough. Determination gets you started and keeps you going for awhile, but it is never enough to bring you across the finish line. Zechariah 4:6 (NKJV) says, "Not by might, nor by power, but by My Spirit, says the Lord of hosts."

What happens if, instead of turning first to willpower in your time of need, you turn to God instead? God releases His power into your willpower and energizes it to bring you across the finish line. Willpower does not get the credit for our success, God does. Jesus said in John 15:5, "apart from Me [cut off from vital union with Me] you can do nothing." This is one of the most important and most difficult lessons we must learn if we want to enjoy the life Jesus died to give us.

Freedom from the Curse of the Law

But then Law came in, [only] to expand and increase the trespass
[making it more apparent and exciting opposition]. But where
sin increased and abounded, grace (God's unmerited favor)
has surpassed it and increased the more and superabounded.

—ROMANS 5:20

The aim of God's law is to restrain the evil tendencies natural to man in his fallen state. But the law in itself is ineffective because it does not regulate humankind's behavior. In other words, the law does not have power to make people *want* to obey it. For example, suppose you have a tendency to eat too much chocolate. You want to be free from this habit, so you make a law for yourself: "I *must not* eat chocolate. I *cannot* eat chocolate. I *will never* eat chocolate again." You even convince yourself that for you it is a *sin* to eat chocolate. This self-made law does not set you free from the desire for chocolate; it actually seems to increase your problem!

Now all you can think about is chocolate. You want chocolate all the time. You have chocolate on your mind from daylight until dark. Eventually, you find yourself sneaking around to eat chocolate because you told everybody you know that you are *never* going to eat chocolate again. You can't eat chocolate in front of people, so you hide when you eat your chocolate. Now you feel really guilty because you have become a "sneaky" sinner.

If you know what I'm talking about, you know the pain that comes from being "under the Law" instead of free in Christ. New believers who may be immature in their faith and weak in the knowledge of God's Word often focus their attention on God's laws in order to control their passions. But as they mature and learn to direct their attention to the leadership of the Holy Spirit, He will set them free from the *desire* to sin.

Accidental Sin

No one born (begotten) of God [deliberately, knowingly, and habitually]
practices sin, for God's nature abides in him [His principle of life, the
divine sperm, remains permanently within him]; and he cannot practice
sinning because he is born (begotten) of God.

—1 JOHN 3:9

I like to put it this way: I used to be a full-time sinner, and once in a while I accidentally slipped up and did something right. But now that I have spent many years developing a deep, personal relationship with God and His Word, I concentrate on being a full-time obedient child of God. I still make mistakes, but not nearly as many as I once did. I am not where I need to be, but *thank God* I am not where I used to be.

There are times when I accidentally make mistakes, but it is not the desire of my heart to do wrong. I do not deliberately, knowingly commit sin. I do not habitually sin. So I don't allow those occasions to make me feel insecure. I don't do everything right, but I do know that the attitude of my heart is right. I can be having an absolutely wonderful day, feeling very close to the Lord and quite spiritual. Then my husband, Dave, comes home and says he does not care for the outfit I am wearing, and I suddenly become angry and defensive, telling him everything I don't like about him either. I don't intend for that to happen; in fact, I plan to be very sweet and submissive when he comes home.

But, as Paul said in Romans 7, the things I want to do, I don't do, and the things I don't want to do, I end up doing. We plan for right behavior because our hearts are right, but like Paul our plans don't always work. Thank God for His mercy that is new every day (SEE LAMENTATIONS 3:22-23).

God Is God—and We Aren't!

For who has known or understood the mind (the counsels and purposes)
of the Lord so as to guide and instruct Him and give Him knowledge?

—I CORINTHIANS 2:16

It is not our job to give God guidance, counsel, or direction. In His Word He makes it clear He doesn't need us to inform Him of what is going on or tell Him what He needs to do about it. "For My thoughts are not your thoughts, neither are your ways My ways, says the Lord. For as the heavens are higher than the earth, so are My ways higher than your ways and My thoughts than your thoughts." (ISAIAH 55:8-9)

It is our job to listen to God and let Him tell us what is going on and what we are to do about it—leaving the rest to Him to work out according to His knowledge and will, not ours. Sometimes we forget that fact, so the Lord has to say to us, "Who do you think you are? Get back in your place of submission and quit trying to be my boss."

I remember one time when I was trying so hard to figure out something while God was trying to free me from the burden of reasoning. Finally, He said to me, "Joyce, don't you realize that if you ever figured Me out, I would no longer be God?"

God is God—and we aren't. We need to recognize that truth and simply trust ourselves to Him, because He is greater than we are in every aspect and area. We are created in His image, but He is still above us and beyond us. His thoughts and ways are higher than ours. If we will listen to Him and be obedient to Him, He will teach us His ways. But we are never going to figure Him out. We shouldn't even try.

In Everything Give Thanks!

Through Him, therefore, let us constantly and at
all times offer up to God a sacrifice of praise, which is the fruit of lips that
thankfully acknowledge and confess and glorify His name.

—HEBREWS 13:15

We should not just praise and offer thanksgiving when there is a reason to do so. It is easy to give thanks and praise if we have a reason. But then it is not a sacrifice. We should, of course, offer up praise and thanksgiving at all times, being mindful to thank God for all the blessings in our lives and for the favor He has shown us.

If we started making a list of blessings we would be quickly enlightened concerning just how good we really have it. There are many things we take for granted because we have an abundance of them, when people in other countries would think they were wealthy if they had them. Clean, fresh water is an example. In India and many other parts of the world, water is a commodity that is not easy to come by. Some people must walk miles just to get a day's supply of it. We take baths in it, swim in it, do dishes in it, wash our hair in it, cook with it, etc. We can have it hot or cold, as often as we like, as much as we desire. There are times while I am taking a hot shower, especially if I am tired, when I stop to give thanks to God for hot water.

There are many things to be thankful for if we decide we are going to be people who continually offer up thanksgiving. The flesh looks for things to complain about, but the spirit searches for reasons to give God glory.

Bear Fruit! Not Just Leaves

> *For this reason we also, from the day we heard of it, have not ceased to pray . . . that you may walk (live and conduct yourselves) in a manner worthy of the Lord, fully pleasing to Him and desiring to please Him in all things, bearing fruit in every good work.*

— COLOSSIANS 1:9-10

People who want to be leaders must have character in their dealings with others. They must keep their word. They must be people of integrity. In Matthew 21:18-19 we read about an incident in the life of Jesus.

> *In the early dawn the next morning, as He was coming back to the city, He was hungry. And as He saw one single leafy fig tree above the roadside, He went to it but He found nothing but leaves on it [seeing that in the fig tree the fruit appears at the same time as the leaves]. And He said to it, Never again shall fruit grow on you! And the fig tree withered up at once.*

I used to feel sorry for that fig tree. I didn't understand this story at all. I thought, *It wasn't the fig tree's fault that it didn't have any figs on it. Why did Jesus curse it?* Some time later God showed me the reason. As this verse in *The Amplified Bible* notes, on a fig tree the fruit appears at the same time as the leaves. So when Jesus from a distance saw the fig tree with leaves on it, He went to it expecting to find fruit on it. When there was none on it, He cursed it. Why? Because it was a phony; it had leaves but no fruit.

In the body of Christ, we must be very careful that we don't have just leaves and no fruit. We are not going to win the world with only a bumper sticker on our car, a Jesus pin on our lapel, a tape recorder slung over our shoulder, and a big Bible and a stack of teaching tapes under our arm. We must have fruit because Jesus has said that it is by our fruit that we will be known.

Living Without Regret

But one thing I do [it is my one aspiration]: forgetting what lies behind and
straining forward to what lies ahead, I press on toward the goal to win the
[supreme and heavenly] prize to which God in Christ Jesus is calling us upward.

—PHILIPPIANS 3:13-14

Many people stay trapped in the past. There is only one thing that can be done about the past, and that is forget it. When we make mistakes, as we all do, the only thing we can do is ask God's forgiveness and go on. Like Paul, we are all pressing toward the mark of perfection, but none of us has arrived. I believe Paul enjoyed his life and ministry and this "one aspiration" of his was part of the reason why. Like us, he was pressing toward the mark of perfection, admitting that he had not arrived, but having insight on how to enjoy his life while he was making the trip.

I spent many years hating myself for each of my failures. I desperately wanted to be a good Christian. I wanted to please God. But I still thought it was my perfect performance that would please Him. I had not yet learned that He was pleased with my faith. In Hebrews 11:6 we read, "But without faith it is impossible to please and be satisfactory to Him."

Even when we make mistakes and waste precious time as a result of those mistakes, being upset when we could be enjoying life, it is useless to continue being miserable for an extended period of time because of the original mistake. Two wrongs never make anything right.

If you made a mistake twenty years ago or ten minutes ago, there is still nothing you can do about it except ask for forgiveness, receive it, forget the past, and go on. There may be some restitution you can make to an individual you hurt; and, if that is the case, by all means do so. But the bottom line is that you still must let go of the past in order to grasp the future. Until you do so, you will not enjoy life the way God intended when He sent Jesus.

How to Live a Holy Life

> *But as the One Who called you is holy, you yourselves also be holy in all your conduct and manner of living. For it is written, You shall be holy, for I am holy.*
>
> —I PETER 1:15-16

Holy living begins with getting rid of selfishness in your life. The paradox of happiness is that it comes when you forget about yourself and live to help somebody else. I found out that you can't be happy if you have yourself on your mind all the time. I spent so many years as an unhappy Christian. If we don't have righteousness, peace, and joy, then we have missed the kingdom.

Prosperity, healing, success, and promotions on our jobs are all kingdom benefits that God wants us to have. He shows us in the Bible how to get them, but those benefits are not the kingdom. We are to seek first the kingdom of God and His righteousness and all these things will be added to us (SEE MATTHEW 6:33).

Years ago, out of my selfish, self-centered lifestyle, I began to cry out to God, "What is wrong?" God showed me how selfish I was. The truth changed my heart. Now I just want to help people. It's the reason I write, travel, and speak. I don't do things to impress people; I just want to please God.

If we can forget about our little aches and pains, our little personal trials and tribulations; if we can get ourselves off of our own minds and go find somebody else to help, our lives are going to get better. This is a marvelous discovery.

Hang on 'til Joy Comes!

Weeping may endure for a night, but joy comes in the morning.

—PSALM 30:5

I gained an excellent piece of wisdom through personal experience: Do not be afraid of pain! As strange as it may seem, the more you dread and resist the pain of healing, the more you increase the effect that pain has upon you.

An example of this truth happened years ago when I went on a fast for the first time in my life. God called me to a twenty-eight-day juice fast. In the beginning, I went through some really hard times. I was very, very hungry. In fact, I was so famished that I was in actual pain. As I cried out to the Lord, complaining that I just could not stand it any longer, He answered me. Deep within me I heard the "still small voice" (1 KINGS 19:12 KJV) of the Lord say to me, "Stop fighting the pain; let it do its work." From that time on, the fast was much easier, even enjoyable, because I knew that every time I felt discomfort, it was a sign of progress.

The rule is that the more pain is resisted, the stronger it becomes. When a pregnant woman goes into labor, the advice she is given by her attendants is, "Relax." They know that the more she fights the pain, the stronger it will become, and the longer the delivery process will take. When you are experiencing pain, do not fight it. Allow it to accomplish its purpose. Remember this promise, "They who sow in tears shall reap in joy and singing." (PSALM 126:5) *Learn to endure whatever you need to, knowing that there is joy on the other side!*

Be a Blessing

> So then, as occasion and opportunity open up to us, let us do good
> [morally] to all people [not only being useful or profitable to
> them, but also doing what is for their spiritual good and advantage].
> Be mindful to be a blessing, especially to those of the household of faith
> [those who belong to God's family with you, the believers].
>
> —GALATIANS 6:10

Our daughter Sandra shared that she was dreading seeing a certain individual because in the past that person had not been very pleasant to her. As she struggled with negative thoughts about the upcoming encounter, God spoke to her heart and said, "You don't need to be concerned about how others treat you; your concern should be how you treat them." This message had a strong impact on Sandra's life as well as on mine.

We are so concerned about our own treatment that we have little or no concern for how we treat others. We are afraid of being taken advantage of, especially if our experience with someone has been painful in the past. The fear and dread we feel probably makes us supersensitive to everything that is said or done. We may even misinterpret things and see them in a negative way because of our expectations. What we fear does come upon us, according to God's Word (SEE JOB 3:25). I agree it is difficult not to be concerned that others will treat us badly if they have done so in the past. That is why it is so important not to think about it at all.

We are to deposit ourselves with God and trust Him to take care of us (SEE 1 PETER 4:19). He is our vindicator (SEE JOB 19:25), and as long as we behave properly toward others, including our enemies, God will bring a reward into our lives. The Bible says we are to be "mindful" to be a blessing (SEE GALATIANS 6:10). That means that we are to have our minds full of ways we can help others. When our minds are filled with ways to be a blessing, we have no time to dwell on our personal problems. It gives God an opportunity to work on them for us.

Dream BIG Dreams!

> *As each of you has received a gift (a particular spiritual talent,*
> *a gracious divine endowment), employ it for one another as [befits]*
> *good trustees of God's many-sided grace [faithful stewards of the extremely*
> *diverse powers and gifts granted to Christians by unmerited favor].*
>
> —I PETER 4:10

The undeveloped, wasted potential in this world is pathetic. Everyone was created to do something great—great in their own realm. Each of us has the potential to become great at something—a great wife, a great mom, a great seamstress, a great husband, a great father, a great businessman. But whatever we do, we should not have little ideas, dreams, or visions. Little things are important, and we should never despise the day of small things. But we ought to have big ideas, dreams, and visions because we serve a big God.

I would rather have a big dream and see half of it come to pass than to have a little dream and see all of it come to pass. I believe that when God created all of us, He formed and fashioned each person, breathed the breath of life into us and then took a little part of Himself and placed it within each of us. One of us may have a musical gift, another may have a speaking gift, another may have a gift of writing. The problem comes when we try to take the gift God has given us and use it to do what someone else is doing instead of developing our own potential. We have a part of God in us. We are not a mistake. We don't have to spend our lives on the back burner.

We are not too old or too young. We have God-given dreams and visions. But the dreams and visions God gives us for the future are possibilities not "positivelies." (That's the way God spoke it to me a long time ago.) With Him, nothing is impossible; but it also takes our cooperation and willingness through determination, obedience, and hard work to develop what He has put in us.

Simply Grace

Through Him also we have [our] access (entrance, introduction) by faith into this grace (state of God's favor) in which we [firmly and safely] stand. And let us rejoice and exult in our hope of experiencing and enjoying the glory of God.

—ROMANS 5:2

Actually, the grace of God is not complicated or confusing. It is simple, and that's why many people miss it. There is nothing more powerful than grace. In fact, everything in the Bible—salvation, the infilling of the Holy Spirit, fellowship with God, and all victory in our daily lives—is based upon it. Without grace, we are nothing, we have nothing, we can do nothing. If it were not for the grace of God, we would all be miserable and hopeless. In Luke 2:40 we are told that as a child, Jesus "grew and became strong in spirit, filled with wisdom; and the grace (favor and spiritual blessing) of God was upon Him." This verse contains everything we need to be happy, healthy, prosperous, and successful in our Christian walk.

We often talk about all the things we need, but in reality there is only one thing that we need, and it is the same thing that Jesus needed: we need to become strong in spirit, filled with God's wisdom and have His grace upon us. If you and I will allow the grace of God to have full reign in our lives, nothing will be impossible to us. Without that grace, nothing is possible to us. As Paul wrote to the believers in his day, everything we are and do and have is by the grace of God. You and I are one hundred percent helpless. Although we often confess as Paul did, ["I can do all things through Christ who strengthens me"] that is only true by the grace of God (SEE; I CORINTHIANS 15:10; PHILIPPIANS 4:13 NKJV).

Sowing and Reaping

Do not judge and criticize and condemn others, so that you may
not be judged and criticized and condemned yourselves. For just as you judge
and criticize and condemn others, you will be judged and criticized and
condemned, and in accordance with the measure you [use to] deal out to others,
it will be dealt out again to you.

—MATTHEW 7:1-2

These scriptures plainly tell us that we will reap what we sow (SEE GALATIANS 6:7). Sowing and reaping applies not only to the agricultural and financial realms, but also to the mental realm. We can sow and reap an attitude as well as a crop or an investment. One pastor I know often says that when he hears someone has been talking about him in an unkind or judgmental way, he asks himself, "Are they sowing, or am I reaping?" Many times we are reaping in our lives what we have previously sown into the life of another.

A Clear Conscience

I am speaking the truth in Christ. I am not lying; my conscience [enlightened and prompted] by the Holy Spirit bearing witness with me.

—ROMANS 9:1

W e see that Paul referred to his conscience being enlightened by the Holy Spirit. Paul could tell by his conscience that his behavior was acceptable to God, and I am sure that he could, likewise, discern when it was not. That is the function of the conscience. Paul spoke of the importance of keeping one's conscience clean. One of the main functions of the Holy Spirit in our lives is to teach us all truth, to convict us of sin, and to convince us of righteousness (SEE JOHN 16:8,13).

Therefore I always exercise and discipline myself [mortifying my body, deadening my carnal affections, bodily appetites, and worldly desires, endeavoring in all respects] to have a clear (unshaken, blameless) conscience, void of offense toward God and toward men.   —ACTS 24:16

We cannot properly worship God with known sin in our lives. The confession of sin should be the prelude to real worship. We must approach God with a clean conscience. There is no peace for the person with a guilty conscience. His faith will not work; therefore, his prayers won't be answered. The two Scriptures that follow bear this out.

Holding fast to faith (that leaning of the entire human personality on God in absolute trust and confidence) and having a good (clear) conscience. By rejecting and thrusting from them [their conscience], some individuals have made shipwreck of their faith.   —1 TIMOTHY 1:16

They must possess the mystic secret of the faith [Christian truth as hidden from ungodly men] with a clear conscience.   —1 TIMOTHY 3:9

Say Yes to God

Also I heard the voice of the Lord, saying, Whom shall I send?
And who will go for Us? Then said I, Here am I; send me.

—ISAIAH 6:8

I would be miserable right now if I had said no to the call of God on my life. I might have stayed home and tried to grow tomatoes and sew my husband's clothes because that's what I thought would cause me to fit into the neighborhood. But I would have been miserable all of my life. Get hold of this truth today for your own life.

When God began showing Dave and me teachings about healing and the baptism of the Spirit and the gifts of the Spirit, we were going to a church where such ideas and practices were not popular or even acceptable. We ended up having to leave that church and all of our friends.

The decision to leave that church was a difficult one. But if I had conformed to their demands, I would have missed the will of God for my life.

Jesus said, Truly I tell you, there is no one who has given up and left house or brothers or sisters or mother or father or children or lands for My sake and for the Gospel's who will not receive a hundred times as much now in this time—houses and brothers and sisters and mothers and children and lands, with persecutions—and in the age to come, eternal life. —MARK 10:29-30

If God calls you to step out, the world will demand that you conform. Decide for God. You will go through trials—that's part of the challenge. You will go through a period of loneliness. There will be other problems. But you will come out on the other side victorious. You will be able to lie down at night and have that peace inside knowing that, even if you may not be popular with everybody else, you are pleasing to God.

I Believe It!

> *Truly I tell you, whoever says to this mountain, Be lifted up and thrown into the sea! and does not doubt at all in his heart but believes that what he says will take place, it will be done for him.*
>
> —MARK 11:23

We say that we live in a complicated society, but I believe we are the complicated ones, and we complicate life. I don't think life is so complicated; I think it is our approach to life that is complicated. Serving God should not be complicated, and yet it can become very complicated and complex. I believe we are the ones who make it that way. Think about the simple, uncomplicated approach a child has to life. Something that children seem to have in common is this: they are going to enjoy themselves if at all possible. They are carefree and completely without concern. And they believe what they are told. It is their nature to trust unless they have had an experience in that area that has taught them otherwise.

Jesus wants us to grow and mature in our behavior, but He also wants us to remain childlike with an attitude of trust and dependence toward Him. Remember, He told us in John 3:16, "God so loved the world that He gave His only begotten Son, that whoever *believes* in Him should not perish but have everlasting life" (NKJV, EMPHASIS MINE). All He wants to hear us say is, "I believe it."

When God says something to you in your heart or when you read something in the Bible, you should say: "I believe it. If God says that He will prosper me, I believe it. If He says that I will reap if I give, I believe it. If He says to forgive my enemies, even though it doesn't make any sense to me, I believe it—and, instead of going to beat them up, I am going to do what He says. If He says to pray for my enemies, I believe it, and I am going to do it. If He says to call 'things that are not as though they were,' I believe it, and I am going to do it."

Lean and Depend on Jesus

My trust and assured reliance and confident hope shall be fixed in Him.

—HEBREWS 2:13

Proverbs 17:1 says that a house full of sacrifices with strife is not pleasing to the Lord. In other words, we could make all kinds of sacrifices of time and effort to try to help people, yet God is not pleased unless we stay in peace. Pursuing peace means making an effort. But we cannot maintain peace simply by our own fleshly effort. We need God's help and we need grace, which is His power assisting us and enabling us to do what needs to be done.

The effort we make must be *in Christ*. So often we just try to do what is right without asking for God's help, and that type of fleshly effort never produces good fruit. The Bible calls this a "work of the flesh." It is man's effort trying to do God's job. What I am saying is, be sure you lean on God and ask for His help. When you succeed, give Him the credit, the honor, and the glory because success is impossible without Him. Jesus said, "Apart from Me [cut off from vital union with Me] you can do nothing." (JOHN 15:5)

It takes most of us a long time to believe this scripture enough to stop trying to do things without leaning on God. We try and fail, try and fail. It happens over and over until we finally wear ourselves out and realize that God Himself is our strength, our success, and our victory. He doesn't just give us strength—He is our Strength. He does not just give us the victory—He is our Victory. Yes, we make an effort to keep peace, but we dare not make an effort without depending on God's power to flow through us—failure is certain if we do.

Counting the Costs

For as by one man's disobedience many were made sinners,
so by the obedience of one shall many be made righteous.

—ROMANS 5:19 (KJV)

Our choice to obey or not to obey affects not only us but multitudes of others. Just think about the Israelites and how much greater their lives would have been if they would have promptly obeyed God. Many of them and their children died in the wilderness because they would not submit to God's ways. Their children were affected by their decisions, and so are ours. Recently, my oldest son said, "Mom, I have something to tell you. I may cry but hear me out." He then went on to say, "I have been thinking about you and Dad and the years you have put into this ministry and all the times you chose to obey God and how it has not always been easy for you. I realize, Mom, that you and Dad have gone through things that nobody knows about, and I want you to know that this morning God made me aware that I am benefiting greatly from your obedience, and I appreciate it."

What he said meant a lot to me and it reminded me of Romans 5:19. Your decision to obey God affects other people and when you decide to disobey God it also affects others. You may disobey God and choose to stay in the wilderness but please keep in mind that if you now have or ever have children, your decision will keep them in the wilderness with you. They may manage to get themselves out when they are grown, but I can assure you they will pay a price for your disobedience.

Faith vs. Feelings

How long will you halt and limp between two opinions?

—I KINGS 18:21

God has blessings and new opportunities in store for us. To receive them we must take steps of faith. That often means doing things we don't feel like doing or in our own minds don't even think will work, but our trust and reverence for God must be greater than what we personally want, think, or feel. We see a perfect example of this in Luke 5. Peter and some of the other disciples of Jesus had been fishing all night; they hadn't caught anything. They were tired and exhausted, and they needed sleep. I am sure they were hungry. They had just finished washing and storing their nets, which was a big job.

Jesus appeared on the bank of the lake and told them if they wanted to catch a haul of fish, they should cast their nets again, only this time in deeper water. Peter explained to the Lord that they were exhausted. They hadn't caught anything all night, but he said, "On the ground of Your word, I will lower the nets [again]." (LUKE 5:5) This is the kind of attitude the Lord wants us to have. We may not feel like doing something, we may not think it is a good idea, or we may feel fearful that none of it will work, but we should be willing to obey God rather than our fears or feelings.

The devil tries to use fear in its many different forms to keep us in shallow water. But even though we may feel fear, we need to focus our attention on God and at His word we should launch out into the deep to receive the blessings God has for us.

Getting Along with YOU!

God's love has been poured out in our hearts through the Holy Spirit Who has been given to us.

—ROMANS 5:5

The Bible teaches us that the love of God has been poured out in our hearts by the Holy Spirit who has been given to us. That simply means that when the Lord, in the form of the Holy Spirit, comes to dwell in our heart because of our faith in His son Jesus Christ, He brings love with Him, because God is love (SEE 1 JOHN 4:8). We all need to ask ourselves what we are doing with the love of God that has been freely given us. Are we rejecting it because we don't think we are valuable enough to be loved? Do we believe God is like other people who have rejected and hurt us? Or are we receiving His love by faith, believing that He is greater than our failures and weaknesses? What kind of relationship do you have with God, with yourself, and ultimately, with your fellow man?

It never occurred to me that I even had a relationship with myself. It was just something I never thought of until God began teaching me in these areas. I now realize that I spend more time with myself than with anyone else and it is vital that I get along well with me. *You are one person you never get away from.* We all know how agonizing it is to work day after day with someone we don't get along with, but at least we don't have to take that person home with us at night. But we are with us all the time, day and night. We never have one minute away from ourselves, not even one second—therefore, it is of the utmost importance that we have peace with ourselves.

Receiving Forgiveness

*If we [freely] admit that we have sinned and confess our sins, He is faithful
and just (true to His own nature and promises) and will forgive our sins
[dismiss our lawlessness] and [continuously] cleanse us from all unrighteousness
[everything not in conformity to His will in purpose, thought, and action].*

—1 JOHN 1:9

Many years ago when I was first developing my relationship with the Lord, each night I would beg His forgiveness for my past sins. One evening as I knelt beside my bed, I heard the Lord say to me, "Joyce, I forgave you the first time you asked, but you have not *received* My gift of forgiveness because you have not forgiven yourself." Have you received God's gift of forgiveness? If you have not, and you are ready to do so, ask the Lord to forgive you for all your sins right now. Then pray this aloud:

*Lord, I receive forgiveness for (name the sin), in Christ Jesus. I forgive myself
and accept your gift of forgiveness as my own. I believe that you remove the
sin from me completely, putting it at a distance where it can never be found
again—as far as the east is from the west. And I believe, Lord, that you remember it no more.*

You will find that speaking aloud is often helpful to you because by doing so you are declaring your stand upon God's Word. The devil cannot read your mind, but he does understand your words. Declare before all the principalities, powers, and rulers of darkness (SEE EPHESIANS 6:12) that Christ has set you free and that you intend to walk in that freedom.

When you speak, sound as though you mean it! If the devil tries to bring that sin to your mind again in the form of guilt and condemnation, repeat your declaration, telling him: "I was forgiven for that sin! It has been taken care of—therefore, I take no care for it."

The Still, Small Voice

> *Let be and be still, and know (recognize and*
> *understand) that I am God. I will be exalted among the*
> *nations! I will be exalted in the earth!*
>
> —PSALM 46:10

While most horses are guided and led by a strap fastened to the bit in their mouths, some horses keep one ear turned to their master's trusted voice for guidance; this is called a *reining ear*. Elijah needed to hear from God, and fortunately he had a reining ear toward Him.

He had just defeated 450 false prophets in a duel of power. Now Queen Jezebel threatened to kill Elijah within the day. Elijah ran for his life, hid in a cave, and prayed to God that he die before Jezebel found him. Then the Lord sent His word to Elijah, asking, "What are you doing here?" Elijah recounted the events and the threats.

So the Lord demonstrated His presence to Elijah once again, telling him to stand on the mountain before Him. A strong wind tore through the mountains, and broke rocks into pieces, but the Lord was not in the wind. After the wind, there was a terrible earthquake; but the Lord was not in the earthquake. After the earthquake, a fire broke out; but the Lord was not in the fire. After the fire, there came "a still, small voice." Then the Lord told Elijah to leave his hiding place and go anoint the next kings to serve over Syria and Israel and the prophet who was to take his place (SEE 1 KINGS 16-19). And Elijah obeyed the still, small voice of the Lord.

Elijah's story helps us understand how to hear God when we need direction. God didn't reassure Elijah with a showy, flashy manifestation of power, although He had already proven that He was capable of doing so. God spoke to His prophet through a still, small voice. And this is one way the Lord still speaks to us today. God chooses to communicate directly to His children through a whisper deep within their spirits.

Giving Aggressively

> Give, and [gifts] will be given to you; good measure, pressed down,
> shaken together, and running over, will they pour into [the pouch formed by]
> the bosom [of your robe and used as a bag]. For with the measure you deal out
> [with the measure you use when you confer benefits on others], it
> will be measured back to you.
>
> —LUKE 6:38

When you and I give, we are to give generously and aggressively. Because the way we give is the way we receive. When we look into our wallet or purse, we are not to pull out the smallest bill we can find. Instead, we are to give as God gives—abundantly.

Now I realize that no offering is too small and none is too great. But at the same time we have got to learn to be as aggressive in our giving as we are in any other aspect of our Christian life. I seek to be a giver. I desire to give all the time.

One time I was in a Christian bookstore and saw a little offering box for one of those ministries that feeds hungry children. There was a sign beside it that read, "For fifty cents two children can eat for two days." I started to open my purse and make a donation when a voice inside said to me, "You don't need to do that; you give all the time."

I immediately got violent—spiritually violent! No one could tell on the outside, but I was aroused on the inside. I reached into my purse, pulled out some money, and placed it in the box just to prove I could give as an act of my free will!

You can do the same. Whenever you are tempted to hold back, give more! Show the devil you are an aggressive giver!

His Glory in Our Weaknesses

God selected (deliberately chose) what in the world is foolish to put the wise to shame, and what the world calls weak to put the strong to shame. And God also selected (deliberately chose) what in the world is lowborn and insignificant and branded and treated with contempt, even the things that are nothing, that He might depose and bring to nothing the things that are, so that no mortal man should [have pretense for glorying and] boast in the presence of God.

—I CORINTHIANS 1:27-29

One time while I was reading about Smith Wigglesworth and his great faith, I was tremendously impressed by all the wonderful things he did, like healing the sick and raising the dead. I thought, "Lord, I know I'm called, but I could never do anything like that." Suddenly the Lord spoke to me and said, "Why not? Aren't you as big a mess as anybody else?" You see, we have it backward. We think God is looking for people who have "got it all together." But that is not true. The Bible says that God chooses the weak and foolish things of the world in order to confound the wise. He is looking for those who will humble themselves and allow Him to work His will and way through them.

Let Your Mess Become Your Message

All of us . . . are constantly being transfigured into His very own image in ever increasing splendor and from one degree of glory to another; [for this comes] from the Lord [Who is] the Spirit.

—2 CORINTHIANS 3:18

I encourage people to let go of their past, but never to run from it. The only way to gain victory over the pain of our past is to let God walk us back through that doorway of pain and into victory. No one can achieve victory for us; we have to work out our own salvation. Paul explained this truth in his letter to the Philippian church, saying:

> *Therefore, my dear ones . . . work out (cultivate, carry out to the goal, and fully complete) your own salvation with reverence and awe and trembling (self-distrust, with serious caution, tenderness of conscience, watchfulness against temptation, timidly shrinking from whatever might offend God and discredit the name of Christ). [Not in your own strength] for it is God Who is all the while effectually at work in you [energizing and creating in you the power and desire], both to will and to work for His good pleasure and satisfaction and delight.* (PHILIPPIANS 2:12-13)

We have to let God take us through things and let Him work in us so our mess becomes our message. Difficult things that we have endured in our past prepare us for God's blessings in our future.

God's Favor to Be Yourself

When a man's ways please the Lord, He makes even
his enemies to be at peace with him.

—PROVERBS 16:7

God will give us favor with people if we ask Him to do so and put our trust in Him. He can cause even our enemies to be at peace with us. In the earlier years of my life, before I allowed God to do a work in me, I did a lot of pretending. Whatever I thought people wanted me to be, that was what I tried to be. I wore many masks, trying to be accepted by everyone.

This type of behavior can become a real problem if it is not addressed and changed. God will never help us be anyone other than ourselves. At times I felt like a vending machine. Everyone who came near pushed a different button, expecting a different thing. My husband wanted a good, adoring, submissive wife. My children wanted an attentive mother. My parents and aunt, who are all elderly and dependent on me, wanted my attention. The call on my life demanded many things. The people I ministered to wanted me to be available for them whenever they felt they needed me. I said yes to everything until I finally became sick from stress and realized that if I did not learn to say no, I was in for serious health issues.

I wanted everyone to love and accept me. I desperately wanted their approval—but I was trying to get it the wrong way. The Lord told me that He would give me favor with people if I would pray for them and trust Him. God can cause people to accept and like us who would normally despise us. The Bible says He changes the hearts of men the way He changes the watercourses (SEE PROVERBS 21:1). If God can make a river flow in a specific direction, surely He can change someone's heart toward us. We wear ourselves out trying to do what only God can do.

It's Okay to Laugh

Be glad in the Lord and rejoice, you [uncompromisingly]
righteous [you who are upright and in right standing with Him];
shout for joy, all you upright in heart!

—PSALM 32:11

Many serious things are going on in this world, and we need to be aware of them and prepared for them. But at the same time we need to learn to relax and take things as they come without getting all nervous and upset about them. We need to learn how to enjoy the good life God has provided for us through the death and resurrection of His Son Jesus Christ (SEE JOHN 10:10). In spite of all the troubling things going on around us in the world, our daily confession should be, "This is the day the Lord has made. I will rejoice and be glad in it."

Something we Christians need to do more of is laugh. We tend to be so heavy about everything—our sin, expecting perfection from ourselves, our growth in God, our prayer life, the gifts of the Spirit, and memorizing Bible verses. We carry around such heavy burdens. If we would just laugh a little more—*be of good cheer,* "cheer up"—we would find that a little bit of laughter makes that load much lighter.

In the world we live in there isn't a great deal to laugh about so we will need to do it on purpose. It is easy to find plenty to worry about. To be happy, we need to work on it a little. We need to laugh and have a good time.

Declare It with Words

Let the redeemed of the Lord say so. —PSALM 107:2

Hebrews 4:12 teaches us that the Word of God is a sharp, two-edged sword. I believe that one edge of the sword defeats Satan, while the other edge slices open the blessings of heaven. We are told in Ephesians 6:17 that the sword the Spirit wields, which is the Word of God, is one of our pieces of armor to be worn in order to effectively do spiritual warfare. David, the psalmist, frequently made statements like, "I will say of the Lord, He is my Refuge and my Fortress, my God; on Him I lean and rely, and in Him I [confidently] trust!" (PSALM 91:2).

Perhaps we should regularly ask ourselves, "What am I saying of the Lord?" We need to *SAY* right things, not just think them. A person may think, "I believe all those good things about the Lord," but are you *saying* anything that is helping you? Often people claim to believe something, yet the opposite comes out of their mouth. We need to talk out loud. We need to do it at proper times and in proper places, but we need to be sure we do it. Let verbal confessions become part of your fellowship time with God.

I often take walks in the morning. I pray, I sing, and I confess the Word out loud. Each time I say something like, "God is on my side. I can do whatever He assigns me to do." Or "God is good, and He has a good plan for my life. Blessings are chasing me and overflowing in my life." It is equivalent to me jabbing Satan with a sharp sword. Verbalize your thanksgiving, your praise, and your worship. Sing songs out loud that are filled with praise and worship. Take some aggressive action against the enemy!

Are You Not Worth Much More Than They?

> *Look at the birds of the air; they neither sow nor reap nor*
> *gather into barns, and yet your heavenly Father keeps feeding*
> *them. Are you not worth much more than they?*
>
> —MATTHEW 6:26

It might do all of us good to spend some time watching birds. That's what our Lord told us to do. If not every day, then at least every now and then we need to take the time to observe and remind ourselves how well our feathered friends are cared for. They literally do not know where their next meal is coming from, yet, I have personally never seen a bird sitting on a tree branch having a nervous breakdown due to worry. The Master's point here is really very simple: *"Are you not worth more than a bird?"* Even though you may be wrestling with a poor self-image, surely you can believe that you are more valuable than a bird, and look how well your heavenly Father takes care of them.

Learn to Wait on God

> *Therefore return to your God! Hold fast to love and mercy, to righteousness*
> *and justice, and wait [expectantly] for your God continually!*
>
> —HOSEA 12:6

When Jesus was betrayed by Judas, He just stood there. Then the mob came up and laid hands on Jesus and arrested Him.

Peter, ready to defend Jesus, drew his sword, struck the servant of the high priest, and cut off his ear. Whack! Old lion-like Peter was full of fleshly zeal. You know what Peter was thinking? "Bless God, we don't have to put up with this! You're messing with God's anointed!"

But Jesus said, "'No more of this!' And he touched the man's ear and healed him." (LUKE 22:51 NIV) Peter was always talking when he didn't need to be talking, doing things when he didn't need to be doing them. Peter needed to learn how to wait on God and he needed to learn humility and meekness. God wanted to use Peter in a mighty way, but if Peter wanted to preach the Good News of the Gospel, he couldn't do it by taking his sword out and chopping off ears when he felt angry.

Our abrasive words can cut off hearing, just as Peter's sword cut off the servant's ear. We just can't come at people whenever we feel like justice is needed. We must be submissive to God; and if He says, "Say nothing," we are to stand there and just let them think they are right even though we know they're not. We have to say, "Yes, Lord," and accept that He doesn't even owe us an explanation. How many times do we prevent somebody's spiritual growth or how many times do we prevent the blessings of God from coming in our own lives simply because we don't have control of the words that come out of our mouths?

None of us would have our names written in the Lamb's Book of Life if Jesus hadn't been submissive or if He had opened His mouth when He shouldn't have. And He is our example. Jesus asks us to trust Him and wait on Him because He loves us.

Finding Peace

Finally, brethren, farewell (rejoice)! Be strengthened (perfected, completed, made what you ought to be); be encouraged and consoled and comforted; be of the same [agreeable] mind one with another; live in peace, and [then] the God of love [Who is the Source of affection, goodwill, love, and benevolence toward men] and the Author and Promoter of peace will be with you.

—2 CORINTHIANS 13:11

One of the stress inducers we face daily in our society is noise. We live in a noisy society. In order to enjoy a peaceful atmosphere, we must create one. Find a place that is quiet, a place where you will not be interrupted, and learn to enjoy simply being quiet for periods of time. I have a certain chair in my living room where I sit and recover. The chair is a white recliner that faces a window to our yard, which is filled with trees.

Sometimes I sit there for several hours. Being still has a soothing effect on us. Peace produces more peace. If we find peaceful places and remain in them for a while, we will begin to feel calmness engulf our souls. We cannot live noisy lives continually and expect to feel peaceful.

Jesus made sure He had seasons of peace and alone time. He ministered to the people, but He slipped away regularly from the crowds to be alone and pray. "But so much the more the news spread abroad concerning Him, and great crowds kept coming together to hear [Him] and to be healed by Him of their infirmities. But He Himself withdrew [in retirement] to the wilderness (desert) and prayed." (LUKE 5:15-16)

Surely if Jesus needed this type of lifestyle, we do also. Waiting on God quietly does more to restore our bodies, minds, and emotions than anything else. We need it regularly. Insist on having it and don't let anyone take it from you. Work your schedule around God—don't try to work Him into your schedule.

You Are God's Favorite

Keep me as the apple of your eye; hide me in the shadow of your wings.

—PSALM 17:8 (NIV)

What does it mean to be a favorite? It means to be particularly favored, esteemed, and preferred. It means to enjoy special attention, personal affection, and preferential treatment, even without being deserving of it. There is nothing about you or me or anyone else that can cause us to become God's favorite. He chooses us for that place of honor and esteem by an act of His sovereign grace. All we can do is to receive His gracious gift in an attitude of thanksgiving and humility.

Now when I talk about being the favorite of God, I must make something clear. Because God is God of all His creation, and because He has a personal relationship with each one of His children, He can say to every single one of us at the same time, and sincerely mean it, "You are the apple of My eye; you are My favorite child." It took a while for me to come to understand that truth. In fact, at first I was afraid to believe it. It was hard for me to imagine myself as God's favorite, even though that is what He was telling me I was.

But then I began to realize that it is what He tells each of His children. He wants to say it to anyone who will believe it, accept it, and walk in it. God assures each of us that we are His favorite child because He wants us to be secure in who we are in Christ Jesus so that we will have the confidence and assurance we need to walk victoriously through this life drawing others to share with us in His marvelous grace.

God Has Plans for You

> *For we are God's [own] handiwork (His workmanship), recreated in Christ Jesus, [born anew] that we may do those good works which God predestined (planned beforehand) for us [taking paths which He prepared ahead of time], that we should walk in them [living the good life which He prearranged and made ready for us to live].*

—EPHESIANS 2:10

God has a good plan for each one of us, but not all of us experience it. Many times we live far below the standard that God intends for us to enjoy. For years I did not exercise my rights and privileges as a child of God. This occurred for two reasons. The first was, I did not even know I had any rights or privileges. Although I was a Christian and believed I would go to heaven when I died, I did not know that anything could be done about my past, present, or future.

The second reason I lived far below the level of life God intended for me was very simply the wrong way I perceived and felt about myself. I had a poor self-image and it affected my day-to-day living as well as my outlook for the future. **GOD HAS PLANS FOR YOU!** "For I know the thoughts and plans that I have for you, says the Lord, thoughts and plans for welfare and peace and not for evil, to give you hope in your final outcome." (JEREMIAH 29:11)

If you have a poor self-image as I did, I recommend that you read the story of Mephibosheth, which is found in the ninth chapter of 2 Samuel. It greatly affected my life and I believe it will do the same for you. It will help you see not only why you are living far below the level that God intends for you now, but also why you are in danger of missing out on what He has in mind for you in the future.

Are You Exhausted?

And Jesus said to them, The Sabbath was made on account and for the sake of man, not man for the Sabbath; so the Son of Man is Lord even of the Sabbath.

—MARK 2:27-28

Are you excessively tired all the time, even after sleeping? Do you go to doctors, but they cannot find anything wrong with you? You may be experiencing some of the symptoms of burnout. Long periods of overexertion and stress can cause constant fatigue, headaches, sleeplessness, gastrointestinal problems, and tension.

Some other signals of burnout are crying, being easily angered, negativity, irritability, depression, cynicism (scornful, mocking of the virtues of others), and bitterness toward others' blessings and even their good health. God established the law of resting on the Sabbath to prevent burnout in our lives. The law of the Sabbath simply says we can work six days; but by the seventh, we need to rest and spend time worshiping God. Even God rested after six days of work. He, of course, never gets tired but gave us this example so we would follow the pattern.

In Exodus 23:10-12, we find that even the land had to rest after six years, and the Israelites were not to sow in it the seventh year. During this rest, everything recovered and prepared for future production. People today are quick to argue that they cannot afford to take a day off, but I say that they cannot afford not to do it. We often hear, "I am too busy to do that. I would never get everything done if I did that."

My answer is, "Then you are too busy and something needs to change in your life." When we are too busy to obey God's ordinances, we will pay the price. Remember, the Bible says we reap only what we sow. If we sow continual stress with no rest to offset it, we will reap the results in our bodies, emotions, and minds.

Getting the Small Things Right

[Remember] this: he who sows sparingly and grudgingly will also reap sparingly and grudgingly, and he who sows generously [that blessings may come to someone] will also reap generously and with blessings.

—2 CORINTHIANS 9:6

Have you ever gone out to breakfast with somebody whose meal cost them eight dollars and watched them torture themselves over the tip? They have two one-dollar-bills in change, but they know leaving just a dollar would be chintzy. Yet do they leave two dollars? Not on your life! That would be too much. Instead, they'll waste ten minutes out of their life getting change on that second dollar so they can leave $1.50 tip and save themselves fifty cents, rather than leave an "exceptionally generous" tip of two dollars.

But what would happen if they left the full two dollars? They'd free up some valuable time—time undoubtedly worth more to them than fifty cents. And they'd make the waitress's day. Not that the actual fifty cents means much to her, either, but the message that goes along with that fifty cents means the world! It says thanks, and it says what she does has value. Maybe this message gets lost—she may just sweep up the tip without counting—but the generous person will always be blessed. He will know instinctively that he has done the better thing.

What an opportunity! We can increase the happiness of others and ourselves for mere pocket change! This is just one tiny example of the many ways in which the small things we do have surprisingly powerful repercussions. Small things set the tone for our days. Going the extra mile for people—whether it's a slightly larger tip, an unexpected compliment or gift, or even holding a door for them—costs you very little and gets you a lot.

Finding the Rest of God

> *Do not let your hearts be troubled, neither let them be afraid. [Stop allowing yourselves to be agitated and disturbed; and do not permit yourselves to be fearful and intimidated and cowardly and unsettled.]*
>
> —JOHN 14:27

Concerning entering God's rest I would like to say this: There is no such thing as "the rest of God" without opposition. To illustrate, let me share a story I once heard involving two artists who were asked to paint pictures of peace as they perceived it. One painted a quiet, still lake, far back in the mountains. The other painted a raging, rushing waterfall that had a birch tree leaning out over it with a bird resting in a nest on one of the branches.

Which one truly depicts peace? The second one does, because there is no such thing as peace without opposition. The first painting represents stagnation. The scene it sets forth may be serene; a person might be motivated to want to go there to recuperate. It may offer a pretty picture, but it does not depict "the rest of God." Jesus said, "Peace I leave with you; My [own] peace I now give and bequeath to you. Not as the world gives do I give to you." (JOHN 14:27) His peace is a spiritual peace, and His rest is one that operates in the midst of the storm—not in its absence.

Jesus did not come to remove all opposition from our lives but rather to give us a different approach to the storms of life. We are to take His yoke upon us and learn of Him (SEE MATTHEW 11:29). That means that we are to learn His ways, to approach life in the same way He did. *Jesus did not worry, and we do not have to worry either!*

Divine Cleansing

*But if we [really] are living and walking in the Light, as He [Himself] is
in the Light, we have [true, unbroken] fellowship with one another, and the
blood of Jesus Christ His Son cleanses (removes) us from all sin and guilt
[keeps us cleansed from sin in all its forms and manifestations].*

—1 JOHN 1:7

I like the last part of this verse which speaks of the blood of Jesus cleansing us from sin and all of its forms and manifestations. Let me give you an example of how this works in our everyday lives. If there is something rotten in your refrigerator, you will know it is there every time you open the door because you will smell it. You may not know what it is or exactly where it is located, but you can be sure that it is in there somewhere.

I believe our lives are like that. If there is something rotten within us, those who come in close contact with us are going to perceive it, whether they know what it is or why it is there. They will "smell" it or sense it. In 2 Corinthians 2:15 the apostle Paul tells us that as believers "we are the sweet fragrance of Christ [which exhales] unto God, [discernible alike] among those who are being saved and among those who are perishing." Unfortunately, it also works in the opposite way.

When there is something within us that has been shut away and become rotten and spoiled, it gives off a totally different aroma—detectable by everyone. That's why we must open up ourselves and allow the Holy Spirit to come in and cleanse our hearts and remove whatever is causing us to give off a foul stench. When we open ourselves to the Lord and let Him begin to cleanse and heal us from within, we will find ourselves coming into better and better fellowship with all those around us. It won't happen overnight, because it is a process. But it will begin to take place, one step at a time.

Don't Fear It, Pray About It

*Fear not [there is nothing to fear], for I am with you; do not look around you
in terror and be dismayed, for I am your God. I will strengthen and harden you
to difficulties, yes, I will help you; yes, I will hold you up and retain you
with My [victorious] right hand of rightness and justice. . . .
For I the Lord your God hold your right hand; I am the Lord,
Who says to you. Fear not; I will help you!*

—ISAIAH 41:10,13

Some time ago the Lord spoke these words to me: "Pray about everything and fear nothing." He said this to me when I had a vague feeling of fear that a new hairdresser I was going to would not do a good job.

The Holy Spirit spoke to me: "Don't fear it, pray about it. Pray that the Lord will anoint this woman so she is able to do for you what needs to be done." Then over the next couple of weeks He continued showing me different things about prayer versus fear. Many of them dealt with little areas in which fear would try to creep into my life and cause me problems. He showed me that in every case, no matter how great or important or how small or insignificant, the solution was to pray.

Your True Value

> *Now therefore, if you will obey My voice in truth and keep My covenant,*
> *then you shall be My own peculiar possession and treasure from*
> *among and above all peoples; for all the earth is Mine.*

> —EXODUS 19:5

In Exodus 19:5, the Lord tells His people that they are His own "peculiar possession and treasure." That word applies to us today as much as it did to the children of Israel. In John 3:18, Jesus told Nicodemus that no one who believes in Him will ever be condemned (rejected). You may not feel treasured, or even acceptable, but you are. In Ephesians 1:6 (KJV), Paul says that all of us who believe in Christ have been "accepted in the beloved." That should give us a sense of personal value and worth.

I remember standing in a prayer line where I overheard a woman next to me telling the pastor who was ministering to her how much she hated and despised herself. The pastor became very firm with her and in a strong manner rebuked her, saying, "Who do you think you are? You have no right to hate yourself. God paid a high price for you and your freedom. He loved you so much that He sent His only Son to die for you, to suffer in your place. You have no right to hate or reject yourself. Your part is to receive what Jesus died to give you!"

The woman was shocked. I was shocked too, just listening. Yet sometimes it takes a strong word to get us to realize the trap that Satan has set for us. Do you lack appreciation for your own value and worth? Surely, you are valuable; otherwise your heavenly Father would not have paid such a heavy price for your redemption.

The Power of Forgiving

The heart knows its own bitterness, and no stranger shares its joy.

—PROVERBS 14:10

Harboring unforgiveness is probably one of the most dangerous heart conditions we can have because the Bible tells us very plainly that if we will not forgive other people, then God cannot forgive us. If we do not forgive others, our faith will not work. And everything that comes from God comes by faith. If our faith doesn't work, we are in serious trouble.

When I preach on the subject of forgiveness, I always ask the audience to stand if they have been offended and need to forgive someone else. I have never had less than 80 percent of the congregation stand up. It doesn't take a genius to figure out why we are lacking the power we need in the body of Christ. Power comes from love—not from hatred, bitterness, and unforgiveness. "But you don't know what was done to me," people always say to try to excuse their bitterness, resentment, and unforgiveness.

Based on what the Bible says, it really doesn't matter how great their offense was. We serve a God who is greater; and if we will handle the offense in the right way, He will bring us justice and recompense if we allow Him to do so. In Isaiah 61:7 the Lord promises us, "Instead of your [former] shame you shall have a twofold recompense." A recompense is a reward. It is a payback for past hurts.

In Romans 12:19 we are told, "Beloved, never avenge yourselves, but leave the way open for [God's] wrath; for it is written. Vengeance is Mine, I will repay (requite), says the Lord." Don't try to get people back for what they have done to you. Leave it in God's hands.

Jesus taught us that we are to forgive those who hurt us, pray for those who despitefully use us, and bless those who curse us. That is hard. But there is something harder—being full of hatred, bitterness, and resentment. Don't spend your life hating someone who is probably out having a good time while you are all upset.

Continue Taking Steps of Obedience

Whatever He says to you, do it.   —JOHN 2:5

Jesus' first recorded miracle took place while He was attending a wedding celebration. When the marriage couple ran out of wine to serve their guests, Mary asked her Son to do something about the situation, telling the servants, "Whatever He tells you to do, do it." Jesus ordered them to fill up several huge water pots. When they had done so, He directed them to draw out of the vessels the water, which by then had been miraculously changed into wine (SEE JOHN 2:1-11). Because of their obedience to Him, the physical needs of many were met that day.

If you are looking for a miracle in your life, make sure you are sowing seeds of obedience, because the Lord has promised us that if we do so in patient confidence and trust in Him, we will eventually reap: "And let us not lose heart and grow weary and faint in acting nobly and doing right, for in due time and at the appointed season we shall reap, if we do not loosen and relax our courage and faint." (GALATIANS 6:9)

Sometimes when things are not working out the way we think they should or we are not receiving the answers to our prayers as quickly as we would like, we get the idea, "Well, since God's not doing anything, why should I? Why should I be obedient if it isn't producing results?" In such times we must realize that God is always working. We just may not be able to see it, because He usually works in secret.

Don't Ignore the Ifs and Buts

If you will listen diligently to the voice of the Lord your God, being watchful to do all His commandments which I command you this day, the Lord your God will set you high above all the nations of the earth. And all these blessings shall come upon you and overtake you if you heed the voice of the Lord your God.

—DEUTERONOMY 28:1-2

Please notice the "ifs" in this passage. So often we choose to ignore the "ifs" and "buts" in the Bible. Consider for example, 1 Corinthians 1:9-10:

God is faithful (reliable, trustworthy, and therefore ever true to His promise, and He can be depended on); by Him you were called into companionship and participation with His Son, Jesus Christ our Lord. But I urge and entreat you, brethren, by the name of our Lord Jesus Christ, that all of you be in perfect harmony and full agreement in what you say, and that there be no dissensions or factions or divisions among you, but that you be perfectly united in your common understanding and in your opinions and judgments.

We see that God is faithful, and we also see that we draw upon that faithfulness by honoring Him with obedience in relationships. Our disobedience does not change God. He is still faithful, but obedience opens the door for the blessing that is already there due to God's goodness to flow to us.

Filled with His Light

And this is the message [the message of promise] which we have heard from Him and now are reporting to you: God is Light, and there is no darkness in Him at all [no, not in any way]. [So] if we say we are partakers together and enjoy fellowship with Him when we live and move and are walking about in darkness, we are [both] speaking falsely and do not live and practice the Truth [which the Gospel presents].

—1 JOHN 1:5-6

So often the things we try to hide by burying them deep inside ourselves become darkness within us. But this passage tells us in God there is no darkness at all. So when we allow Him full entrance into our hearts and minds, there will be no darkness there. I am so glad that God fills every room in my heart, so that I am filled with His light. There are no places in my heart that I know of that are blocked off from Him and the light that comes with His presence. Often one of the signs that we are walking in the light of the Gospel is that we have good relationships with everyone with whom we come in contact in our daily lives—including our spouses and our children.

I can truthfully say that right now I do not know of any person in my life with whom I have a major problem. And it is not because *they* have all changed. The reason is that I have allowed the Lord to come into those dark recesses of my heart and fill them with His marvelous light. When I was one person on the inside and another person on the outside, I had to wear masks and be phony. I am so glad that now I can stand before God and be at peace with myself and with others.

I no longer have to live in fear of what anyone thinks of me, because I have opened my heart to God's Holy Spirit and He has lighted up the dark places within me so I can live free! You can say the same thing if you will open your heart to God and allow Him to fill every part of you with His life-giving Spirit.

Letting God Take the Lead

> *When they had eaten, Jesus said to Simon Peter, Simon, son of John, do you*
> *love Me more than these [others do—with reasoning, intentional, spiritual*
> *devotion, as one loves the Father]? He said to Him, Yes, Lord, You know that I love*
> *You [that I have deep, instinctive, personal affection for You, as for a close*
> *friend]. He said to him, Feed My lambs.*
>
> —JOHN 21:15

Three times Jesus asked Peter, "Do you love Me? Peter, do you love Me? Do you love Me, Peter?" Finally, by the third time, Peter was grieved that Jesus kept asking him the same thing. He said, "Yes, Lord, You know that I love You." Then we discover the solemn reason Jesus was asking Peter that question. "I assure you, most solemnly I tell you, when you were young you girded yourself [put on your own belt or girdle] and you walked about wherever you pleased to go. But when you grow old you will stretch out your hands, and someone else will put a girdle around you and carry you where you do not wish to go." (JOHN 21:18)

God challenged me with that Scripture because I had my own plan and was walking in my own way. If we really want God's perfect will, He may ask us to do things that we do not want to do. If we really love Him, we will let Him have His way in our lives.

Dealing with Disappointment

Do not [earnestly] remember the former things; neither consider the things of old.

—ISAIAH 43:18

All of us must face and deal with disappointment at different times. No person alive has everything happen in life the way they want or in the way they expect.

When things don't prosper or succeed according to our plan, the first thing we feel is disappointment. This is normal. There is nothing wrong with feeling disappointed. But we must know what to do with that feeling, or it will move into something more serious. In the world we cannot live without disappointment, but in Jesus we can always be given re-appointment!

In Philippians 3:13 the apostle Paul says, "But one thing I do [it is my one aspiration]: forgetting what lies behind and straining forward to what lies ahead." Paul stated that one thing of greatest importance to him was to let go of what lay behind and press toward the things that were ahead! When we get disappointed, then immediately get re-appointed, that's exactly what we're doing. We're letting go of the causes for the disappointment and pressing toward what God has for us. We get a new vision, a plan, an idea, a fresh outlook, a new mind-set, and we change our focus to that. *We decide to go on!*

A Different Viewpoint

Do not be conformed to this world (this age), [fashioned after and adapted to its external, superficial customs], but be transformed (changed) by the [entire] renewal of your mind [by its new ideals and its new attitude].

—ROMANS 12:2

It requires a constant vigilance not to become like the world in its ways and attitudes. The news media frequently delivers negative reports, often with unemotional accounts of tragic events, and many times we listen with unemotional responses. We hear of so much violence nowadays that we hardly notice it or pay any attention to it. This is understandable, but not acceptable. Evil is progressive and will continue to increase if we don't aggressively come against it.

I believe this is all part of Satan's overall plan for the world. He wants us to have a hard-hearted viewpoint, not really caring about people or their needs. As Christians we should pray for those who are hurting and vow to fight against the apathetic ways of the world's attitudes. Single-handedly we may not be able to solve all the problems in the world today, but we can care—and we can pray.

Jesus said, "The Spirit of the Lord is upon me to preach good news." (LUKE 4:18) I believe there are still more good things going on than bad if somebody would report them. I am not saying that we should never turn on the news or read the newspaper, but I am saying that we should not dwell on the world's reports or conform to its viewpoint. We need to listen to what God says about current events in our lives and pray as He leads us to intercede for others who are affected by them.

Love: Your First Priority

*But earnestly desire and zealously cultivate the greatest and best
gifts and graces (the higher gifts and the choicest graces). And yet I will
show you a still more excellent way [one that is better by far and the
highest of them all—love].*

—I CORINTHIANS 12:31

Where does love fit into your list of priorities? Jesus said, "A new commandment I give to you, that you love one another, as I have loved you." (JOHN 13:34 NKJV) It seems to me that Jesus was saying love is the main thing on which we should concentrate. The apostle Paul states that "faith, hope, love abide . . . but the greatest of these is love." (I CORINTHIANS 13:13)

Love should be number one on our spiritual priority list. We should study love, pray about love, and develop the fruit of love by practicing loving others. God is love, so when we walk in His love we abide in Him.

Because we walk in God's love by receiving and expressing it, we should not deceive ourselves into thinking we can love God while we hate other people (SEE I JOHN 4:20). It took me about forty-five years to realize that my priorities were mixed up and that I was not making love the main thing in my life. The commitment to learn how to walk in love has been the single best decision I have ever made as a Christian.

We All Have a Limp

And He said, Your name shall be called no more Jacob [supplanter],
but Israel [contender with God]; for you have contended and have power with
God and with men and have prevailed.

—GENESIS 32:28

Jacob was a man with many weaknesses, yet he pressed on with God; he was determined to get God's blessing. God likes that kind of determination. Because Jacob was so aggressive, God could be glorified in him. God can gain glory for Himself through those who will not let their personal weaknesses get in the way of God's work in them. For God to do that through us, we must first come face to face with the fact that we have weaknesses, and then we must determine not to let them bother us. Our imperfections are not going to stop God unless we let them do so.

I'm going to ask you to do something, and it's very important. Stop right now, wrap your arms around yourself, give yourself a big hug, and say out loud: "I accept myself. I love myself. I know I have weaknesses and imperfections, but I will not be stopped by them." Try doing that several times a day, and you will soon develop a new attitude and outlook.

Jacob wrestled with the angel of the Lord who touched the hollow of his thigh, and as a result, he had a limp from that day forward (SEE GENESIS 32:24-32). I always say that Jacob limped off from the fight, but he limped away with his blessing. Another way to say it is this: "God will bless us even though all of us have a limp (an imperfection)." Remember, God sees our heart. If we have our faith in Him and a heart that wants to do right, we have all we need to receive God's blessings.

You Are One of a Kind!

*The sun is glorious in one way, the moon is glorious
in another way, and the stars are glorious in their own
[distinctive] way; for one star differs from and
surpasses another in its beauty and brilliance.*

—1 CORINTHIANS 15:41

God has created us to be different from one another; and He has done it on purpose. Each of us meets a need, and we are all part of God's overall plan. When we struggle to be like others, we not only lose ourselves, but also grieve the Holy Spirit. God wants us to fit into His plan, not to feel pressured trying to fit into everyone else's plans. Different is okay; it is all right to be different.

We are all born with different temperaments, different physical features, different fingerprints, different gifts and abilities, etc. Our goal should be to find out what we are good at and then throw ourselves wholeheartedly into it.

Some people feel they are not good at anything, but that is not true. When we make an effort to do what others are good at doing, we often fail because we are not gifted with those things. But that does not mean we are good at nothing. We all have limitations and we must accept them. That is not bad; it is just a fact. It is wonderful to be free to be different, and to not feel that something is wrong with us because we are different.

We should be free to love and accept ourselves and one another without feeling pressure to compare or compete. Secure people who know God loves them and has a plan for them are not threatened by the abilities of others. They enjoy what other people can do and they enjoy what they can do. When I stand before God, He will not ask me why I wasn't like Dave, or the apostle Paul, or my pastor's wife, or my friend. I don't want to hear Him say to me, "Why weren't you Joyce Meyer?" I want to hear Him say, "Well done, good and faithful servant." (MATTHEW 25:23 KJV)

Testing the Motive of the Heart

After these events, God tested and proved Abraham and said to him, Abraham!
And he said, Here I am. [God] said, Take now your son, your only son Isaac,
whom you love, and go to the region of Moriah; and offer him there as a burnt
offering upon one of the mountains of which I will tell you. So Abraham
rose early in the morning, saddled his donkey, and took two of his young men
with him and his son Isaac; and he split the wood for the burnt offering, and
then began the trip to the place of which God had told him.

—GENESIS 22:1-3

I believe God was testing Abraham's priorities. Isaac had probably become very important to Abraham, so God tested Abraham to see if he
would give up Isaac to Him in faith and obedience. When God saw Abraham's willingness to obey, He provided a ram for Abraham to sacrifice in
place of Isaac.

Remember, we all go through tests. As with Abraham, these tests are
designed to try, prove, and develop our faith. One of the tests I had to face
was, "What if I never have the ministry I've dreamed about for so long?
What if I never get to minister to more than fifty people at a time? Can I
still love God and be happy?"

What about you? If you don't get whatever it is you want, can you still
love God? Will you still serve Him all the days of your life? Or are you
just trying to get something from Him? A fine line divides the motives of
the heart between selfish and selfless; and we must always make sure we
understand which side of the line we are standing on.

Are You Enjoying Your Trip?

*I came that they may have and enjoy life, and
have it in abundance (to the full, till it overflows).*

—JOHN 10:10

I cannot imagine that God does not lead a thoroughly enjoyable life. To even begin to have an understanding of the quality of life that God enjoys, we must change our modern perspective of what constitutes real life. Our society has fallen into the trap of believing that quantity is greater than quality, but this is not true. This lie from Satan has been fuel for the spirit of greed that prevails in our world today.

It is becoming more and more difficult to find anything that is of excellent quality. In most industrialized nations of the world, especially in America, there is an abundance of everything; and yet there are more unhappy people than ever before. I believe that if we had more quality and a little less quantity, we would experience more real joy in our everyday lives. It would be far better to live forty years to the fullest, truly enjoying every aspect of life, than to live a hundred years and never enjoy anything.

Thank God, we can have both a long life and a quality life; but I am trying to make a point. As believers, you and I have available to us the quality of life that God has. His life is not filled with fear, stress, worry, anxiety, or depression. God is not impatient and He is in no hurry. He takes time to enjoy His creation—the works of His hands. Learn to enjoy not only your work and your accomplishments but even the ride to work in the morning. Don't get so frustrated about traffic and have your mind on what you need to do when you arrive that you fail to enjoy the trip.

Choose Life!

I call heaven and earth to witness this day against you that I have set before you life and death, the blessings and the curses; therefore choose life, that you and your descendants may live.

—DEUTERONOMY 30:19

We will never enjoy life unless we make a quality decision to do so. Satan is an expert at stealing and our joy is one of his favorite targets. Nehemiah 8:10 tells us that the joy of the Lord is our strength. In John 10:10 we are told that "the thief" comes to kill, steal, and destroy, but that Jesus came that we might have and enjoy life. Satan is the thief, and one of the things he seeks to steal is our joy. If he can steal our joy from us, we will be weak; and when we are weak, the enemy takes advantage of us.

Weak believers are no threat to him and his work of destruction. In order to live as God intends for us to live, the first thing we must do is truly believe that it is God's will for us to experience continual joy. Then we must decide to enter into that joy. Experiencing enjoyment in our souls is vitally important to our physical, mental, emotional, and spiritual health. Proverbs 17:22 says, "A happy heart is good medicine and a cheerful mind works healing, but a broken spirit dries up the bones." It is God's will for us to enjoy life! Now it is time to decide to enter into the full and abundant life that God wills for us.

Joy and enjoyment are available just as misery is available. Righteousness and peace are available and so are condemnation and turmoil. There are blessings and curses available, and that is why Deuteronomy 30:19 tells us to choose life and blessings.

Fishing on the Wrong Side of the Boat

Simon Peter said to them, I am going fishing! They said to Him, And we are coming with you! So they went out and got into the boat.

—JOHN 21:3

Peter wasn't sure what he should do after Jesus rose from the dead and proved Himself alive to him and the disciples. So he went back to what he was doing before he met Jesus: fishing. The others decided to join with Peter, and fished throughout the night but caught nothing.

John 21:4-5 says, "Morning was already breaking when Jesus came to the beach and stood there. However, the disciples did not know that it was Jesus. So Jesus said to them, Boys (children), you do not have any meat (fish), do you?...They answered Him, No!" Emotional decisions usually leave us "catching nothing." In other words, they don't provide satisfying results.

The passage continues in verse 6: "And He said to them, Cast the net on the right side of the boat and you will find [some]. So they cast the net, and now they were not able to haul it in for such a big catch ... [was in it]." It's interesting that Jesus didn't call the disciples men, but rather He called them children. He asked them, "Are you doing any good at what you are trying to do?" That is a question we might ask ourselves when we have no fruit (or fish) to show for the long hours we work.

When we fish outside the will of God, it's equivalent to fishing on the wrong side of the boat. Sometimes we struggle, strive, work, and strain, trying to make something great happen. We try to change things, or change ourselves. We try to get more money. We try to get healed. We try to change our spouse or even try to find a spouse. We can work and work, but still have nothing to show for our labor. Have you caught anything? Have you accomplished anything besides getting worn out? If your answer is no, you may be fishing on the wrong side of the boat. If you listen for God's voice, He will tell you where to throw your net.

Lay It on the Altar

> *God tested and proved Abraham and said to him, Abraham! And he*
> *said, Here I am. [God] said, Take now your son, your only son Isaac, whom you*
> *love, and go to the region of Moriah; and offer him there as a burnt offering*
> *upon one of the mountains of which I will tell you.*
>
> —GENESIS 22:1-2

Recently the Lord said to me, "Joyce, do you love Me? If so, will you still love Me and serve Me even if I don't do everything just the way you want or just when you think I should?" At the time of the Lord's visitation, I had been asking God for a huge ministry. He also said, "Joyce, if I asked you to go down to the riverfront here in St. Louis and minister to fifty people for the rest of your life and never be known by anyone, would you do it?" My response was, "But, Lord, surely you can't really be asking me to do that!"

We always have such grandiose plans for ourselves. If God asks us to do something that isn't prominent, we aren't always sure we are hearing Him correctly or that it is His will for us! When God asked me those questions about my ministry, I felt the way I imagined Abraham must have felt when the Lord asked him to sacrifice his son Isaac through whom He had promised to bless him and all nations of the earth (SEE GENESIS 22).

It seemed God was asking me to give up the very work He had given me through which He blessed many others as well as me. But God wasn't asking me to give up that ministry. He was just asking me to lay it on the altar, just like Abraham laid Isaac on the altar before the Lord. We must not let anything—even our work for God—become more important to us than God Himself. To keep that from happening, from time to time God calls upon us to lay it all on the altar as proof of our love and commitment. He tests us by asking us to lay down our most treasured blessing as proof of our love for Him.

Don't Give Up

And let us not lose heart and grow weary and faint in acting nobly and doing right, for in due time and at the appointed season we shall reap, if we do not loosen and relax our courage and faint.

—GALATIANS 6:9

No matter how bad the condition of your life or your circumstances, don't give up! Regain the territory the devil has stolen from you. If necessary, regain it one inch at a time, always leaning on God's grace and not on your own ability to get the desired results. In Galatians 6:9 the apostle Paul simply encourages us to keep on keeping on! Don't be a quitter! Don't have that old "give up" spirit. God is looking for people who will go all the way through with Him. "When you pass through the waters, I will be with you, and through the rivers, they will not overwhelm you. When you walk through the fire, you will not be burned or scorched, nor will the flame kindle upon you" (ISAIAH 43:2). Whatever you may be facing or experiencing right now in your life, I am encouraging you to go through it and not give up! It's easy to quit—it takes faith to go through with something.

Joy and Peace Are Found in Believing

May the God of your hope so fill you with all joy and peace in believing [through the experience of your faith] that by the power of the Holy Spirit you may abound and be overflowing (bubbling over) with hope.

—ROMANS 15:13

Joy is never released through unbelief, but it is always present where there is belief. Believing is so much simpler than not believing. If we do not believe God, His Word, and His promises, then we are left with the labor of reasoning and attempting to work out matters ourselves. The writer of Hebrews 4:3 noted that we who have believed enter the rest of God. In Hebrews 4:10 he wrote, "For he who has once entered [God's] rest also has ceased from [the weariness and pain] of human labors."

In Matthew 11:28 Jesus said, "Come to Me, all you who labor and are heavy-laden and overburdened, and I will cause you to rest. [I will ease and relieve and refresh your souls.]"

Jesus instructed us to come to Him, but *how* are we to come to Him? In Hebrews 11:6 we read, "But without faith it is impossible to please and be satisfactory to Him. For whoever would come near to God must [necessarily] believe that God exists and that He is the rewarder of those who earnestly and diligently seek Him [out]."

That means that when we come to God, we must do so believing. When we do, we will have joy; and where there is joy, there will also be enjoyment. This is God's will for us, that we might have and enjoy life. Jesus did not die for you and me that we might be miserable. He died to deliver us from every kind of oppression and misery. His work is already finished, and the only thing that remains to be accomplished is for us to *believe.*

God Helps the Helpless

[God] gives grace (favor, blessing) to the humble.   —1 PETER 5:5

The world says, "God helps those who help themselves." That statement is totally unscriptural. In some matters we do help ourselves: God won't send an angel to clean our cars and houses for instance. We need to be in charge of that. We also need to go out and look for a job to earn our own living. God gives us wisdom and strength, but we need to use our own arm of the flesh in these matters.

Saying that God helps those who help themselves is not only unscriptural but misleading. This statement tends to make people feel as though they need to do all they possibly can for themselves before ever asking God to help. No wonder it is a "worldly statement" frequently accepted as Scripture.

Satan, the god of this world's system (SEE 2 CORINTHIANS 4:4) would like nothing better than for us to believe that lie and spend our lives in frustration trying to take care of ourselves rather than leaning on God.

God does not help those who help themselves. Rather, He helps those who know they cannot help themselves, those who realize they are totally dependent upon Him for their deliverance.

Mountains into Molehills

For who are you, O great mountain [of human obstacles]? Before Zerubbabel
[who with Joshua had led the return of the exiles from Babylon and
was undertaking the rebuilding of the temple, before him] you shall become a
plain [a mere molehill]! And he shall bring forth the finishing gable stone [of
the new temple] with loud shoutings of the people, crying, Grace, grace to it!

—ZECHARIAH 4:7

The Samaritans who came against the Israelites as they were building the temple of the Lord had become like a mountain of human obstacles, frustrating them and preventing them from doing what God had commanded them to do. That may be the situation in which you find yourself right now as you read these words. You may feel that the Lord has told you to do something but that the enemy has thrown up a mountain in your path to frustrate you and prevent you from carrying out the Lord's will. If so, I know just how you feel because that is exactly the way I used to feel. The problem is one of perspective. In this passage the Lord tells Zechariah that the problem facing the Israelites, although it may appear to be a mountain, is actually a molehill. How would you like for all your mountains to become molehills? They can, if you will do what God is saying here and look not at the problems but at the Lord and His power. If God has told you to do something, it is certainly His will not only that you begin it but also that you finish it.

You Were Made to Be a Blessing

I will bless you [with abundant increase of favors] and . . .
you will be a blessing [dispensing good to others].

—GENESIS 12:2

Every time you think anything good about anyone, verbalize it. People cannot read your mind. Your thoughts have power and may affect other's confidence level in a minor way, but your words can really lift them up and encourage them. All people need affirmation, especially those who have been emotionally wounded or hurt by someone. We have more power than we realize we do. We can help people! Right words spoken at the right time have the power to heal: "A man has joy in making an apt answer, and a word spoken at the right moment—how good it is!" (PROVERBS 15:23).

Not only are right words spoken at the right time good for others, they are good for us. We experience joy in building others up. We are created by God to be a blessing. He told Abraham, "I will bless you and make you a blessing." We are blessed in being a blessing. God made you to be a blessing. Start being what you were made to be and you will start receiving what you are meant to receive!

If It Be Thy Will

*You do not have, because you do not ask. [Or]
you do ask [God for them] and yet fail to receive, because you ask with
wrong purpose and evil, selfish motives. Your intention is [when you get what
you desire] to spend it in sensual pleasures.*

—JAMES 4:2-3

There are some things in the Word of God that are so clear that we never have to pray, "if it be Thy will." Salvation is a good example. In 1 Timothy 2:3-4 the Bible states that it is God's desire that all should be saved and come to a knowledge of Him. I would never pray, "Dear Father in heaven, I ask in Jesus' name that you save _____, if it be Thy will." I already know it is His will to save that person.

James 4:2 says we have not because we do not ask. Verse 3 says that sometimes we ask and yet fail to receive because we ask with wrong purpose and evil, selfish motives. I realize that sometimes it is hard to believe that of ourselves; but, nonetheless, it is true. It is especially true of the believer who has not allowed the purification process of God to take place in his life. In that state, a person has God in him, but he also has an abundance of "self" in him.

I believe that in those instances when what we are asking for is not clearly spelled out in the Word and we are not positive that we have heard from God about the issue, it is wise and an act of true submission to pray, "if it be Thy will."

I do not personally feel that I am weak in faith if I pray, "Lord, I want this thing—if it is Your will, *if it* fits in with Your plan, *if it* is Your best for me, and *if it* is Your timing." Proverbs 3:7 says, "Be not wise in your own eyes." I have taken this verse to heart and believe it has saved me a great deal of agony. We must resist the temptation to play "Holy Ghost Jr." Instead, we must let God be God.

The Negative Effect of Judging Others

Therefore you have no excuse or defense or justification, O man, whoever you are who judges and condemns another. For in posing as judge and passing sentence on another, you condemn yourself, because you who judge are habitually practicing the very same things [that you censure and denounce].

—ROMANS 2:1

In other words, the very same things that we judge others for, we do ourselves. The Lord gave me a very good example once to help me understand this principle. I was pondering why we would do something ourselves and think it was perfectly all right, but judge someone else who does it. He said, "Joyce, you look at yourself through rose-colored glasses, but you look at everyone else through a magnifying glass."

We make excuses for our own behavior, but when someone else does the same thing we do, we are often merciless. Doing unto others as we want them to do to us (SEE MATTHEW 7:12) is a good life principle that will prevent a lot of judgment and criticism, if followed. A judgmental mind is an offshoot of a negative mind—thinking about what is wrong with an individual instead of what is right. *Be positive and not negative!* Others will benefit, but you will benefit more than anyone.

Submit to the Potter's Hands

Yet, O Lord, You are our Father; we are the clay, and You our Potter, and we all are the work of Your hand.

—ISAIAH 64:8

I like the story about the couple who went into an antique shop one day and found a beautiful teacup sitting on a shelf. They took it off the shelf so they could look at it more closely, and they said, "We really want to buy this gorgeous cup."

All of a sudden, the teacup began to talk, saying, "I wasn't always like this. There was a time when I was just a cold, hard, colorless lump of clay. One day my master picked me up and said, 'I could do something with this.' Then he started to pat me, and roll me, and change my shape. I said, 'What are you doing? That hurts. I don't know if I want to look like this! Stop!' But he said, 'Not yet.'

"Then he put me on a wheel and began to spin me around and around and around, until I screamed, 'Let me off, I am getting dizzy!' 'Not yet,' he said. Then he shaped me into a cup and put me in a hot oven. I cried, 'Let me out! It's hot in here, I am suffocating.' But he just looked at me through that little glass window and smiled and said, 'Not yet.'

"When he took me out, I thought his work on me was over, but then he started to paint me. I couldn't believe what he did next. He put me back into the oven, and I said, 'You have to believe me; I can't stand this! Please let me out!' But he said, 'Not yet.' Finally he took me out of the oven and set me up on a shelf where I thought he had forgotten me. Then one day he took me off the shelf and held me before a mirror. I couldn't believe my eyes, I had become a beautiful teacup that everyone wants to buy."

There may be things going on inside of us that we do not understand. But when we finally arrive at the place where God wants to bring us, we will see how it has prepared us for what God wanted for us all along.

Releasing Joy

But the fruit of the [Holy] Spirit [the work which His presence
within accomplishes] is love, joy (gladness), peace, patience (an even temper,
forbearance), kindness, goodness (benevolence), faithfulness, gentleness
(meekness, humility), self-control (self-restraint, continence).

—GALATIANS 5:22-23

Doubt and unbelief are thieves of joy, but simple childlike believing releases the joy that is resident in our spirits because of the Holy Spirit Who lives in us. As we see in Galatians 5:22-23, one of the fruits of the Holy Spirit is joy. Therefore, since we are filled with God's Holy Spirit, we believers should express joy and enjoy our lives. We might look at it like this: Joy is in the deepest part of the person who has accepted Jesus as his Savior—joy is in his spirit. But if his soul (his mind, will, and emotions) is filled with worry, negative thoughts, reasoning, doubt, and unbelief, these negative things will become like a wall that holds back the release of the fruit of joy resident in him.

The apostle Peter says to cast all our care (anxieties, worries, concerns) on the Lord (SEE 1 PETER 5:7). Paul exhorted the believers of his day, "Be anxious for nothing, but in everything by prayer and supplication, with thanksgiving, let your requests be made known to God; and the peace of God, which surpasses all understanding, will guard your hearts and minds through Christ Jesus." (PHILIPPIANS 4:6-7 NKJV) Keep your mind filled with happy, glad thoughts and, as you trust God, He will take care of your problems.

Walking in the Spirit

But I say, walk and live [habitually] in the [Holy] Spirit [responsive to and controlled and guided by the Spirit]; then you will certainly not gratify the cravings and desires of the flesh (of human nature without God).

—GALATIANS 5:16

When God speaks, He divides the thoughts of our soul from the truth in our spirit and brings to life His purposes in us. When I became a student of the Word, I didn't know when I was operating in the soul and when I was operating in the spirit. I didn't know when I was operating emotionally until I studied God's Word and learned to operate by faith in His promises.

When I wanted something, I just tried to make it happen. I tried in all the wrong ways. If I wasn't getting my way, I pouted and threw fits. Sometimes I wouldn't talk to Dave for days on end, hoping to manipulate him to give in and give me what I wanted. All I cared about was what *I* wanted. I was carnal, selfish, self-centered, and extremely miserable because I was all wrapped up in myself.

Many people get into a relationship with God hoping He will give them what they want. Their life prayer is a list of everything *they* want. Consequently, they remain baby Christians all their lives. They slip in the door of heaven when they die, but they never have victory in this life. They never learned to listen to God and hear what He wants for them. We cannot walk in the flesh and have victory or be truly happy! We cannot spend our lives seeking to satisfy our own appetites and still affect anybody else's life in a positive way. It is not possible. If we follow the leading of the Holy Spirit, we will not fulfill the lusts of our flesh.

People Are More Important Than Things

Do not love or cherish the world or the things that are in the world. If anyone loves the world, love for the Father is not in him.

—1 JOHN 2:15

One day my previous housekeeper was cooking a roast for us in the pressure cooker. She did something wrong and the valve blew off the top, shooting steam, roast, grease, potatoes, and carrots straight up into the air. The ceiling fan above the stove was on full speed. It caught the food and grease and sent them flying all over the kitchen walls, ceiling, floor, furniture—and the housekeeper. When I came home from work, she was sitting in a corner of the kitchen, crying. She looked so bad I thought she had received some tragic news. I finally got her to tell me what had happened; and when she did, I started laughing. By the time Dave came in, she and I were both laughing hysterically.

She said, "I've destroyed your kitchen!"

I remember telling her, "The kitchen can be replaced, but you can't. You're more important than the kitchen. Thank God you're not hurt." There was a time in my life when that would not have been my response. Before I learned that people are more important than things, I would have become angry and said things to make the housekeeper feel stupid and guilty.

If we love people, God can replace things; but if we love things excessively, we may lose people who cannot be replaced.

Seek God All the Time

Keep on asking and it will be given you; keep on seeking and you will find; keep on knocking [reverently] and [the door] will be opened to you.

—MATTHEW 7:7

In 2 Chronicles 20, King Jehoshaphat proclaimed a fast to show his sincerity to God. Missing a few meals and taking that time to seek God is not a bad idea. Turning the television off and spending the time you would normally spend watching it with God is not a bad idea either. Stay home a few evenings and spend extra time with the Lord instead of going out with your friends and repeating your problem over and over to them. These things and others show that we know hearing from God is vital.

I have learned the word *seek* means to pursue, crave, and go after with all your might. In other words, we act like a starving man in search of food to keep us alive. I would also like to add that we need to seek God all the time, not just when we are in trouble. Once, God told me the reason so many people had problems all the time was because that was the only time they would seek Him. He showed me that if He removed the problems, He would not get any time with the people. He said, "Seek Me as if you were desperate all the time and then you won't find yourself desperate as often in reality." I think this is good advice, and I highly recommend that we all follow it.

A Wounded Heart

For I am poor and needy, and my heart is wounded and stricken within me.

—PSALM 109:22

Is it wrong to have a wounded heart? No, a wounded heart is not wrong, but you need to get it healed and go on. In Old Testament days, if a priest had a wound or a bleeding sore, he could not minister. I think today we have a lot of wounded healers. By that I mean there are a lot of people in the body of Christ today who are trying to minister to other people but who themselves still have unhealed wounds from the past. These people are still bleeding and hurting themselves.

Am I saying such people cannot minister? No, but I am saying they need to get healed. Jesus said that the blind cannot lead the blind; because if they do, they will both fall into a ditch. There is a message in that statement. What is the use of my trying to minister victory to others if I have no victory in my own life? How can I minister emotional healing to others if I still have unresolved emotional problems from my past?

In order to minister properly, we need to go to God and let Him heal us first. I think we need to wake up and realize that God is not looking for wounded healers. He wants people with wounds He can heal who will then go and bring healing to others. God loves to use people who have been hurt and wounded, because nobody can minister to someone else better than one who has had the same problem or been in the same situation as that person.

If we are still bleeding and hurting from our own wounds, we are not going to be able to come against other people's problems with the same kind of aggressive faith we would have if we had already worked through that problem ourselves. The bottom line is that we need to let God heal us so He can use us to bring healing to other people.

No One Is Useless to God

God chose the foolish things of the world to shame the wise; God chose the weak things of the world to shame the strong. He chose the lowly things of this world and the despised things—and the things that are not—to nullify the things that are, so that no one may boast before him.

—I CORINTHIANS 1:27-29 (NIV)

Christ's teachings are the best I know for learning to ignore ego (the flesh) and embrace spirit. They are what did it for me.

God chooses what the world throws away as useless. There are no hopeless cases, no useless people in God's eyes. Each of us is His special creation. We are not an accident; and if we will give Him the opportunity, He will restore everything that has been damaged and help us be someone even we can be delighted to be. Ego thrives on competition and striving to be first, but what is the point of competition? What does it get you? Not contentment. Not joy.

It can't get you the one thing that matters—eternal salvation and peace with God. To get that, you have to forsake ego and embrace spirit; and often the ones who have the easiest time doing this are not the powerful or the rich, but the meek. These are the ones who know they are nothing without God and have no problem with it. They are the ones through whom God has chosen to work. Instead of competition, spirit thrives on cooperation and love; because the only true goal is to know God, and then to help others, through love, to do the same.

The Only Right Kind of Fear

In the reverent and worshipful fear of the Lord there is strong confidence, and His children shall always have a place of refuge.

—PROVERBS 14:26

There is only one right kind of fear described in the Bible—the reverential fear and awe of God. Fearing God doesn't mean being afraid of Him or believing He is going to hurt you. Being afraid of God or what He might do is a perversion of the kind of fear God meant for you to have. The fear of God the Bible talks about is the kind of fear we would have for anyone in authority. It is the kind of fear children should have for their parents, wives for their husbands, and students for their teachers. It is a type of godly respect that involves reverential fear and awe. In our society there isn't a lot of respect for authority anymore. Instead, there is a lot of rebellion.

Proverbs 14:26 is an interesting scripture: "In the reverent and worshipful fear of the Lord there is strong confidence." Why? If you have a reverent and worshipful fear, you will obey. You will *do* what God says to do, and your confidence and trust in Him will continue to grow. Having a reverential fear and awe of God has a positive effect on our relationships with other people. I've noticed that the more reverential fear and awe I have of God and the more I realize who God is, the more careful I am in my dealings with other people. I know I'm accountable to Him for my actions and those other people are just as valuable to Him as I am.

Building Bridges, Not Walls

For He is [Himself] our peace (our bond of unity and harmony). He has made us both [Jew and Gentile] one [body], and has broken down (destroyed, abolished) the hostile dividing wall between us.

—EPHESIANS 2:14

One day while I was praying, the Holy Spirit showed me that my life had become a bridge for others to pass over and find their place in God. For many years, I erected only walls in my life; but now where there were walls, there are bridges instead. All the difficult and unfair things that have happened to me have been turned into highways over which others can pass to find the same liberty I have found. *I have learned to build bridges instead of walls.*

In Hebrews 5:9 Jesus is referred to as "the Author *and* Source of eternal salvation." He pioneered a pathway to God for us. He became a highway for us to pass over. It is as though He faced a giant forest and went in ahead of us so that when we came along we could drive right through it without having to fight all the elements and the density of the forest. He sacrificed Himself for us; and now that we are benefiting from His sacrifice, He is giving us a chance to sacrifice for others so they can reap the same benefits we enjoy.

Hebrews 12:2 says that Jesus endured the cross for the joy of obtaining the prize that was set before Him. I like to remind myself of that fact when the way seems hard. I tell myself, "Keep pressing on, Joyce. There is joy ahead."

Make a decision to tear down your walls and build bridges. There are many, many people who are lost in their messes and need someone to go before them and show them the way. Why not be that person for them? Walls or bridges? The choice is yours.

Be Quick to Forgive

Let all bitterness and indignation and wrath (passion, rage, bad temper) and resentment (anger, animosity) and quarreling (brawling, clamor, contention) and slander (evil-speaking, abusive or blasphemous language) be banished from you, with all malice (spite, ill will, or baseness of any kind). And become useful and helpful and kind to one another, tenderhearted (compassionate, understanding, loving-hearted), forgiving one another [readily and freely], as God in Christ forgave you.

—EPHESIANS 4:31-32

The Bible teaches us to forgive "readily and freely." We are to be quick to forgive. According to 1 Peter 5:5 we are to clothe ourselves with the character of Jesus Christ, meaning that we are to be longsuffering, patient, and filled with mercy. My definition of the word *mercy* is the ability to look beyond what is done to discover the reason why it was done. Many times people do things even they don't understand themselves, but there is always a reason why people behave as they do.

The same is true of us as believers. We are to be merciful and forgiving, just as God in Christ forgives us our wrongdoing—even when we don't understand why we do what we do. The Bible teaches that we are to forgive in order to keep Satan from getting the advantage over us. So when we forgive others, not only are we doing them a favor, we are doing ourselves an even greater favor. The reason we are doing ourselves such a favor is because unforgiveness produces in us a root of bitterness that poisons our entire system. The longer we allow it to grow and fester, the more powerful it becomes, and the more it infects our entire being: our personality, our attitude and behavior, our perspective, and our relationships—especially our relationship with God.

To keep Satan from getting the advantage over you, forgive! Do yourself a favor and let the offense go! Forgive to keep yourself from being poisoned—and imprisoned.

Delegate or Fall Apart

You will surely wear out both yourself and this people with you, for the thing is too heavy for you; you are not able to perform it all by yourself.

—EXODUS 18:18

I've learned from experience that it is wise to set proper limits and margins. It is a sign of strength, not weakness. Asking for help is a good thing to do also. God has placed certain people in each of our lives to help us. If we do not receive their help, we become frustrated and overworked, and they feel unfulfilled because they are not using their gifts. Remember that God has not called you to do everything for everybody in every situation. You cannot be all things to all people all the time. You have legitimate needs.

It is not wrong to need help and ask for it. However, it is wrong to need help and be too proud to ask for it. In Exodus 18:12-27, we see that Moses was a man with many responsibilities. The people looked to him for everything, and he tried to meet all their needs. Moses' father-in-law suggested that Moses delegate some of his authority to others. He said Moses should let them make the less-important decisions and Moses should deal only with the hard cases.

Moses did what his father-in-law suggested, and it enabled him to endure the strain of his task. And the others had the benefit of a sense of accomplishment for the decisions they made on their own. Many people either complain all the time about what they are expected to do or they end up falling apart emotionally and physically because they won't let anyone help them do anything. They don't think anyone is as qualified for the job as they are.

It is easy to think you are more important than you actually are. Learn to delegate. Let as many people help you as possible. If you do, you will last a lot longer and enjoy yourself a lot more.

You Are Responsible for You

By this we come to know (progressively to recognize, to perceive, to understand)
the [essential] love: that He laid down His [own] life for us; and we ought to
lay [our] lives down for [those who are our] brothers [in Him].

—1 JOHN 3:16

The Holy Ghost has your desires in mind when He tells you to demonstrate love toward someone. A lot of times I have felt prompted, "Just do it. Just do it." I would argue, "Well, God, You are always saying something to me. When are You going to say something to Dave?!!" I felt as though I were the only one who was ever corrected. If God wasn't dealing with Dave, too, I couldn't stand it!

A couple of times I even went to Dave and said, "Dave, is God dealing with you about anything?" Invariably, Dave would shrug and say, "No, nothing that I can think of."

One time God dealt very strongly with me about showing Dave respect, yet I felt as though there were plenty of times that Dave wasn't respectful to me! If I interrupted Dave when he was talking, the Holy Ghost would say, "That is disrespectful." I would think in retaliation, *Well, he interrupts me when I'm talking! Why can he be rude and I can't?!*

It's a flesh burner when God wants you to stop doing something that the other person is doing too. But we are each responsible to do what God shows us to do. Do the hard things now, and your reward will surely come later.

Trust in Christ to Lead You

You will guide me with Your counsel, and afterward receive me to honor and glory.

—PSALM 73:24

We believe that God is inherently good and that He is also in control of our lives. Therefore, when tragedy strikes or loss occurs, we don't understand why God does not prevent such things from happening to us and hurting us so badly.

Faced with tragic loss, often we become angry and ask, "If God is good and all-powerful, why does He allow bad things to happen to good people?" This question becomes a major issue when it is we, God's own children, who are the ones suffering.

At such times, reasoning wants to scream out, "This makes no sense at all!" Over and over the question, "Why, God, why?" torments those who are grieving over losses in their life, just as it also tortures the lonely and the dejected. Excessive reasoning, trying to figure out things for which we will not be able to find an answer, torments and brings much confusion; but Proverbs 3:5-6 tells us that trust in the Lord brings assurance and direction: "Lean on, trust in, and be confident in the Lord with all your heart and mind and do not rely on your own insight or understanding. In all your ways know, recognize, and acknowledge Him, and He will direct and make straight and plain your paths."

When we face a time of crisis in life, we need direction. These scriptures tell us that trusting God is the way to find that direction. *Trust requires allowing some unanswered questions to be in your life!*

No matter how badly you may be hurting from a loss or tragedy, the Holy Spirit can give you a deep peace that somehow everything will be all right. Being angry at God is useless, because He is the only One Who can help.

There's POWER in the Name of Jesus

Up to this time you have not asked a [single] thing in My Name [as presenting all that I AM]; but now ask and keep on asking and you will receive, so that your joy (gladness, delight) may be full and complete.

—JOHN 16:24

As you and I come before the throne of God's grace asking in faith according to His Word and in the name of His Son Jesus Christ, we can know we have the petitions that we ask of Him. Not because we are perfect or worthy in ourselves or because God owes us anything, but because He loves us and wants to give us what we need to do the job He has called us to do.

There is power in the name of Jesus. At the very mention of it, every knee has to bow in heaven, on earth, and beneath the earth (SEE PHILIPPIANS 2:10). By the power of that name, you and I are to lay hands on the sick and they will recover, cast out demons and they will flee, and do the same works Jesus did and even greater works than these for the glory of God (SEE MARK 16:17-18 AND JOHN 14:12).

Jesus has purchased a glorious inheritance for us by the shedding of His blood. We are now heirs with Him (SEE ROMANS 8:17). Everything He has earned by His sacrifice is in the heavenlies stored up for us. We have the keys to that storehouse, and the keys are prayer.

We do not have to live in fear and lack. Let's start using those keys and opening those doors so that heavenly blessings may be showered down upon us for the glory of God, so that His divine will may be done on earth as it is in heaven, and so that our joy may be made complete.

I Understand

> *For we do not have a High Priest Who is unable to understand*
> *and sympathize and have a shared feeling with our weaknesses and infirmities*
> *and liability to the assaults of temptation, but One Who has been tempted in*
> *every respect as we are, yet without sinning.*
>
> —HEBREWS 4:15

As human beings, we have a deep need to be understood. When we don't receive it, we feel lonely. In listening to people share their hurt and pain, I find that the words "I understand" have a very soothing effect. I have told my husband, "Even if you don't have a clue about what I am talking about, just tell me you understand, and it will make me feel a lot better." A man could not possibly understand PMS, but it is better for him if he appears to have understanding of his wife's plight. She needs to be understood. She does not want to feel alone in her pain and struggle.

One day my husband came in from trying to play golf. He had not had a good experience because his leg was hurting and swollen. He was not too happy about it. His golf game is really important to him, so I said, "I understand how you feel." I offered him whatever help I could give physically, but my understanding seemed to help more than anything.

There have been times in the past when my attitude has been, "What's the big deal? It's only one round of golf. After all, you play all the time." That attitude has started arguments and driven a wedge between us. He wants me to understand his needs, and I want him to understand mine.

One of my favorite scriptures in the Bible is Hebrews 4:15, which teaches that Jesus is a High Priest Who understands our weaknesses and infirmities because He has been tempted in every respect just as we have, yet He never sinned. Just knowing that Jesus understands makes me feel closer to Him. It helps me be vulnerable and trust Him. It helps me feel connected rather than lonely.

Don't Let Selfishness Win the War

> *And falling on his knees, he cried out loudly, Lord, fix not*
> *this sin upon them [lay it not to their charge]! And when he had*
> *said this, he fell asleep [in death].*
>
> —ACTS 7:60

Purposely forgetting about ourselves and our problems and doing something for someone else while we are hurting is one of the most powerful things we can do to overcome evil. When Jesus was on the cross in intense suffering, He took time to comfort the thief next to Him (SEE LUKE 23:39-43). When Stephen was being stoned, he prayed for those stoning him, asking God not to lay the sin to their charge (SEE ACTS 7:59-60).

When Paul and Silas were in prison, they took time to minister to their jailer. Even after God came on the scene with a powerful earthquake that broke their chains and opened the door for them to come out, they remained just for the purpose of ministering to their captor. How tempting it must have been to run away quickly while the opportunity was there. How tempting to take care of themselves and not worry about anyone else. Their act of love moved the man to ask how he might be saved, and he and his entire family were born again (asked Jesus into their hearts) (SEE ACTS 16:25-34).

I believe if we, as the church of Jesus Christ, His body here on earth, will wage war against selfishness and walk in love, the world will begin to take notice. We will not impress the world by being just like them. But how many unsaved friends and relatives might come to know Jesus if we genuinely loved them instead of ignoring, judging, or rejecting them? I believe it is time to find out, don't you?

The Growing Times

Enfolded in love, let us grow up in every way and in all things into Him Who is the Head, [even] Christ (the Messiah, the Anointed One).

—EPHESIANS 4:15

If you look back over your life, you will see that you never grow during easy times; you grow during hard times. During the easy times that come, you are able to enjoy what you have gained during the hard times. This is really a life principle; it is just the way it works. You work all week, then you receive your paycheck and enjoy your weekend off.

You exercise, eat right, and take good care of yourself, then you enjoy a healthy body. You clean your house, or basement, or garage, and then you enjoy your neat, clean surroundings each time you walk through them. I am reminded of Hebrews 12:11: "For the time being no discipline brings joy, but seems grievous and painful; but afterwards it yields a peaceable fruit of righteousness to those who have been trained by it."

To be truly victorious, we must grow to the place where we are not afraid of hard times but are actually challenged by them. Because it is during these hard times that we grow.

Work Now, Play Later

Pay your debt.

—2 KINGS 4:7

We have seen that the Bible teaches us that we are to owe no man anything except to love him. When we allow debt to overwhelm us, it can bring discouragement and even depression. When Dave and I were young marrieds, we got into trouble with debt. We did it by running up our credit cards to the maximum, buying things we wanted for ourselves and our children. We were making the minimum payment on the balance each month, but the interest was so high we never seemed to make any progress toward paying off what we owed. In fact, we just kept getting deeper and deeper into debt.

If you and I are ever going to get anywhere in the kingdom of God, we must learn to live by wisdom and not by our carnal desire, which is human emotion (SEE PROVERBS 3:13). The Bible teaches that Jesus has been made unto us wisdom, and that the Holy Spirit is wisdom within us (SEE 1 CORINTHIANS 1:30 AND EPHESIANS 1:17). If we will listen to the prompting of the Spirit, we will not get into trouble. But if we live by the dictates of the flesh, we are headed for destruction.

Wisdom makes the decision today that it will be comfortable with tomorrow. Emotion does what feels good today and takes no thought of tomorrow. When tomorrow arrives, the wise enjoy it in peace and security, but the foolish end up in discouragement and depression. Why? Because the wise have prepared for tomorrow and are able to enjoy the fruits of their labor, while the foolish who have put pleasure first must now pay for yesterday.

To live a disciplined life, we have to be willing to invest today so that we can reap tomorrow. To relieve the discouragement and depression that come from being in debt, we must get out of debt by becoming self-disciplined to think not of today's sacrifices but of tomorrow's rewards.

Entering the Rest of God

Behold, I long for Your precepts; in Your righteousness give me renewed life. . . . I will keep Your law continually, forever and ever [hearing, receiving, loving, and obeying it]. And I will walk at liberty and at ease, for I have sought and inquired for [and desperately required] Your precepts.

—PSALM 119:40, 44-45

If you truly love the Word of God—if you hear it, receive it, and *obey it*—you will have freedom and live "at ease." In other words, life will not be hard, frustrating, or difficult. Your joy is full when you believe God's promises for your life and obey *His* commands.

The Bible teaches that those who disobey God's instructions, who don't listen to His Word, do not enter into the place of rest He offers to them. So when you feel frustrated or upset or if you have lost your peace and your joy, ask yourself, "Am I believing God's Word?"

The only way we will ever be free from struggling is to believe the Word and obey whatever Jesus puts in our hearts to do. Believing God's Word delivers us from struggling so that we rest in the promises of God. The Word says, "For we who have believed (adhered to and trusted in and relied on God) do enter that rest" (HEBREWS 4:3).

If your thoughts have become negative and you are full of doubt, it is because you have stopped hearing, receiving, and obeying God's Word. As soon as you start believing God's Word, your joy will return and you will be "at ease" again. And that place of rest in Him is where God wants you to be *every day* of your life.

Our Number One Goal in Life

For those whom He foreknew [of whom He was aware and loved beforehand], He also destined from the beginning [foreordaining them] to be molded into the image of His Son [and share inwardly His likeness], that He might become the firstborn among many brethren.

—ROMANS 8:29

Our number one goal in life as Christians should be Christlikeness. Jesus is the express image of the Father, and we are to follow in His footsteps. He came as the pioneer of our faith to show us by example how we should live and conduct ourselves. We should seek to behave with people the way Jesus did. Our goal is not to see how successful we can be in business or how famous we can be. It is not prosperity, popularity, or even building a big ministry, but to be Christlike.

The world doesn't only need a sermon preached to them; they also need to see actions backing up what we say we believe as Christians. Our lives should make other people hungry and thirsty for what we have in Christ. The Bible refers to us as salt, which makes people thirsty, and light, which exposes darkness.

Many Christians have bumper stickers on their cars, or they wear some kind of jewelry that indicates they are believers in Jesus Christ. The world is not impressed by our bumper stickers and Christian jewelry; they want to see fruit of godly behavior. They want to see people who claim to be Christians living what they preach, not just preaching to others while it doesn't seem to be working in their own lives.

Just Do It

For all who are led by the Spirit of God are sons of God.

—ROMANS 8:14

I have discovered that if I want to be happy and if I want to have an anointing on my life, then I must be obedient to the voice of God. I don't always have to know *why* God wants me to do something. I just need to know *what* He tells me to do—and then do it!

When our feelings run amuck, we need to keep them from running our lives. We need to submit our will to what God tells us to do through His Word to us. If we don't feel like going to church, we go anyway. If we don't feel like giving that hundred-dollar offering God told us to give, we do it anyway. If God tells us to give away items we feel like keeping, we give them away with joy.

"Walking in the Spirit" is a phrase that charismatic believers have used loosely in the past few decades. What it means to me is to hear God speak and do whatever He tells me to do. We can point our finger when we see that other people aren't obeying God, but all He wants from us is our own obedience.

Only God Can Really Help

You are He Who took me out of the womb; You made me hope and trust when I was on my mother's breasts. I was cast upon You from my very birth; from my mother's womb You have been my God. Be not far from me, for trouble is near and there is none to help.

—PSALM 22:9-11

I have been walking with God now for a long time, so I have some experience behind me and have been through some hard times. But I have never forgotten the many years the devil controlled and manipulated me. I remember the nights I used to spend walking the floor crying, feeling like I just couldn't make it.

I remember running to my friends and others I thought might be able to help me. Eventually I got smart enough to stop running to people—not because I didn't like them or trust them, but because I knew they really could not help me—only God could.

I heard one speaker say, "If people can help you, you don't really have a problem."

I used to get so aggravated at my husband because when he would be having problems or going through rough times, he wouldn't tell me about it. Then two or three weeks after he had won the victory, he would say, "I was really going through a rough time a few weeks ago."

Before he would finish, I would ask, "Why didn't you tell me?"

Do you know what he would say?

"I knew you couldn't help me, so I didn't even ask!"

I am not saying it is wrong to share with someone you love and trust what is going on in your life, but Dave understood a truth that I needed to put into practice in my own life. There are times when only God can help. Although I would have liked to have been able to help my husband, I really couldn't. Only God could, and he needed to go to Him.

Know Your Enemy

We are not wrestling with flesh and blood [contending only with physical opponents], but against the despotisms, against the powers, against [the master spirits who are] the world rulers of this present darkness.

—EPHESIANS 6:12

Satan uses people and circumstances, but they are not our real enemy; he is. He finds things and people through whom he can work and delights in watching us fight and war without ever realizing he is the source. When Satan used Peter to try to divert Jesus from going to Jerusalem to complete the task God had sent Him to do, "Jesus *turned away* from Peter and said to him, Get behind Me, Satan! You are in My way [an offense and a hindrance and a snare to Me]." (MATTHEW 16:23, EMPHASIS MINE) Satan used Peter, but Jesus knew that Peter was not His real problem. He *turned away* from Peter and addressed the source of His temptation.

We need to look beyond what we see or initially feel and seek to know the source of our problems too. Usually we blame people and become angry with them, which only complicates and compounds the problem. When we behave in this manner, we are actually playing right into Satan's hands and helping his plans succeed. We also blame circumstances and sometimes even God, which also delights Satan.

Yes, we need to know our enemy—not only who he is but what his character is like. The Bible encourages us to know the character of God so we can place faith in Him and what He says. Likewise, we should know Satan's character so we do not listen to or believe his lies.

More Than Conquerors

Yet amid all these things we are more than conquerors and
gain a surpassing victory through Him Who loved us.

—ROMANS 8:37

We need to have a sense of triumph. In Romans 8:37 Paul assures us that through Christ Jesus we are more than conquerors. Believing that truth gives us confidence. I once heard that a woman is more than a conqueror if her husband goes out, works all week, and brings his paycheck home to her. But God spoke to me and said, "You're more than a conqueror when you know that you already have the victory before you ever get a problem."

Sometimes our confidence is shaken when trials come, especially if they are lengthy. We should have so much confidence in God's love for us that no matter what comes against us, we know deep inside that we are more than conquerors. If we are truly confident, we have no need to fear trouble, challenges, or trying times, because we know they will pass. Whenever a trial of any kind comes against you, always remember: *This, too, shall pass!* Be confident that during the trial you will learn something that will help you in the future.

Without confidence we are stifled at every turn. Satan drops a bomb, and our dreams are destroyed. Eventually we start over, but we never make much progress. We start and get defeated over and over again. But those who are consistently confident, those who know they are more than conquerors through Jesus Christ, make rapid progress.

We must take a step of faith and decide to be confident in all things. God may have to correct us occasionally, but that is better than playing it safe and never doing anything. Confident people get the job done; they have the ministries that are making a difference in the world today. They are fulfilled because they are succeeding at being themselves.

Give Away Your Salt

You are the salt of the earth, but if salt has lost its taste (its strength, its quality . . . it is not good for anything any longer.

—MATTHEW 5:13

For much of our lives, many of us try to find happiness the wrong way. We attempt to find it in getting, but it is found in giving. Love must give; it is the nature of love to do so: "For God so greatly loved and dearly prized the world that He [even] gave up His only begotten (unique) Son, so that whoever believes in (trusts in, clings to, relies on) Him shall not perish (come to destruction, be lost) but have eternal (everlasting) life." (JOHN 3:16)

We show love to others by meeting their needs—practical needs as well as spiritual needs. Generosity is love in action. Love is seen through edification and encouragement, patience, kindness, courtesy, humility, unselfishness, good temper, gentleness (believing the best), and sincerity. We should actively pursue ways to show love, especially in little things.

"You are the salt of the earth, but if salt has lost its taste (its strength, its quality), how can its saltness be restored? It is not good for anything any longer but to be thrown out and trodden underfoot by men." (MATTHEW 5:13) In this verse, Jesus tells us we are the salt of the earth; but if salt has lost its flavor, it is not good for anything.

I say that all of life is tasteless without love. Even acts of generosity done out of obligation but devoid of sincere love leave us empty. Love is the salt, the energy of life, the reason to get up every morning.

Every day can be exciting if we see ourselves as God's secret agents, waiting in the shadows to sprinkle some salt on all the tasteless lives we encounter.

Be Decisive

A man of two minds (hesitating, dubious, irresolute), [he is] unstable and unreliable and uncertain about everything [he thinks, feels, decides].

—JAMES 1:8

Whatever the problem or situation, decision is always better than doubt and indecision. For example, if you have had a quarrel with someone, it is much easier to *decide* to apologize than it is to stay angry and be filled with unforgiveness, bitterness, and resentment while you are waiting for the other person to apologize to you. Be a peacemaker, and you will have a lot of joy. I spent many years making war; and believe me, the price I paid was high. It cost me my peace and my joy and sometimes my health. Jesus has a way, and we can do it His way and enjoy life. Indecision wastes a lot of time, and time is too precious to waste.

Become a decisive person, and you will accomplish a lot more with less effort. No one learns to hear from God without making mistakes. Don't be overly concerned about errors. Don't take yourself too seriously. You are a fallible human being, not an infallible god. Learn from your mistakes, correct the ones you can, and continue being decisive. Don't fall back into a pattern of indecision and double-mindedness just because you are wrong a few times. If you feel that God is prompting you to give something away, do it! Get it off your mind. Take some action and sow the seed. If you believe it is right, then do it. That is how you will find out for sure.

Devote a reasonable amount of time to waiting on God. Don't follow fleshly zeal, but do follow your heart. Don't be afraid of yourself! You will not be the first person to make a mistake, nor will you be the last. The fear of failure keeps thousands trapped in indecision, which definitely steals joy and complicates life. Don't be afraid to make a decision and follow through with it. *Just do it!*

Receiving Correction

A fool despises his father's instruction and correction,
but he who regards reproof acquires prudence.

—PROVERBS 15:5

Ask yourself how you react to correction or criticism. Try to be honest in your evaluation. Confident people who have validated themselves as valuable can receive correction without anger or a defensive attitude. God says only a fool hates correction (SEE PROVERBS 15:5). Why is that? Because he should be wise enough to want to learn everything he can about himself.

Confident people can listen objectively to another point of view. They can pray about what is said and either receive or reject it according to what God places in their hearts. During the years I was filled with shame and guilt, I could not receive even a tiny word of correction from my husband. If he said anything that even remotely suggested he felt I needed to change in any way, I became emotionally upset, angry, and defensive. Dave would repeatedly say, "I am only trying to help you."

But I could not get past how I felt when I was given his or anyone else's help. If I asked him whether he liked an outfit I was wearing, I would get defensive if he said no. I could not even allow him to give me his honest opinion. If his opinion did not agree with mine, I felt rejected. I am grateful that those days are over. Everyone does not have to like what I like in order for me to feel secure.

It is absolutely wonderful to be able to approve of ourselves, because we believe God approves of us, even though others do not. It is good to be humble enough to receive correction, yet confident enough not to let the opinions of others control us.

A Forgiving Heart

But if you do not forgive, neither will your
Father in heaven forgive your failings and shortcomings.

—MARK 11:26

Jesus taught us to pray, "Forgive us our trespasses as we forgive those who trespass against us." God is a God of mercy, but this issue of forgiveness is very important to Him. In His Word He tells us repeatedly that if we want mercy, we have to give mercy. We are willing to keep taking and taking forgiveness from God, but it is amazing how little we want to give forgiveness to others.

In Matthew 18:23-35 Jesus told a story about a servant who owed a tremendous amount of money to his master and was forgiven of it. But then the servant went out and began to choke another servant who owed him only a small sum of money, threatening to have him thrown in prison if he didn't pay up immediately. The other servant begged for more time to come up with the money but was thrown in prison anyway. When the other servants heard about it, they told the master, who called in the merciless servant and said to him, "How dare you leave my presence after receiving my forgiveness for such a huge amount and go directly out and be unforgiving with someone else for such a paltry amount!"

In verse 34 of Matthew 18, Jesus said that the master turned the unforgiving servant over to the torturers, or the jailers, until he paid his debt in full. I believe that when we refuse to forgive other people, we are the ones who end up in a prison of emotional torment.

We hurt ourselves much more than we hurt anyone else because when we harbor bitterness, resentment, and unforgiveness toward a person, we are miserable. At the end of that story, Jesus warned His audience, "So also My heavenly Father will deal with every one of you if you do not freely forgive your brother from your heart his offenses." If you want to be used by God in ministry, you must learn to be forgiving.

Tear Down Your Walls with Faith

For I will restore health to you, and I will heal your wounds,
says the Lord, because they have called you an outcast, saying, This is Zion,
whom no one seeks after and for whom no one cares!

—JEREMIAH 30:17

To avoid pain, some of us build walls around ourselves so we will not get hurt, but that is pointless. God has shown me that it is impossible to live in this world if we are not willing to get hurt. People are not perfect; therefore, they hurt and disappoint us, just as we hurt and disappoint others.

I have a wonderful husband, but occasionally he has hurt me. Because I came from such a painful background, the moment that kind of thing happened, I used to put up walls to protect myself. *After all,* I reasoned, *no one can hurt me if I don't let anyone get close to me.* However, I learned that if I wall others out, I also wall myself in. The Lord has shown me that He wants to be my protector, but He cannot do that if I am busy trying to protect myself.

He has not promised that I will *never* get hurt, but He has promised to heal me if I come to Him rather than try to take care of everything myself. If you build walls around yourself out of fear, then you must tear them down out of faith. Go to Jesus with each old wound and receive His healing grace. When someone hurts you, take that new wound to Jesus. Do not let it fester. Take it to the Lord and be willing to handle it His way and not your own. Receive this scripture as a personal promise from the Lord to you: "For I will restore health to you, and I will heal your wounds, says the Lord, because they have called you an outcast, saying, This is Zion, whom no one seeks after and for whom no one cares!" (JEREMIAH 30:17). With the help of the Lord, you can survive hurt and disappointment and find your completion "in Him."

Jesus' Tough Love Tactics

He then said to the paralyzed man, Get up! Pick up
your sleeping pad and go to your own house.

—MATTHEW 9:6

Although Jesus had compassion for hurting people, He never merely felt sorry for them. And whenever possible he helped them help themselves. He instructed them to take some particular action, and frequently His instructions were shocking. For instance, He told a crippled man to rise, take up his bed, and go home (SEE MATTHEW 9:6). He told a man who had just received a report that his daughter was dead not to be afraid (SEE MARK 5:35-36). When Jesus saw a blind man, He spat on the ground, made some mud by mixing dirt with it, and then rubbed it on the blind man's eyes. He then instructed the man to walk to the Pool of Siloam and wash himself in it. When the man did as Jesus had commanded, he was able to see (SEE JOHN 9:1-7).

We see that Jesus often told people to do things that were not only surprising but seemingly impossible. How could a crippled man rise, take up his bed, and walk? After all, he was a cripple. How could a man who had just received a report of his daughter's death be expected not to fear? How could a blind man see to get to a certain pool of water when he was blind? Instead of merely feeling sorry for these people, Jesus moved them to action. He helped them get their minds off of themselves and their problems, and He motivated them to do something about them. Jesus was *moved* with pity (SEE MATTHEW 9:36). He was moved to do something besides enable people to stay the way they were.

At times we feel we are being mean if we confront people who have problems, when in reality "tough love" is what Jesus often used to set people free.

Trusting the Leadership of the Holy Spirit

So if the Son liberates you [makes you free men],
then you are really and unquestionably free.

—JOHN 8:36

I once read that we believers are like ships that God wants to turn out to sea to sail wherever the wind and waves carry us. That sea represents the freedom we have in God, and the wind is a symbol of the Holy Spirit. But as new believers, we are tied to the dock because that is the only place we can avoid becoming shipwrecked until we learn how to follow Him. When we learn to follow those inner promptings of the Holy Spirit, we can be untied from the dock and sail the seas of life under His leadership without the fear of becoming lost.

Paul explains, *We [Jewish Christians] also, when we were minors, were kept like slaves under [the rules of the Hebrew ritual and subject to] the elementary teachings of a system of external observations and regulations. But when the proper time had fully come, God sent His Son, born of a woman, born subject to [the regulations of] the Law, to purchase the freedom of (to ransom, to redeem, to atone for) those who were subject to the Law, that we might be adopted and have sonship conferred upon us [and be recognized as God's sons]. And because you [really] are [His] sons, God has sent the [Holy] Spirit of His Son into our hearts, crying, Abba (Father)! Father!*

(GALATIANS 4:3-6)

When the Spirit of God is in you, the law of God is written in your heart. You no longer have to memorize the law, because you can follow the leadership of the Holy Ghost, Who will lead you in the right direction.

The Simple Approach

> *Come to Me, all you who labor and are heavy-laden and overburdened, and*
> *I will cause you to rest. [I will ease and relieve and refresh your souls.] Take*
> *My yoke upon you and learn of Me, for I am gentle (meek) and humble (lowly)*
> *in heart, and you will find rest (relief and ease and refreshment and recreation*
> *and blessed quiet) for your souls. For My yoke is wholesome (useful, good—not*
> *harsh, hard, sharp, or pressing, but comfortable, gracious, and pleasant), and*
> *My burden is light and easy to be borne.*
>
> —MATTHEW 11:28-30

One of the definitions of *simple* is "easy." With that in mind, take a look at Jesus' words in the passage above. Notice how often the words "ease" and "easy" appear.

First of all, Jesus said, "Learn of Me." I believe He meant, "Learn how I handle situations and people. Learn what My response would be to any given circumstance and follow My ways." Jesus was not stressed out or burned out. He was not controlled by circumstances and by the demands of other people. In John 14:6, He said, **"I am the Way."** His way is the right way—the way that will lead us into righteousness, peace, and joy.

Remember that in John 15:11 Jesus prayed that His enjoyment would fill our souls. That is not going to happen unless we learn a different approach to life and its many different circumstances. I could write about various things we need to simplify, and the list would be endless. But if we can learn to have the simple approach to everything, that is far better than learning to be simple in some things.

No matter what you face, if you will ask yourself what the simple approach would be, I believe you will be amazed at the creative ideas you will have. The Holy One lives in you; and although He is awesomely powerful, He is also awesomely simple. The Holy Spirit will teach you simplicity if you truly wish to learn.

Invite Christ into Your Relationships

> *(Lead a life) worthy of the [divine] calling to which you have been called*
> *[with behavior that is a credit to the summons to God's service, living as*
> *becomes you] with complete lowliness of mind (humility) and meekness*
> *(unselfishness, gentleness, mildness), with patience, bearing with one another*
> *and making allowances because you love one another.*
>
> —EPHESIANS 4:1-2

God loved us first, and we loved Him back. He reaffirms us concerning His love; and we start loving others, and eventually, the love becomes so intertwined in us that it no longer matters who was first to love the other. Ephesians 5:1 says, "Therefore be imitators of God [copy Him and follow His example], as well-beloved children [imitate their father]."

The book of Ephesians explains this lesson of love by saying that we are to be useful and helpful and kind to one another, tenderhearted, compassionate, and understanding with the other. In becoming like Christ, we will naturally turn our attention to the needs of others. Christ is the role model to whom we must adapt.

It is sometimes painful to work at relationships; but it is more painful to reap failure, dissension, and separation from those we love because we have simply neglected them and sown bad seed. So, to foster good relationships, we must first come into agreement with God by drawing near to Christ and becoming like Him. Once we invite Jesus into our relationships and do what He says to do, we become like Him in our thoughts and deeds; and consequently, we become loving like He is and we develop and maintain good relationships.

Remember, "There is [now no distinction] neither Jew nor Greek, there is neither slave nor free, there is not male and female; for you are all one in Christ Jesus." (GALATIANS 3:28)

Follow God, Not People

And yet [in spite of all this] many even of the leading men (the authorities and the nobles) believed and trusted in Him. But because of the Pharisees they did not confess it, for fear that [if they should acknowledge Him] they would be expelled from the synagogue.

—JOHN 12:42

The Bible teaches us in John 12:42-43 that many of the leading men believed in Jesus but would not confess it for fear that if they did, they would be expelled from the synagogue. "They loved the approval and the praise and the glory that come from men [instead of and] more than the glory that comes from God" (v. 43). In this example we see that some people were hindered from a relationship with Jesus because they were addicted to approval. Although they wanted a relationship with the Lord, they loved the approval of man more. That is sad, but it happens all the time.

The people mentioned in John 12 knew that Jesus was real. They believed in Him, but the love of approval would not permit them to have a true relationship with Him. I wonder how their lives turned out. What did they miss because they said yes to people and no to God? I wonder how many of them were never mentioned in the Bible again. I wonder if they faded into oblivion and never fulfilled their destiny because they loved the approval of men more than the approval of God. How many of them spent their lives disrespecting themselves because they were people-pleasers? Follow God, not people!

Trying vs. Trusting

Commit your way to the Lord [roll and repose each care of your load on Him];
trust (lean on, rely on, and be confident) also in Him and He will bring it to pass.

—PSALM 37:5

Do you realize that the word *try* is unscriptural? I know that is true because I checked in the largest concordance I could find. Oh, the word is there all right, but not in the sense that we are using it in today's devotion. The only way *try* is used in the Bible is in the sense of putting someone or something to the test. The Bible speaks of the "trying of our faith" (SEE JAMES 1:3 KJV). We are told not to believe everything that we hear, but to "try the spirits" (SEE 1 JOHN 4:1 KJV). The psalmist says, "Try me, O Lord, and know my thoughts" (SEE PSALM 139:23). The Bible also talks about fiery trials which will "try" us (SEE 1 PETER 4:12).

In the scriptural sense then, the word *try* refers to a test or trial to determine the value and worth of a person or thing. But that is totally different from the way we usually use the word *try*—which refers to human effort. We say we are "trying" when we are attempting to achieve or accomplish something by our own means or ability. Now I am not saying that we should never make any effort to achieve or accomplish anything in life. Not at all. One of the messages I often preach is on the subject of the proper effort we are to put out as believers—an effort that is made through the power and by the grace of God at work within us.

In other words, we don't attempt anything without asking for God's help. We lean on Him the whole way through each project. We maintain an attitude that says, "Apart from Him I can do nothing." But we are not to be involved in natural, carnal efforts because the result is only fatigue and frustration, disappointment, and destruction. Be willing to exchange trying for trusting. That's what I learned to do as the Lord opened to me a whole new realm of revelation about His marvelous grace.

No Condemnation

*Therefore, [there is] now no condemnation . . . for those
who are in Christ Jesus, who live [and] walk not after
the dictates of the flesh, but after the dictates of the Spirit.*

—ROMANS 8:1

Don't receive condemnation when you have setbacks or bad days. Just get back up, dust yourself off, and start again. When a baby is learning to walk, he falls many, many times before he enjoys confidence in walking. However, one thing in a baby's favor is the fact that, even though he may cry a while after he has fallen, he always gets right back up and tries again.

The devil will try hard to stop you through discouragement and condemnation. When condemnation comes, use your "Word weapon." Quote Romans 8:1, reminding Satan and yourself that you do not walk after the flesh but after the Spirit. Walking after the flesh is depending on yourself; walking after the Spirit is depending on God. When you fail (which you will), that doesn't mean you are a failure. It simply means you don't do everything right. We all have to accept the fact that along with strengths we also have weaknesses. Just let Christ be strong in your weaknesses; let Him be your strength on your weak days.

Avoid Worldly Competition

> *Let us not become vainglorious and self-conceited, competitive and challenging and provoking and irritating to one another, envying and being jealous of one another.*
>
> —GALATIANS 5:26

According to the world's system, the best place to be is ahead of everyone else. Popular thinking would say that we should try to get to the top no matter who we have to hurt on the way up. But the Bible teaches that there is no such thing as real peace until we are delivered from the need to compete with others.

Even in what is supposed to be considered "fun games," we often see competition get so out of balance that people end up arguing and hating one another rather than simply relaxing and having a good time together. Naturally, human beings don't play games to lose; everyone is going to do his best. But when a person cannot enjoy a game unless he is winning, he definitely has a problem—possibly a deep-rooted one that is causing other problems in many areas of his life.

We should definitely do our best on the job; there is nothing wrong with wanting to do well and advance in our chosen professions. But I encourage you to remember that promotion for the believer comes from God and not from man. You and I don't need to play worldly games to get ahead. God will give us favor with Him and with others if we will do things His way (SEE PROVERBS 3:3-4).

What God does for you or for me may not be what He does for someone else, but we must remember what Jesus said to Peter: "Don't be concerned about what I choose to do with someone else—you follow Me!" (SEE JOHN 21:22).

This, Too, Shall Pass

And it shall come to pass. —GENESIS 4:14 (KJV)

In the beginning chapters of the book of Genesis we see a prophetic word that things will "come to pass." In fulfillment of this word, the expression "it came to pass" is used hundreds of times throughout the *King James Version* of the Bible. For example, in Genesis 39 (KJV), which describes some of Joseph's experiences in Egypt where he was sold into slavery and rose to second in command of the entire nation, the phrase "and it came to pass" appears eight times. The last book of the Bible, Revelation, speaks of "things which must shortly come to pass" (SEE REVELATION 1:1 KJV).

That should tell us in this life whatever exists now, or will exist in the future, is not permanent but temporary. The good news is, no matter how dismal our current situation or outlook, we are assured by God, "This, too, shall pass."

Life is a continual process in which everything is constantly changing. If we can grasp that truth, it will help us make it through the difficult times in which we find ourselves. It will also help us not to hold on too tightly to the good times, thinking, *If I ever lose all this, I just can't make it.*

God wants us to enjoy all of life—not just its destination but also the trip itself.

Faith as a Channel, Not a Source

My help comes from the Lord, Who made heaven and earth. —PSALM 121:2

We need to know about faith. Faith is a wonderful thing. The Bible says that without faith it is impossible to please God (SEE HEBREWS 11:6). The reason it is so important and so vital is because it is the means through which we receive from God all the good things He wants to provide us. That is why the Lord trains His people in faith. He wants them to get their eyes on Him and learn to believe Him so He can do for and through them what He wants done in the earth. The same is true of prayer, praise, meditation, Bible study, confession, spiritual warfare, and all the other precepts we have been hearing about and engaging in.

But in all our spiritual activity, we must be careful that we don't start worshiping—adhering to, trusting in, and relying on—these things instead of the Lord Himself. It is possible to worship our prayer time, our Bible study, our confession, our meditation, our praise, our good works. *It is possible to develop faith in our faith rather than faith in our God.* It is almost frightening because there is such a fine line between the two. But the thing we must remember is that as good as all these things are, they are only channels to receiving from the Lord.

God Chooses the Unlikely

> *God selected (deliberately chose) what in the world is foolish to put the wise to shame, and what the world calls weak to put the strong to shame. And God also selected (deliberately chose) what in the world is lowborn and insignificant and branded and treated with contempt, even the things that are nothing, that He might depose and bring to nothing the things that are, so that no mortal man should [have pretense for glorying and] boast in the presence of God.*
>
> —I CORINTHIANS 1:27-29

God purposely chooses those who are the most unlikely candidates for the job. By doing so, He has a wide-open door to show His grace, mercy, and power to change human lives. When God uses someone like me or many others He is using, we realize that our source is not in ourselves but in Him alone: "[This is] because the foolish thing [that has its source in] God is wiser than men, and the weak thing [that springs] from God is stronger than men." (I CORINTHIANS 1:25) Each of us has a destiny, and there is absolutely no excuse not to fulfill it. We cannot use our weakness as an excuse, because God says that His strength is made perfect in weakness (SEE 2 CORINTHIANS 12:9). We cannot use the past as an excuse, because God tells us through the apostle Paul that if any person is in Christ, he is a new creature, old things have passed away, and all things have become new (SEE 2 CORINTHIANS 5:17).

How God sees us is not the problem. It is how we see ourselves that keeps us from succeeding. Each of us can succeed at being everything God intends us to be.

Believers Are Achievers

Stop toiling and doing and producing for the food that perishes and decomposes [in the using], but strive and work and produce rather for the [lasting] food which endures [continually] unto life eternal; the Son of Man will give (furnish) you that, for God the Father has authorized and certified Him and put His seal of endorsement upon Him. They then said, What are we to do, that we may [habitually] be working the works of God? [What are we to do to carry out what God requires?] Jesus replied, This is the work (service) that God asks of you: that you believe in the One Whom He has sent [that you cleave to, trust, rely on, and have faith in His Messenger].

—JOHN 6:27-29

I cannot tell you how many times I have said to the Lord, "Father, what do You want me to do? If You will just show me, I'll do it."

I was a doer. All anybody had to do was to show me what needed to be done, and I did it—and I did it right. But what frustrated and confused me was when I did something right and it still didn't work.

"What must we do to work the works of God?" these people wanted to know. Nobody had told them to work the works of God; that was their idea. God is big enough to work His own works. That is the way we are. We hear about the mighty works of God, and immediately our reaction is, "Lord, just show me what I can do to work those works." What was Jesus' answer to these people? "This is the work that God requires of you, that you *believe*."

Now when the Lord first revealed this passage to me, I thought He was going to show me what to do to finally be successful in doing His works. And in a sense He did. He told me, "Believe."

"You mean that's it?" I asked.

"Yes," He answered, "that's it."

You and I think we are supposed to be achievers, and we are. But the way we achieve is to believe.

He Increases Your Strength

> *He gives power to the faint and weary, and to him who has no might*
> *He increases strength [causing it to multiply and making it to abound].*
>
> —ISAIAH 40:29

When we are tired, the Lord can strengthen and refresh us. He will refresh our body and soul.

I remember times when I would minister to a very long prayer line, and I could feel myself just starting to cave in physically and even mentally. I would stop for a second and inside I would say, "Lord, I need help here—I need You to refresh me." And as the scripture above promises, He increased my strength, causing it to multiply and abound.

If you are sitting at your desk or cleaning your house, if you have worked all day then need to go home and cut the grass or change the oil in the car, the Lord can refresh you. Lean back for a minute and let Him give you that power. "Have you not known? Have you not heard? The everlasting God, the Lord, the Creator of the ends of the earth, does not faint or grow weary; there is no searching of His understanding. He gives power to the faint and weary, and to him who has no might He increases strength [causing it to multiply and making it to abound]." (ISAIAH 40:28-29)

It's Time to Declare New Things

*Behold, the former things have come to pass, and new things
I now declare; before they spring forth I tell you of them.*

—ISAIAH 42:9

Here in this confirming verse in which God speaks to His people Israel, we see that the Lord declares new things before they happen. If you are like me, I am sure you are ready and waiting for some new things in your life. You need some changes, and reading this book is God's will and timing for you. Even though I know these principles, I, too, need to be reminded of them occasionally. Sometimes we all need to be "stirred up" in things we already know. It encourages us to begin operating once again in powerful principles that we have let slip away.

If you are tired of the old things, then stop speaking the old things. Do you want some new things? Then start speaking some new things. Spend some time with God. Set aside some special time to study His Word. Find out what His will is for your life. Don't let the devil push you around anymore. *Don't be the devil's mouthpiece.* Find out what God's Word promises you and begin to declare the end from the beginning. Instead of saying, "Nothing will ever change," say, "Changes are taking place in my life and circumstances every day."

I heard the story of a doctor who was not a believer but who had discovered the power of the principle I am sharing with you. His prescription to his patients was to go home and repeat several times daily: "I am getting better and better every day." He had such marvelous results that people traveled from all over the world to avail themselves of his services. Amazing! God said it first, and a man gets the credit. **Do it God's way!** Jesus said, "I am the way, follow Me" (SEE JOHN 12:26; 14:6). We never see Jesus being negative or speaking negatively. You and I should follow His example. Say about your situation what you believe Jesus would say, and you will open the door for the miracle-working power of God.

Pressing On

> *Not that I have now attained [this ideal], or have already been made*
> *perfect, but I press on to lay hold of (grasp) and make my own, that for which*
> *Christ Jesus (the Messiah) has laid hold of me and made me His own.*
>
> —PHILIPPIANS 3:12

In the next verse, Paul goes on to say that he forgot what lay behind and strained forward to what lay ahead. We see this principle in many places in God's holy Word. The prophet Isaiah had the same revelation when he brought forth the message of the Lord, "Do not [earnestly] remember the former things; neither consider the things of old. Behold, I am doing a new thing!" (ISAIAH 43:18-19).

Almost every one of us could use some improvement in our self image. It takes time to grasp the hope for ourselves that God has for us. To realize how much hope God has for me, all I need to do is remember what I was like when God called me into full-time ministry. I certainly was not the kind of material the world would have picked to be doing what I am doing today. As a matter of fact, I firmly believe most people would have given up on me.

It is so wonderful and comforting to know that when everyone else only sees our faults, God still sees our possibilities. The Lord did not wait for me to get all fixed up before He got involved with me. He started with me where I was then and has been responsible for getting me to where I am today. I am convinced He will do the same for you.

Watch Your Countenance

> *And the Lord said to Moses, Say to Aaron and his sons, This is the way*
> *you shall bless the Israelites. Say to them, The Lord bless you and watch,*
> *guard, and keep you; The Lord make His face to shine upon and enlighten you*
> *and be gracious (kind, merciful, and giving favor) to you; The Lord lift up His*
> *[approving] countenance upon you and give you peace (tranquility of heart*
> *and life continually).*
>
> —NUMBERS 6:22-26

Jesus' countenance was changed on the mountain as He was transfigured. Our countenance is simply the way we look. It refers to our face. In the church today, we need to be concerned about our countenance. One of the blessings that was pronounced upon God's people was that God's face would shine upon them and that He would lift up His countenance upon them.

When the world looks at us, they need to see something about us that is different from them. They can't read our minds or see into our hearts, so our countenance is the only way we can show them that we have something they do not have but really want and need. I believe we look better when we worship God. Worship puts a smile on our face. It is very hard to keep a scowl on our face while we are being thankful, praising, and worshiping God.

If we regularly do these things, our countenance will carry His presence, not the expression of inner frustration and turmoil. Christians are supposed to be joyful people who walk in love. We must ask ourselves, "Would people know that I am a Christian by looking at my countenance most of the time?"

Let God Build Your Reputation

Now am I trying to win the favor of men, or of God? Do I seek to please men? If I were still seeking popularity with men, I should not be a bond servant of Christ (the Messiah).

—GALATIANS 1:10

The apostle Paul said that in his ministry he had to choose between pleasing men and pleasing God. That is a choice each of us must make. In Philippians 2:7, we read that Jesus made Himself of "no reputation." Our Lord did not set out to make a name for Himself, and neither should we.

The Lord once commanded me, "Tell My people to stop trying to build their own reputations, and let Me do it for them." If it is our goal to build a name for ourselves, it will cause us to live in fear of man rather than in fear of God. We will try to win favor with people rather than with the Lord.

There is nothing the devil uses more to keep people out of the will of God than the threat of rejection. In my own case, when I made a full commitment to follow the will of God for my life, many of my former friends abandoned me and some even turned against me. Like Paul, I soon learned I had to choose between pleasing people and pleasing God. If I had chosen to be popular with people, I would not be standing in the place of ministry I occupy today.

Today you and I are faced with a decision. Are we going to go on trying to build ourselves, our ministries, and our reputations, or are we willing to give up all our own human efforts and simply trust God?

The Keeping Power of God

For He will give His angels [especial] charge over you to accompany and defend and preserve you in all your ways [of obedience and service].

—PSALM 91:11

A lady who works for me says that she doesn't have a "big" testimony. She just grew up in the church, loving God. She got married, was filled with the Holy Spirit, then came to work for us. Through our ministry, she was moved by the testimonies of drug addicts and people who have suffered abuse. One day she asked God, "Lord, why don't I have a testimony?"

He said, "You do have a testimony. Your testimony is that I kept you from all of it." God had kept her from the pain that results from being separated from Him. The keeping power of God is a great testimony! Psalm 91 teaches that He will give His angels charge over us, and they will protect and defend us.

It's true that a few things happen in our lives that we don't like, but what has God kept us from that we never even knew Satan had planned against us? I marvel at the fact that we can drive in traffic and stay alive. We need to thank God for His keeping power. We can relax knowing that He is our Keeper. Daily, God protects us and keeps us from the power of the enemy. We are sealed in the Holy Spirit and preserved for the final day of redemption when Jesus will return.

God's Boundaries

Do you not know that your body is the temple (the very sanctuary)
of the Holy Spirit Who lives within you, Whom you have received [as a Gift]
from God? You are not your own, You were bought with a price [purchased with
a preciousness and paid for, made His own]. So then, honor God
and bring glory to Him in your body.

—1 CORINTHIANS 6:19-20

The word *stress* was originally an engineering term used to refer to the amount of force a beam or other physical support could bear without collapsing under the strain.

In our time, the word has been expanded to refer not only to physical pressure but also to mental and emotional tension. As human beings, you and I are built to handle a normal amount of stress. God has created us to withstand a certain amount of pressure and tension. The problem comes when we push ourselves beyond our limitations, beyond what we were intended to bear without permanent damage. But like so many people, because I have things to do, I just keep pushing myself even though it is causing me physical damage.

Of course, when sickness tries to come on Dave or me, we immediately pray for healing. But if you become sick as a result of running your body down by pushing it beyond the limits God set for you to operate in good health, you need rest as well as prayer to restore your health. The boundaries He has set for us are for our own good.

God's Good Plan for Your Life

For we are God's [own] handiwork (His workmanship), recreated in Christ Jesus, [born anew] that we may do those good works which God predestined (planned beforehand) for us [taking paths which He prepared ahead of time], that we should walk in them [living the good life which He prearranged and made ready for us to live].

—EPHESIANS 2:10

Since before we were born, God has had a unique plan for each of us. It is not a plan of failure, misery, poverty, sickness, and disease. God's plan is a good plan, a plan for life and health, happiness, and fulfillment. In Jeremiah 29:11 we read, "For I know the thoughts and plans that I have for you, says the Lord, thoughts and plans for welfare and peace and not for evil, to give you hope in your final outcome."

It would benefit every one of us if we would say to ourselves several times a day, "God has a good plan for my life." Each of us needs to be firmly convinced of that truth to keep us from being affected by our changing circumstances and emotions. You may be asking, "If God has such a wonderful plan for my life, why am I not living in it?" I understand why you would ask that question. It does seem strange that if God loves us so much and has such good plans for us, we should have to suffer and go through pain.

What you must remember is that we have an enemy who is out to destroy God's wonderful plan. Although God had a good plan for my life, I ended up in an abusive environment because the devil came and disrupted that good plan. But there is something else, something really awesome about God, we need to understand. God doesn't like it when someone hurts us and tries to undermine His plan for us. While He is making us lie down in green pastures to restore our soul (SEE PSALM 23:2-3), He is getting up to do something about our situation!

It should be a great comfort to us to know that what we cannot do for ourselves, the Lord will do for us—if we will trust ourselves to Him.

Pray and Obey

Sacrifice and offering You do not desire, nor have You delight in them; You have given me the capacity to hear and obey [Your law, a more valuable service than] burnt offerings and sin offerings [which] You do not require.

—PSALM 40:6

God delights in our obedience. Naturally, it doesn't do God any good to talk to us if we aren't going to listen and obey.

For many years, I wanted God to talk to me, but I wanted to pick and choose what to obey. I wanted to do what He said if I thought it was a good idea. If I didn't like what I was hearing, then I would act like it wasn't from God. God has given us the capacity both to hear Him and to obey Him. He does not require a higher sacrifice than obedience. Some of what God says to you will be exciting. Some things God tells you might not be so thrilling to hear. But that doesn't mean that what He tells you won't work out for good if you will just do it His way. If you want God's will for your life, I can tell you the recipe in its simplest form: *Pray and obey.* God has given you the capacity to do both.

But God . . .

But God shows and clearly proves His [own] love for us by the fact that while we were still sinners, Christ (the Messiah, the Anointed One) died for us.

—ROMANS 5:8

There is a little phrase in the Bible that I get excited about every time I come across it. It is just two little words, but it is found throughout the Bible and is probably one of the most powerful two-word phrases in it. It is simply this: **But God** . . .

As we go through the Bible, we constantly read disastrous reports of the terrible things the devil had planned for God's people. Then we come to this little phrase, **But God** . . . , and the next thing we read about is a victory. In the above scripture, the fact is mentioned that we are all sinners, a condition that deserves punishment and death. The phrase **But God** . . . interrupts the process. God's love is brought into the situation and changes everything.

While we were sinners, Christ died for us and, by doing so, proved His love for us. He proved that His love interrupts the devastation of sin. When God called me into the ministry, people told me, "Joyce, a group of us have been talking, and we feel that there is no way you are ever going to be able to do what you say God has told you that you are going to do. We don't feel your personality is suitable for such a job." I still remember how awful I felt when they said those things to me.

I was hurt and discouraged . . . **But God** had called me, and He qualified me. What others thought was not even usable, God saw value in. He helped me, and He will do the same thing for you.

Love Aggressively

This is My commandment: that you love one another [just]
as I have loved you. No one has greater love [no one has shown stronger
affection] than to lay down (give up) his own life for his friends.

—JOHN 15:12-13

As the children of God, we must love others as God loves us. And that means aggressively—and sacrificially.

Love is an effort. We will never love anybody if we are not willing to pay the price.

One time I gave a woman a nice pair of earrings. My flesh wanted to keep them for myself, but my spirit said to be obedient to the Lord and give them away.

Later that woman stood up in a meeting and told how she had been given the earrings she was wearing as "a free gift."

The Lord spoke to me and said, "Yes, it was a free gift to her, but it cost you, just as salvation is a free gift to you but it cost Jesus His life."

Love is the greatest gift of all. When you show forth the love of God, do it freely, sacrificially—and aggressively!

Know What Your *Peace Stealers* Are

Seek, inquire for, and crave peace and pursue (go after) it!

—PSALM 34:14

To enjoy a life of peace, you will need to examine your own life to learn what your "peace stealers" are. Satan uses some of the same things on everyone, but we also have things that are particular to each one of us. For example, one person may be very disturbed by having to do two things at one time, while another person may actually be challenged and energized by multitasking and doing several projects at once. We are all different, and we must learn to know ourselves.

My husband is not the least bit concerned about hearing that someone is talking unkindly about him, but he is easily disturbed when a driver does not stay in his lane of traffic or cuts in front of us. I am just the opposite. Although I do not appreciate unsafe driving, it does not disturb me as much as hearing I am being accused unjustly. When our children are going through hard things, Dave says it is good for them and will help build their character; on the other hand, I want to rescue them.

Since we are all different, Satan uses different things on each of us, and he usually has studied us long enough to know exactly what buttons to push at what time. I can endure things better when I am not tired, and the devil knows this, so he waits to attack until I am worn out. I learned by pursuing peace what Satan already knew about me, and now I try not to get overly tired because I know I am opening a door for Satan when I do. It will be virtually impossible to enjoy a life of peace if you don't study to know what your peace stealers are. Keep a list of each time you get upset. Ask yourself what caused the problem, and write it down. Be honest with yourself, or you will never break free.

Your Worth Is Based on the Blood

To Him Who ever loves us and has once [for all]
loosed and freed us from our sins by His own blood.

—REVELATION 1:5

We need to come to the place where we are secure enough in who we are in Christ that we will not allow our sense of worth to be based on the opinions or actions of others.

Don't try to find your worth in how you look. Don't try to find your worth in what you do. Don't try to find your worth in how other people treat you. You are worth something because Jesus shed His blood for you.

You may have faults, and there may be things about you that need to be changed, but God is working on you the same as He is on everybody else. Don't let somebody else dump their problems off on you. Don't allow someone else to make you feel worthless or useless just because they don't know how to treat you right and love you as you deserve to be loved as a blood-bought child of God.

Don't spend all your life trying to win somebody else's acceptance or approval. Remember that you have already been accepted and approved by God. Make sure your affirmation, your validation, and your sense of self-worth come from Him.

Only God Can Satisfy

One thing have I asked of the Lord, that will I seek, inquire for, and [insistently] require: that I may dwell in the house of the Lord [in His presence] all the days of my life.

—PSALM 27:4

I went to church for years without knowing the importance of spending regular fellowship time with the Lord. I was really doing all that I knew to do at the time, but it wasn't enough to satisfy my longing for God. I could have spent every moment in church or in Bible study, but it wouldn't have quenched the thirst I had for a deeper fellowship with the Lord. I needed to talk to Him about my past and hear Him talk to me about my future. But nobody taught me that God wanted to talk directly to me. No one offered a solution for the dissatisfied feelings I endured.

Through reading the Word, I learned that God does want to talk to us and that He has a plan for our lives that will lead us to a place of peace and contentment. Isaiah expressed well our own hunger for God when he wrote, "My soul yearns for You [O Lord] in the night, yes, my spirit within me seeks You earnestly." (ISAIAH 26:9) Nothing can satisfy our longing for God, except communion and fellowship with Him.

Conviction vs. Condemnation

And when He comes, He will convict and convince the world and bring demonstration to it about sin and about righteousness (uprightness of heart and right standing with God) and about judgment.

—JOHN 16:8

Often when we are convicted of sin, we become grouchy while God is dealing with us. Until we admit our sin, become ready to turn from it, and ask for forgiveness, we feel a pressure that squeezes out the worst we have in us. As soon as we come into agreement with God, our peace returns, and our behavior improves.

The devil knows that condemnation and shame keep us from approaching God in prayer so our needs can be met and we can once again enjoy fellowship with God. Feeling bad about ourselves or thinking that God is angry with us separates us from His presence. He doesn't leave us, but in fear we withdraw from Him.

That's why it is so important to discern the truth and know the difference between conviction and condemnation. Remember, if you heed conviction, it lifts you up and out of sin. Condemnation only makes you feel bad about yourself.

When praying, ask regularly for God to convict you of your own sin, realizing that conviction is a blessing, not a problem. If only perfect people could pray and receive answers, nobody would be praying. We don't need to be perfect, but we do need to be cleansed of sin. As I begin my prayer time I almost always ask my heavenly Father to cleanse me of all sin and unrighteousness. When we pray in Jesus' name, we are presenting to our Father all that Jesus is, not all that we are.

An Open Heart

One of those who listened to us was a woman named Lydia, from the city of Thyatira, a dealer in fabrics dyed in purple. She was [already] a worshiper of God, and the Lord opened her heart to pay attention to what was said by Paul.

—ACTS 16:14

In the city of Philippi, to which God had directed Paul and those traveling with him, there was a group of women who gathered together on the bank of a river for prayer. Paul began to speak to these women, telling them some things they had never heard before. They were used to living under the Jewish Law, and Paul was delivering a message of grace. One of the women named Lydia had an open heart to receive what Paul had to say.

The reason an open heart is so important is that without it, we won't listen to anything new or different. It is amazing the things in the Bible we will refuse to believe because they are not part of what we have been taught in the past. Why can't our believing be progressive? Why can't we accept that there may be a few things we don't know? That doesn't mean we should be so open that we believe anything the devil wants to dump on us, but it does mean that we should not be so narrow-minded that nobody can teach us anything new.

We should not be afraid to listen to what is being said and check it out for ourselves by reading the Bible and talking to God about it to see if it is really true. I get concerned about people who think there is only one way to do things, and it is their way. We must have an open heart. It will tell us when what we are hearing is true.

Enjoy Yourself

*I came that they may have and enjoy life, and have
it in abundance (to the full, till it overflows).*

—JOHN 10:10

When I was growing up, I did not enjoy myself. I was never really allowed to act like a child. I can remember getting into trouble and being corrected for playing. Our house was not enjoyable. It was filled with fear. As an adult Christian, I began to realize I felt guilty if I attempted to enjoy myself. I felt safe if I was working, but enjoyment was something I denied myself. I did not feel it was a legitimate need for me. I resented other people who were not working as long and hard as I was.

My husband really enjoyed his life, and it made me angry. I felt he could accomplish so much more in life if he would just be more serious. I realize now I was not angry because Dave enjoyed his life; I was angry because I did not enjoy mine. It was foolish of me to resent Dave and other people, because the enjoyment they had in life was also available to me for the taking.

I did not like myself. Deep down inside I believed I was no good, and I punished myself for being bad by refusing to enjoy anything. After all, bad people don't deserve to enjoy life! The Holy Spirit worked with me a long time before I finally understood God wanted me to enjoy my life. Jesus actually said, "I came that you might have and enjoy your life" (SEE JOHN 10:10).

We need enjoyment. Without it, life is unbalanced, and a door is opened for Satan to devour us (SEE 1 PETER 5:8). The joy of the Lord is our strength (SEE NEHEMIAH 8:10). There is a time to work and a time to play, a time to cry and a time to laugh (SEE ECCLESIASTES 3:1-8). Make sure you are not denying your legitimate needs. It is good to help others; as Christians, it is our call. But it is not wrong to do things for ourselves. Be sure you take time for yourself. Take time to do things you enjoy.

Doing Things God's Way

I am the Way. —JOHN 14:6

Many people are hurting so badly, and they are crying out for help. The problem is, they are not willing to receive the help they need from God. No matter how much we may want or need help, we are never going to receive it until we are willing to do things God's way. In John 14:6, Jesus said, "I am the Way." What Jesus meant when He said, "I am the Way," is that He has a certain way of doing things; and if we will submit to *His* way, everything will work out for us.

But so often we wrestle and struggle with Him, trying to get Him to do things our way. It just won't work. Countless times have people stood in front of me at the altar and told me all kinds of terrible things that are going on in their lives and how badly they are hurting, yet they absolutely refuse to do what they are told to do to receive the help they need. Too often people are trying to find some other way to get help rather than by doing things God's way.

The Bible plainly teaches that if we will learn and act on the Word, God will bless our lives. Let me give you an example. The Bible teaches that we are to live in harmony and peace with others and to forgive those who have done us wrong. If we refuse to do that, what hope do we have of receiving what we need?

I remember how difficult it was for me the first time the Lord told me I had to go to my husband and tell him I was sorry for being rebellious against him. I thought I would die on the spot! I realize that one reason we don't always do what we are told to do in the Word of God is because it is hard.

If we don't do what we can do, then God won't do what we can't do. If we will do what we can do, God will do what we can't do. It's just that simple.

Obey the Word

But be doers of the Word [obey the message], and not merely listeners to it, betraying yourselves [into deception by reasoning contrary to the Truth].

—JAMES 1:22

A woman who attended one of my seminars had a lot of emotional wounds that left her insecure and fearful. She desperately wanted to be free, but nothing seemed to work. At the conclusion of the seminar she told me that she now understood why she had never experienced any progress. She said, "Joyce, I sat with a group of ladies who all had a lot of the same problems that I did. Step-by-step God had been delivering them. As I listened to them, I heard them say, 'God led me to do this, and I did it. Then He led me to another thing, and I did it.' I realized that God had also told me to do the same things. The only difference was they did what He said to do, and I didn't."

To receive from God what He has promised us in His Word, we must obey the Word. There will be times when doing what the Word says is not easy. Obeying the Word requires consistency and diligence. There must be a dedication and commitment to do the Word whatever the outcome. "Yes," you may say, "but I have been doing the Word for a long time, and I still don't have the victory!" Then do it some more. Nobody knows exactly how long it is going to take for the Word to begin to work in this life. If you keep at it, sooner or later it will work.

I know it's a fight. I know Satan tries to keep you out of the Word; and once you do get into the Word, he tries everything in his power to keep you from putting the Word into practice in your life. I also know that once you do start putting the Word into practice, he does everything he can to make you think it won't work. That's why you must keep at it. Ask God to help by giving you a desire to get into His Word and to do it no matter how hard it is or how long it takes to produce any results in your life.

Do You Want to Get Well?

> *There was a certain man there who had suffered with a deep-seated*
> *and lingering disorder for thirty-eight years. When Jesus noticed him lying*
> *there [helpless], knowing that he had already been a long time in that*
> *condition, He said to him, Do you want to become well? [Are you really in*
> *earnest about getting well?]*
>
> —JOHN 5:5-6

Isn't this an amazing question for Jesus to ask this poor man who had been sick for thirty-eight long years: "Do you want to become well?" That is the Lord's question to you as you read these words right now. Do you know there are people who really don't want to get well? They just want to talk about their problem. Are you one of those people?

Sometimes people get addicted to having a problem. It becomes their identity, their life. It defines everything they think and say and do. If you have a "deep-seated and lingering disorder," the Lord wants you to know that it does not have to be the central focal point of your entire existence. He wants you to trust Him and cooperate with Him as He leads you to victory over that problem one step at a time. Don't try to use your problem as a means of getting sympathy.

When I used to complain to my husband, he would tell me, "Joyce, I'm not going to feel sorry for you, because if I do, you will never get over your problems." That used to make me so mad I could have beaten him to a pulp. We get angry at those who tell us the truth. And the truth is that before we can get well, we must really *want* to be well—body, soul, and spirit. We must want to enough that we are willing to hear and accept truth.

Each of us must learn to follow God's personal plan for us. Whatever our problem may be, God has promised to meet our need and to repay us for our loss. Facing truth is the key to unlocking prison doors that may have held us in bondage.

Choosing Approval from God

Then Peter and the apostles replied, We must obey God rather than men.

—ACTS 5:29

Any of us who intend to do very much in life will have to accept the fact that there will be times when we will not receive approval from everyone. The need to be popular will steal our destiny. I deal with and minister to a wide variety of people. There is no way humanly possible that I can please all of them all the time. We have more than five hundred employees at Joyce Meyer Ministries. We almost never make one decision that suits all of them.

The Bible says Jesus made Himself of "no reputation" (SEE PHILIPPIANS 2:7). That is a significant statement. He was not well thought of by many people; but His heavenly Father approved of Him and what He was doing, and that was all that really mattered to Him. As long as you and I have God's approval, we have what we need most. In the Philippians passage, the apostle Paul is saying that if he had been trying to be popular with people, he would not have been a servant of the Lord Jesus Christ. He says that needing people's approval in an unbalanced way can steal our destiny.

We cannot always be God-pleasers and people-pleasers at the same time.

Keeping Your Mind on Track

Keep your foot [give your mind to what you are doing].

—ECCLESIASTES 5:1

I believe the expression "keep your foot" means "don't lose your balance or get off track." The amplification of this phrase indicates that one stays on track by keeping his mind on what he is doing. I had a wandering mind and had to train it by discipline. Sometimes I still have a relapse.

While trying to complete some project, I will suddenly realize that my mind has just wandered off onto something else that has nothing to do with the issue at hand. I have not yet arrived at a place of perfect concentration, but at least I understand how important it is not to allow my mind to go wherever it wishes, whenever it desires.

If you are like me, you can be sitting in a church service listening to the speaker, really enjoying and benefiting from what is being said, when suddenly your mind begins to wander. After a while you "wake up" to find that you don't remember a thing that has been going on. Even though your body stayed in church, your mind has been at the shopping center browsing through the stores or home in the kitchen cooking dinner.

Remember, in spiritual warfare the mind is the battlefield. That is where the enemy makes his attack. He knows very well that even though a person attends church, if he can't keep his mind on what is being taught, he will gain absolutely nothing by being there. The devil knows that a person cannot discipline himself to complete a project if he cannot discipline his mind and keep it on what he is doing.

Remember, Satan wants you to think that you are mentally deficient— that something is wrong with you. But the truth is, you just need to begin disciplining your mind. Don't let it run all over town, doing whatever it pleases. Begin today to "keep your foot," to keep your mind on what you're doing. You will need to practice for a while. Breaking old habits and forming new ones always takes time, but it is worth it in the end.

God Will Do the Impossible

And Jesus said, [You say to Me], If You can do anything? [Why,]
all things can be (are possible) to him who believes!

—MARK 9:23

It is impossible for me to be doing what I am doing today. When God called me into ministry, to say I was a mess does not even begin to describe it. But I loved God, and I did not want to continue being the way I was. I just did not know how to change the way I was and be different and better. It took years for God to get me where He needed me to be, but I believe that He is doing a quicker work of righteousness in these last days.

You may feel the way Martha felt when her brother Lazarus died. She said to Jesus, "Master, if You had been here, my brother would not have died." (JOHN 11:21) Jesus could have arrived on the scene sooner, but the Bible says that He purposely waited until Lazarus was dead and laid in the grave. He waited until the situation was so impossible that if anything good came of it, everybody would know that it had to be a work of God (SEE JOHN 11:1-45).

We need to understand that when God does not move in our circumstances or when He does not move as quickly as we would like for Him to move, He may be waiting on purpose. Just when we think there is no way out of our mess, God will prove to us how strong and wonderful He is on our behalf (SEE 2 CHRONICLES 16:9).

I had been trying to serve God for years. Why did He wait so long to touch me with the power of the Holy Ghost? Why didn't He do it two years before? Four years before? I think He was just waiting until it would take a miracle to prove that He was working in my life. The fact that God could use my life for ministry is a miracle in itself.

Turn and Face the Truth

Have mercy upon me, O God, according to Your steadfast love; according to the multitude of Your tender mercy and loving-kindness blot out my transgressions. Wash me thoroughly [and repeatedly] from my iniquity and guilt and cleanse me and make me wholly pure from my sin! For I am conscious of my transgressions and I acknowledge them; my sin is ever before me. Against You, You only, have I sinned and done that which is evil in Your sight, so that You are justified in Your sentence and faultless in Your judgment. Behold, I was brought forth in [a state of] iniquity; my mother was sinful who conceived me [and I too am sinful]. Behold, You desire truth in the inner being; make me therefore to know wisdom in my inmost heart.

—PSALM 51:1-6

In Psalm 51, King David was crying out to God for mercy and forgiveness because the Lord had been dealing with him about his sin with Bathsheba and the murder of her husband. Believe it or not, David's sin had occurred one full year prior to the writing of this psalm, but he had never really faced it and acknowledged it. He was not facing truth; and as long as he refused to face truth, he could not truly repent. And as long as he could not truly repent, God could not forgive him. Verse 6 of this passage is a powerful scripture. It says that God desires truth "in the inner being." That means if we want to receive God's blessings, we must be honest with Him about ourselves and our sins.

Our Confidence Is in Jesus

I have strength for all things in Christ Who empowers me
[I am ready for anything and equal to anything through Him Who infuses
inner strength into me; I am self-sufficient in Christ's sufficiency].

—PHILIPPIANS 4:13

Satan does not want you to fulfill God's plan for your life because he knows that you are part of his ultimate defeat. If he can make you think and believe that you are incapable, then you will not even try to accomplish anything worthwhile. Even if you do make an effort, your fear of failure will seal your defeat, which, because of your lack of confidence, you probably expected from the beginning. This is what is often referred to as the "failure syndrome." The devil wants you and me to feel so bad about ourselves that we have no confidence in ourselves.

But here is the good news: *We do not need confidence in ourselves—we need confidence in Jesus!* I have confidence in myself only because I know that Christ is in me, ever present and ready to help me with everything that I attempt to do for Him. A believer without confidence is like a jumbo jet parked on the runway with no fuel; it looks good on the outside but has no power on the inside. With Jesus inside us, we have the power to do what we could never do on our own.

Once you learn this truth, when the devil lies and says, "You can't do anything right," your response to him can be, "Perhaps not, but Jesus in me can; and He will, because I am relying on Him and not on myself. He will cause me to succeed in everything that I put my hand to" (SEE JOSHUA 1:7). Or should the enemy say to you, "You're not able to do this, so don't even try, because you will only fail again, just as you have in the past," your response can be, "It is true that without Jesus I am not able to do one single thing, but with Him and in Him I can do all that I need to do" (SEE PHILIPPIANS 4:13).

Stay Focused

Wherefore seeing we also are compassed about with so great a cloud of witnesses, let us lay aside every weight, and the sin which doth so easily beset us, and let us run with patience the race that is set before us.

—HEBREWS 12:1 (KJV)

In the days when this verse was written, the writer was drawing a parallel that was much better understood than it is today. In those days, runners conditioned their bodies for a race just as we do today. But at the time of the race, they stripped off their clothing so that when they ran there would be nothing to hinder them. They also oiled their bodies with fine oils. In the same way, we need to be well oiled or anointed with the Holy Spirit if we are going to win our race. We also need to remove anything from our lives that would hinder us in running the race set before us. There are many different hindrances to running a race.

Too many commitments will keep us from developing our potential. Letting other people control us will keep us from developing our potential. Not knowing how to say no will keep us from developing our potential. Getting overly involved in someone else's goals and vision or becoming entangled in someone else's problems instead of keeping our eyes on our own goals will keep us from fulfilling our potential.

If we are going to do what God has called us to do, we are going to have to stay focused; because the world we live in is filled with distractions and entanglements. We try to read our Bible, and somebody stops by. We try to pray, and the phone rings. There is distraction after distraction. Sooner or later we have to learn to say no. We have to be determined that nothing is going to hinder us from fulfilling God's plan and purpose for us.

Seeking God's Face

You have said, Seek My face [inquire for and require My presence as your vital need]. My heart says to You, Your face (Your presence), Lord, will I seek.

—PSALM 27:8

It is a sign of maturity to seek God for who He is, not just for what He can do for us. If my husband returned from a long trip away from home, I would meet him at the airport thrilled to see *him*. Because I care about him, he delights in giving me things to show me his love. However, if I met him at the airport excited—not over his being home, but over finding out what *gift* he had brought me—he might be hurt and offended. I have found that when I seek God's face (His presence) to get to know my wonderful, loving heavenly Father better, His hand is always open to me.

We need to seek after one thing, and one thing only, and that is to dwell in God's presence, because only there can we experience the fullness of joy (SEE PSALM 16:11; 27:4).

Peace Is the "Umpire"

> *And let the peace (soul harmony which comes) from Christ rule (act as umpire continually) in your hearts [deciding and settling with finality all questions that arise in your minds, in that peaceful state] to which as [members of Christ's] one body you were also called [to live].*
>
> —COLOSSIANS 3:15

Peace is our inheritance from Jesus, but we have to choose to follow Him daily. Colossians 3:15 teaches us that peace is to be the "umpire" in our lives, settling every issue that needs a decision. To gain and maintain peace in our hearts, we may have to learn to say no to a few things.

For example, if we don't feel peace about something, we should never go ahead and do it. And if we don't have peace *while* we are doing something, then we shouldn't expect to have peace *after* we have done it. Many people marry others they didn't have peace about marrying, and then they wonder why they don't have peace in their marriages. Many people buy expensive items they didn't have peace about buying, then continue to lose their peace every month when they have to make payments on them.

Colossians 3:15 says to let the peace from Christ "rule (act as umpire continually)" in our hearts. The presence of peace helps us decide and settle with finality all questions that arise in our minds. If you let the Word have its home in your heart and mind, it will give you insight *and* intelligence *and* wisdom (SEE v. 16). You won't have to wonder, *Should I or shouldn't I? I don't know if it's right. I don't know what to do.* If you are a disciple of Christ, He has called you to follow peace.

Faith and Grace: Working Together

For it is by free grace (God's unmerited favor) that you are saved (delivered from judgment and made partakers of Christ's salvation) through [your] faith. And this [salvation] is not of yourselves [of your own doing, it came not through your own striving], but it is the gift of God.

—EPHESIANS 2:8

Let me give you an illustration of the way that faith and grace work together to bring us the blessings of God. In my meetings I often take along a large electric fan that I set up on the speaker's platform. I call up a member of the audience and have her stand in front of the fan, telling her that I am going to cool her off. When the fan doesn't run even though I turn it on, I ask the audience, "What's wrong? Why is this fan not running?"

Of course, the audience sees right away what's wrong: "It's not plugged in!" they yell. "That's right," I say, "and that's exactly what's wrong many times when our prayers are not answered." I explain that we get our eyes on faith (the fan), expecting it to do the work, but we fail to look beyond the fan to its source of power, which is the Lord.

Jesus had faith all the time He was suffering. He had faith while in the Garden of Gethsemane. He had faith before the high priest and Pilate. He had faith when He was being ridiculed, abused, and mistreated. He had faith on the way to Golgotha. He had faith while hanging on the cross. He even had faith while His body lay in the tomb; He had absolute faith that God would not leave Him there but would raise Him up, as He had promised. But do you realize that for all His faith, nothing happened until the power of God came forth to bring about the Resurrection?

His faith kept Him stable until the Father's appointed time for His deliverance. We can have all the faith in the world; but it will avail us nothing until it is "plugged in" to the source of power, which is the grace of God. Keep your eyes on God to deliver you—not your faith.

It Is What It Is!

Do not conform any longer to the pattern of this world,
but be transformed by the renewing of your mind.

—ROMANS 12:2 (NIV)

My body is shaped so that I wear a size eight top and a size ten bottom. I have always been that way. There are lots of beautiful suits I can't buy because they don't come in split sizes. I could buy two suits and take what I needed, but then I'd feel like I had to find someone who was a size eight bottom and a size ten top, so I wasn't being wasteful! The whole situation used to frustrate me until I decided, "It is what it is!"

Now I mostly laugh about it—and laughing is a very important habit to have, especially as you age. If your feet are larger than you would like them to be, your body is not proportioned perfectly, or you are shorter than you wish you were, don't ever let it frustrate you. Decide right now, "It is what it is!"

I am going to be happy with what I have been given and do the best I can with it. Never forget that God wants you to love your body and yourself. He *expects* it, no matter what messages the world has given you. As the Bible says, "Do not conform any longer to the pattern of this world, but be transformed by the renewing of your mind." (ROMANS 12:2 NIV) Think about yourself in a new way. Determine to be the best "you" that you can, and stop trying to be what the world says you should be.

The world can tell you lots of things. It whispers untruths in your ear, many of them cruel. It also changes its views and fashions by the month. If you start following its lead, you are lost. Your friendship with yourself will be lost. But instead, if you see yourself as God sees you, then you will not only love yourself but also have the confidence and faith to be a powerful force for good in the world.

Judge Not

Why do you criticize and pass judgment on your brother? Or you, why do you look down upon or despise your brother? For we shall all stand before the judgment seat of God. For it is written, As I live, says the Lord, every knee shall bow to Me, and every tongue shall confess to God [acknowledge Him to His honor and to His praise]. And so each of us shall give an account of himself [give an answer in reference to judgment] to God. Then let us no more criticize and blame and pass judgment on one another, but rather decide and endeavor never to put a stumbling block or an obstacle or a hindrance in the way of a brother.

—ROMANS 14:10-13

When I stand before the judgment seat of God, He is not going to ask me about you, just as He is not going to ask you about me when you appear before Him. God is not going to hold me accountable for anybody else on earth other than Joyce Meyer.

I don't know how much time I have left to work with God to get myself straightened out, but I do want to be able to answer the questions He asks me about me. If I stand before Him and He says, "Joyce, why didn't you pay attention to Me when I was dealing with you about your faults?" I don't want to have to answer, "Well, Lord, I didn't have time because I was too busy working to get my husband, Dave, straightened out."

According to this passage, each of us is going to give an account of our own self to God the Father. That is why we need to learn to work on our own sanctification and quit putting stumbling blocks, obstacles, and hindrances in the way of our brothers and sisters in Christ. We will never all believe exactly alike on everything. That is why we are told to follow our own convictions—and let everyone else do the same.

Melted by Love

Love never fails [never fades out or becomes obsolete or comes to an end].

—1 CORINTHIANS 13:8

The God-kind of love bears up under anything and everything that comes. It endures everything without weakening. It is determined not to give up on even the hardest case. The hard-core individual who persists in being mean can be eventually melted by love.

It is hard to keep showing love to someone who never seems to appreciate it or even respond to it. It is difficult to keep showing love to those individuals who take from us all we are willing to give but who never give anything back. But we are not responsible for how others act, only how we act. Our reward does not come from man but from God. Even when our good deeds seem to go unnoticed, God notices and promises to reward us openly for them: "Your deeds of charity may be in secret; and your Father Who sees in secret will reward you openly." (MATTHEW 6:4)

Love knows that if it refuses to quit, it will ultimately win the victory: "And let us not lose heart and grow weary and faint in acting nobly and doing right, for in due time and at the appointed season we shall reap, if we do not loosen and relax our courage and faint." (GALATIANS 6:9) *Don't, fail to walk in love, because love never fails!*

Trust God More Than Yourself

Believe in the Lord Jesus Christ [give yourself up to Him, take yourself out of your own keeping and entrust yourself into His keeping] and you will be saved.

—ACTS 16:31

This is what Paul and Silas told the Philippian jailer who asked them, "What must I do to be saved?" This is what salvation really means—giving ourselves up to God, taking ourselves out of our own keeping, and entrusting ourselves into His keeping. God wants to take care of us. He can do a much better job of that if we will avoid a problem called independence, which is really self-care.

The desire to take care of ourselves is based on fear. Basically, it stems from the idea that if *we* do it, we can be sure it will be done right. We are afraid of what might happen if we entrust ourselves totally to God and He doesn't "come through" for us. *The root problem of independence is trusting ourselves more than we trust God.*

We love to have a back-up plan. We may pray and ask God to get involved in our lives, but if He is the least bit slow in responding (at least, to our way of thinking), we are quick to take control back into our own hands. What we fail to realize is, God has a plan for us too—and His plan is much better than ours.

God Is Speaking, Are You Listening?

But when He, the Spirit of Truth (the Truth-giving Spirit) comes, He will guide you into all the Truth (the whole, full Truth). For He will not speak His own message [on His own authority]; but He will tell whatever He hears [from the Father; He will give the message that has been given to Him], and He will announce and declare to you the things that are to come [that will happen in the future].

—JOHN 16:13

God's greatest desire for His children is that they experience His best in their lives, and that includes being able to hear clearly from Him in an intimate, personal way.

God longs to have a people who worship Him in Spirit and in truth (SEE JOHN 4:23-24), who follow Him and know His voice (SEE JOHN 10:2-14). The depth of our personal relationship with God is based upon intimate communication with Him. He speaks to us so that we are guided, refreshed, restored, and renewed regularly.

Listening is the first step toward hearing. I encourage you to turn your ear toward Him and be still. He will speak to you and tell you He loves you. God cares about your life and wants to meet your needs and do more than you could ever think or imagine in order to bless you abundantly (SEE EPHESIANS 3:20).

You are one of His sheep, and the sheep know the Shepherd's voice— the voice of a stranger they will not follow. You *can* hear from God; it is part of your inheritance—don't ever believe otherwise! Listen to Him, then follow Him all of the days of your life.

Childlikeness

Just [Jesus] *called a little child to Himself and put him in the midst of them, And said, Truly I say to you, unless you repent (change, turn about) and become like little children [trusting, lowly, loving, forgiving], you can never enter the kingdom of heaven [at all]. Whoever will humble Himself therefore and become like this little child [trusting, lowly, loving, forgiving] is greatest in the kingdom of heaven.*

—MATTHEW 18:2-4

In Luke 18:17 Jesus expressed this same message about the spiritual importance of being childlike when He said, "Truly I say to you, whoever does not accept and receive and welcome the kingdom of God like a little child [does] shall not in any way enter it [at all]." As we see, *The Amplified Bible* translation of Matthew 18:3 states that the defining attributes of a child are: trusting, lowly, loving, and forgiving. Oh, how much more we would enjoy our lives if we operated in those four virtues.

Children believe what they are told. Some people say children are gullible, meaning they believe anything no matter how ridiculous it sounds. But children are not gullible; they are trusting. *It is a child's nature to trust* unless he has experienced something that teaches him otherwise. One thing we all know about children is that they enjoy life. A child can literally enjoy anything. A child can turn work into a game so he is able to enjoy it.

I recall asking my son to sweep the patio when he was about eleven or twelve years old. I looked outside and saw him dancing with the broom to the music playing on the headset he was wearing. I thought, *Amazing! He has turned sweeping into a game. If he had to do it—he was going to enjoy it.* We should all have that attitude. We may not choose to dance with a broom, but we should choose an attitude of enjoying all aspects of life.

Magnify the Lord

O magnify the Lord with me, and let us exalt His name together.

—PSALM 34:3

The word *magnify* means "to enlarge." When we tell God, "I magnify You," we are literally saying, "I make You bigger in my life than any problem or need that I have." I have sung many songs over the years that talked about magnifying the Lord without even realizing what the word meant. We do this a lot. We sing and talk about things we don't even really understand. They are just phrases we have learned in church.

We should magnify the Lord, and that means we should make Him larger than anything else in our life. When we worship and praise Him, we are doing just that. We are saying, "You are so big, so great, that I want to worship You." By putting God first, we are also saying, "You're bigger than any need I have."

Faith Is for the Middle

*And a furious storm of wind [of hurricane proportions] arose, and the
waves kept beating into the boat, so that it was already becoming filled. But
He [Himself] was in the stern [of the boat], asleep on the [leather]
cushion; and they awoke Him and said to Him, Master, do You not
care that we are perishing?*

—MARK 4:37-38

The disciples probably were not nearly as excited in the middle as they
may have been in the beginning. Although God often calls us to launch
out to a new destination, He usually does not let us know what is going to
happen on the way to it. We leave the security of where we are and start
out for the blessings of the other side, but it is often in the middle where
we encounter the storms. *The middle is often a place of testing.* The storm
was in full force, and Jesus was asleep! Does that sound familiar?

Have you ever had times when you felt that you were sinking fast—
and Jesus was asleep? You prayed and prayed and heard nothing from God.
You spent time with Him and tried to sense His Presence, and yet you felt
nothing. You searched for an answer, but no matter how hard you struggled against the wind and waves, the storm raged on—and you didn't
know what to do about it.

This storm the disciples found themselves facing was no little April
shower or harmless summer squall, but *a storm of hurricane proportions.*
The waves were not gently rolling and tossing; they were beating into the
boat with such fury that it was quickly becoming filled up with water. It
is at times like this, when it looks as if the boat is sinking with us in it, that
we must "use" our faith. We can talk about faith, read books about it, hear
sermons about it, sing songs about it; but in the storm, we must *use* it. It is
also at such times when we discover just how much faith we really have.

Letting Go of Offenses

> *[You should] be exceedingly glad on this account, though now for a little while you may be distressed by trials and suffer temptations, so that [the genuineness] of your faith may be tested, [your faith] which is infinitely more precious than the perishable gold which is tested and purified by fire. [This proving of your faith is intended] to redound to [your] praise and glory and honor when Jesus Christ (the Messiah, the Anointed One) is revealed.*
>
> —1 PETER 1:6-7

Understand that every time you are tempted to be offended and upset, your faith is being tried. Peter was saying, "Don't be amazed at the fiery trials that you go through, because they are taking place to test your quality." Every relationship test is an opportunity to glorify the work of God in you as a testimony to those watching you endure the offense.

There is a right and a wrong way to handle the storms of life. But until I was filled with the Holy Spirit and began to learn about the power that is available to me as a believer to do the right thing, I never handled offenses right.

Jesus' economy is upside down from what the world teaches us. He says that we can have peace in the midst of the storm. Now just think about how awesome that would be, if *no matter what happened,* you could remain full of peace.

Jesus said that He gives us power even "to trample upon serpents and scorpions, and [physical and mental strength and ability] over all the power that the enemy [possesses]." (LUKE 10:19) He promised that nothing will harm us in any way. If we have the power over the enemy, surely we can overlook the offenses of others. He gives us the energy we need to treat people right.

There's Joy in Believing

*May the God of your hope so fill you with all joy and peace in
believing [through the experience of your faith] that by the power of the Holy
Spirit you may abound and be overflowing (bubbling over) with hope.*

—ROMANS 15:13

I remember an evening when I was feeling strongly dissatisfied and dis-
contented. I had no peace or joy and was absolutely miserable. I read
Romans 15:13, and it was indeed "a word in season" for me (SEE ISAIAH
50:4). My problem was simple, I was doubting instead of believing. I was
doubting God's unconditional love, doubting that I could hear from Him,
doubting His call on my life, doubting that He was pleased with me. I was
filled with doubt . . . doubt . . . doubt. When I saw the problem, I got
back into faith and out of doubt. My joy and peace returned immediately.

I have found the same thing to be true again and again in my life. When
joy and peace seem to be gone, I check my believing—usually it is gone
also.

The Highest Position of All

> *He who is greatest among you shall be your servant. Whoever exalts*
> *himself [with haughtiness and empty pride] shall be humbled (brought low),*
> *and whoever humbles himself [whoever has a modest opinion of himself*
> *and behaves accordingly] shall be raised to honor.*

—MATTHEW 23:11-12

Jesus was able to wash His disciples' feet because He was free. Only a person who is truly free, one who is not insecure, can do menial tasks and not feel insignificant as a result.

So much of our worth and value is connected to what we do that it makes it very difficult for us to enjoy serving. Serving others is not viewed as a high position, and yet Jesus said it is the highest of all. Serving others also sets them free to love. It disarms even the most hateful individual. It is actually fun to watch that person's amazement when he realizes he is being served through love. If someone knows full well he has done us wrong, and we return his evil with good, it begins to tear down the walls he has built around himself. Sooner or later he will begin to trust us and start learning from us what real love is. That is the whole purpose behind being a servant, to show others the love of God that He has shown us so that they, too, can share in it—and then pass it on.

Depending on Him Alone

Then Jerubbaal, that is, Gideon, and all the people who were with him rose early and encamped beside the spring of Harod; and the camp of Midian was north of them by the hill of Moreh in the valley. The Lord said to Gideon, The people who are with you are too many for Me to give the Midianites into their hands, lest Israel boast about themselves against Me, saying, My own hand has delivered me. So now proclaim in the ears of the men, saying, Whoever is fearful and trembling, let him turn back and depart from Mount Gilead. And 22,000 of the men returned, but 10,000 remained.

—JUDGES 7:1-3

Instead of telling Gideon, who was facing a major battle, that He would give him more men, God told him that he had too many for God to give him the victory. Interestingly enough, sometimes God works through our weaknesses better than through our strengths. There are times when we have too much going for us in the natural for God to give the victory. We are not in line for a miracle if anyone but God can help us. God was telling Gideon that they were too strong in themselves, that He wanted them in a position where they would have to depend entirely on Him. Pride and boasting ruin the best of men so God has to help us stay humble and, under His mighty hand, totally dependent on Him.

Living a Life of Prayer

Be unceasing in prayer [praying perseveringly].

—I THESSALONIANS 5:17

I could not even begin to tell you now how much I pray during any given day. I really don't know. I just talk with God all through the day. I talk to Him when I'm doing my hair. I talk to Him in the middle of the night. I talk to Him about everything. I talk to Him about little things. I talk to Him about big things. And talking to Him always brings joy to my life.

I used to hear about different problems and situations in people's lives and determine that I would remember to pray for them. In a short time, I would accumulate a bunch of things that I needed to pray about. Now, as soon as I hear that someone has a need, I stop and pray right then. Prayer needs to be like breathing—just a natural part of our lives. We are to be constantly in fellowship with God so He can lead us in the way that we should go. This is what Paul meant when he wrote, "Pray without ceasing" (SEE I THESSALONIANS 5:17 NKJV). This doesn't mean we are to go sit in the corner somewhere and not do anything but concentrate on a formalized program of prayer all day long. It simply means that we *live* a life of prayer.

False Evidence Appearing Real

> *The devil . . . was a murderer from the beginning and does not
> stand in the truth, because there is no truth in him. When he speaks a false-
> hood, he speaks what is natural to him, for he is a liar [himself] and the father
> of lies and of all that is false.*
>
> —JOHN 8:44

It is said that the letters in the word *fear* actually stand for *False Evidence
Appearing Real*.

Jesus said the devil is a liar and the father of all lies. The truth is not in
him. He tries to use falsehood to deceive God's people into fear so they
will not be bold enough to be obedient to the Lord and reap the blessings
He has in store for them.

Most of the time the fear of something is worse than the thing itself.
Usually, if we will be courageous and determined enough to do whatever
it is we fear, we will discover it is not nearly as bad as we thought it would
be. Throughout the Word of God we find the Lord saying to His people
again and again, "Fear not." I believe the reason He did that was to encourage them so they would not allow Satan to rob them of their blessing.

In the same way, because He knows we are fearful, the Lord continues
to exhort and encourage us to press through what lies before us to do
what He is telling us to do. Why? Because He knows that great blessings
await us on the other side.

A Fun, Generous, Wonderful God

> *In Him we have redemption (deliverance and salvation) through His blood, the remission (forgiveness) of our offenses (shortcomings and trespasses), in accordance with the riches and the generosity of His gracious favor, which He lavished upon us in every kind of wisdom and understanding (practical insight and prudence) . . . in accordance with His good pleasure (His merciful intention) which He had previously purposed and set forth in Him.*
>
> —EPHESIANS 1:7-9

It's amazing what God will do for you if you just love Him. We complicate Christianity to the point of losing the joy of our salvation. The primary thing we need to do is receive the love of God, learn how to love ourselves in a balanced way, love God back, and then let that love flow through us to the world full of hurting, dying people. God will not only give back to us what we give away but will also give us a great deal of joy with it.

The world is full of rich people who have "things" but are miserable. It's good to be materially prosperous, but it's even better to be happy and biblically blessed along with prosperity. We are amazed at the doors God has opened for us. I can't figure it out; but I am determined that as long as I can breathe, I will keep walking through them by trying to help as many people receive God's joy in their lives as I can.

Our society today is in a major, major, major mess, and people don't realize that they need God! So many people have an impression of God that is just not true, and they don't know to turn to Him to solve their problems. God called Dave and me to a ministry in which we can show the world an exciting God Who is fun, generous, and wonderful, and Who can solve their problems.

Mercy, Mercy, Mercy!

> *It is because of the Lord's mercy and loving-kindness that we are not consumed, because His [tender] compassions fail not. They are new every morning; great and abundant is Your stability and faithfulness.*
>
> —LAMENTATIONS 3:22-23

In Noah Webster's 1828 *American Dictionary of the English Language*, he defines *mercy* as: "That benevolence, mildness or tenderness of heart which disposes a person to overlook injuries, or to treat an offender better than he deserves; the disposition that tempers justice, and induces an injured person to forgive trespasses and injuries, and to forbear punishment, or inflict less than law or justice will warrant.

"In this sense, there is perhaps no word in our language precisely synonymous with *mercy*. That which comes nearest to it is *grace*. It implies benevolence, tenderness, mildness, pity or compassion, and clemency, but exercised only towards offenders. *Mercy* is a distinguishing attribute of the Supreme Being."

I don't know about you, but I am extremely happy about God's mercy. I cannot possibly imagine where I would be today without it. I know for sure I would not be anywhere pleasant. We all deserve punishment, but instead God gives us mercy. What an awesome God we serve! The Psalms are filled with references to His mercy. Psalm 107:1 is an example: "O give thanks to the Lord, for He is good; for His mercy and loving-kindness endure forever!" David was a man who loved God very much, yet he made serious mistakes. I believe David talked so much about the mercy of God because he had experienced it firsthand in his life and ministry.

God's mercy forgives and restores, and only a person like David who has been honest in his evaluation of himself can truly say, "O give thanks to the Lord, for He is good; for His mercy and loving-kindness endure forever!"

The Power of Rejoicing

> *About midnight, as Paul and Silas were praying and singing hymns of praise to God . . . Suddenly there was a great earthquake, so that the very foundations of the prison were shaken; and at once all the doors were opened and everyone's shackles were unfastened.*
>
> —ACTS 16:25-26

Throughout the Bible, God instructs His people to be filled with joy and to rejoice. For example, Philippians 4:4 says: "Rejoice in the Lord always [delight, gladden yourselves in Him]; again I say, Rejoice!"

Any time the Lord tells us twice to do something—the Philippians were told twice in this verse to rejoice—we need to pay careful attention to what He is saying. Many times people see or hear the word *rejoice* and think, *That sounds nice, but how do I do that?* They would like to rejoice but don't know how!

Paul and Silas, who had been beaten and thrown into prison and had their feet put in stocks, rejoiced by simply singing praises to God. We don't often realize the "rejoicing" that can release so much power can be just as simple as smiling and laughing, having a good time, and enjoying ourselves. And doing that in itself often makes the problem go away!

If you have a personal relationship with the Lord—if you are saved—the Holy Spirit dwells within you (SEE JOHN 14:16-17 AND 1 CORINTHIANS 12:3). If joy is a fruit of the Spirit, and the Spirit is in you, joy is in you. You're not trying to get joy or manufacture it—it is already there, just as are the ability to love and the other fruit of the Spirit—because the Spirit is there.

It is very important to understand that we as believers are not to try to *get* joy—we *have* joy. Joy is in our spirit. What we need to do is learn how to release it.

Suffering Now, Glory Later

And if we are [His] children, then we are [His] heirs also; heirs of
God and fellow heirs with Christ [sharing His inheritance with Him]; only we
must share His suffering if we are to share His glory.

—ROMANS 8:17

Anytime our flesh wants to do one thing and the Spirit of God wants us
to do something else, if we choose to follow the Spirit of God, our flesh
is going to suffer. We don't like that; but the Bible simply says that if we
want to share Christ's glory, we have to be willing to share His suffering. I can still remember suffering through those early years of walking in
obedience when I thought: *Dear God, am I ever going to get over this? Am I ever*
going to get to the point where I can obey God and not hurt while I'm doing it?

I like to encourage those who are just beginning to heed the voice of
God that once the fleshly appetite is no longer in control they will get to
the point where it is easy to obey God—the place where they actually
enjoy obeying God. In Romans 8:18 Paul says, "I consider that the suffer-
ings of this present time (this present life) are not worth being compared
with the glory that is about to be revealed to us and in us and for us and
conferred on us!" In modern language Paul is saying, "We suffer a little
now, but so what! The glory that will come from our obedience far out-
shines the suffering we endure now." That is good news. Whatever we may
go through is absolutely nothing compared to the good things that God is
going to do in our lives as we continue to press on with Him.

Humble Yourself and Be Exalted

Therefore humble yourselves [demote, lower yourselves in your own estimation]
under the mighty hand of God, that in due time He may exalt you.

—I PETER 5:6

The apostle Peter is a good example of a man who had to be humbled. In Matthew 26:31-35 we see that Peter thought more highly of himself than he should have. In this passage, we read that just before the crucifixion Jesus told His disciples they would all be offended and fall away from Him. In verse 33, Peter declared to the Lord that he would never do such a thing. In response, Jesus warned Peter that before that very night was over, his fears would cause him to deny Him three times; but Peter could not conceive that he would ever be that weak.

Peter really did not know himself, and many of us are the same way. We look at others and judge them, thinking, *I would never do that.* Then when we find ourselves in a similar situation, we do things we would have never believed possible. Peter needed to go through the experience of failing, of falling apart in the crisis hour. He had to see his weaknesses before he could bring them to the cross and find God's strength. Yes, Peter failed miserably. He denied Jesus three times. He fell apart in a crucial time, but the end result was good. The experience humbled him and brought him to the place where God could use him greatly. God can only use humble men and women. We must humble ourselves and He will exalt us (SEE I PETER 5:6).

Religion vs. Relationship

[It is He] Who has qualified us [making us to be fit and worthy and sufficient] as ministers and dispensers of a new covenant [of salvation through Christ], not [ministers] of the letter (of legally written code) but of the Spirit; for the code [of the Law] kills, but the [Holy] Spirit makes alive.

—2 CORINTHIANS 3:6

I feel sometimes that religion is killing people. There are so many precious people who are seeking to have relationship with God, and the religious community continues to tell them something else they need to "do" in order to be acceptable to Him.

Jesus talked of His personal relationship with the Father, and the religious leaders of His day persecuted Him. It amazes me how certain people always want to come against anyone who talks about God in a personal way or who thinks he has any power from God. It is obvious that Satan hates our personal relationship with God and the power it makes available in our lives.

In certain religious circles, if you and I were to talk about God as if we knew Him, we would be judged and criticized. People would ask, "Who do you think you are?" Religion wants us to picture God as being far away—somewhere up in the sky—unapproachable by any except the elite of the church. And, further, they want us to believe that He can only be reached through rule-keeping and good behavior. This "religious spirit" was alive in Jesus' day; and even though He died to put an end to it and bring people into close personal relationship with Himself, the Holy Spirit, and the Father, that same spirit still torments people to this day—if they do not know the truth.

Religion says, "You have to find a way, no matter how impossible it may seem. You had better do it . . . keep the rules or take the punishment." But relationship says, "Do your best because you love Me. I know your heart. Admit your faults, repent of your mistakes, and just keep loving Me."

Exercise

> For the time being no discipline brings joy, but seems grievous and
> painful; but afterwards it yields a peaceable fruit of righteousness to those who
> have been trained by it [a harvest of fruit which consists in righteousness—in
> conformity to God's will in purpose, thought, and action, resulting in right
> living and right standing with God].
>
> —HEBREWS 12:11

Human beings were made to exercise. Our body is fit together with joints because God expected we would move a lot. Admittedly, we don't hear much in the Bible about Noah's workout routine or Moses' Pilates session. Does that mean the people back then didn't get much exercise? Quite the opposite! Everything they did in life involved exercise. Before vehicles, electricity, and machines, everything in the world ran by human power or animal power. If you wanted to get somewhere, you walked.

If you needed to bring something with you, you carried it. You did laundry by hand, chopped your own firewood, and milled your own grain. This physically active lifestyle may have been one of the reasons for the incredible longevity of these biblical characters. The best walker of all may be Jesus. He routinely walked from His home in Galilee to Jerusalem—a distance of about 120 miles! Over the course of His ministry, He must have walked thousands of miles.

In Jesus' day, people thought little of walking ten miles. And because they did it all their lives, they had the well-developed bodies to accomplish such long walks with ease. Yes, regular exercise will help you lose weight and look your best, but there are so many health benefits from regular exercise that go beyond the value of looks. Just a few of the conditions you can help prevent through exercise are heart disease, stroke, diabetes, cancer, Alzheimer's, arthritis, asthma, depression, and gastrointestinal ills. You'll get fewer colds, feel less stress, and look great too!

Your Future Is in the Lord

The Spirit of the Lord is upon me, because he hath anointed me to preach the gospel to the poor; he hath sent me to heal the brokenhearted, to preach deliverance to the captives, and recovering of sight to the blind, to set at liberty them that are bruised, to preach the acceptable year of the Lord.

—LUKE 4:18-19 (KJV)

I come from a background of abuse, raised in a dysfunctional home. My childhood was filled with fear and torment. Experts say a child's personality is formed within the first five years of his life. My personality was a mess! I lived in pretense behind walls of protection that I built to keep people from hurting me. I was locking others out, but I was also locking myself in. I was so filled with fear that the only way I could face life was to feel that I was in control, and then no one could hurt me.

As a young adult trying to live for Christ and follow the Christian lifestyle, I knew where I had come from, but I did not know where I was going. I felt that my future would always be marred by my past. I thought, *How could anyone who has the kind of past I do ever be really all right? It's impossible!* However, Jesus said that He came to make well those who were sick, brokenhearted, wounded, and bruised—those broken down by calamity.

Jesus came to open the prison doors and set the captives free. I did not make any progress until I started to believe that I could be set free. I had to have a positive vision for my life. I had to believe that my future was not determined by my past or even my present.

You may have had a miserable past; you may even be in current circumstances that are very negative and depressing. You may be facing situations that are so bad it seems you have no real reason to hope. But I say to you boldly, *your future is not determined by your past or your present!*

Don't Be Afraid of the Light

God is Light, and there is no darkness in Him at all [no, not in any way].

—1 JOHN 1:5

The light of God exposes things (SEE JOHN 3:20 AND 1 CORINTHIANS 4:5). When the light is turned on in a room, we can see the dirt and the bugs that begin to scurry. God is Light (SEE 1 JOHN 1:5). When He gets involved in our lives, He begins to show us things we may prefer not to look at, things we have kept hidden, even from ourselves. We are frequently deceived, especially about ourselves. We prefer not to deal with our faults, nor do we delight in having them exposed. We may feel condemned about them, but at least we feel they are hidden. Anything hidden has power over us because we fear it may be found out. The best and most freeing thing we can do is face up to what God wants to expose and get beyond the fear of it.

Taking Responsibility for Yourself

But they will have to give an account to Him Who is ready
to judge and pass sentence on the living and the dead.

—I PETER 4:5

I once had an employer who took advantage of me. He required me to work so many hours that it kept me from spending proper time with my family. I was worn out and never had time for myself. He never showed appreciation and always expected more. If I even mildly indicated that I might not be able to comply with one of his requests, his anger would start to surface, and I would cave in and agree to do what he had asked of me.

As I was praying about the situation one day and moaning to God about how unfair it was, He said, "What your boss is doing is wrong, but you not confronting him is just as wrong." This was hard for me to hear. Like most people I wanted to blame someone else for my lack of courage. Had I not been a people-pleaser and had I not been afraid, I would have saved myself about five years of being so stressed that it eventually made me very sick. My boss wasn't my problem; I was my problem.

It is important to realize that God has given you authority first and foremost over your own life. If you don't accept and exercise that authority, you may spend your life blaming others for things you should be doing something about. You should make your own decisions according to what you believe God's will is for you.

On Judgment Day God will not ask anyone else to give an account of your life; He will ask only you (SEE MATTHEW 12:36 AND I PETER 4:5)! What if Jesus asks you on Judgment Day why you never got around to fulfilling His call on your life? Are you going to tell Him people took advantage of you and you just couldn't do anything about it? Are you going to tell Him you were so busy pleasing people you just never got around to pleasing Him? If you do offer those types of excuses, do you really believe they will be acceptable?

Taking the Time to Listen

Let be and be still, and know (recognize and understand) that I am God.

—PSALM 46:10

If we really want to hear from God, we can't approach Him with selective hearing, hoping to narrow the topics down to only what we want to hear. People take time to listen for God's voice when they have issues *they* want solved. If they have a problem or concerns about their jobs or need wisdom on how to have more prosperity or how to deal with a child, then they are all ears to hear what God has to say.

Don't just go to God and talk to Him when you want or need something; spend time with Him just listening. He will open up many issues if you will be still before Him and simply listen.

For many people, listening is an ability that must be developed by practice. I have always been a talker and have never had to try to talk. But I have had to learn to listen on purpose. The Lord says, "Be still, and know that I am God." (PSALM 46:10) Our flesh is full of energy and usually wants to be active doing something, so it can be difficult for us to be still.

When you do ask God something, take some time and listen. Even if He does not respond right at that moment, He will in due time. You may be doing some ordinary task when God decides to speak to you, but if you have honored Him by listening as part of your fellowship with Him, He will speak at the right time.

Don't Make Small Plans

Any enterprise is built by wise planning, becomes strong through common sense, and profits wonderfully by keeping abreast of the facts.

—PROVERBS 24:3-4 (TLB)

I hope you have a dream or a vision in your heart for something greater than what you have now. Ephesians 3:20 tells us that God is able to do exceedingly abundantly above and beyond all that we can hope or ask or think. If we are not thinking, hoping, or asking for anything, we are cheating ourselves. We need to think big thoughts, hope for big things, and ask for big things. I always say, I would rather ask God for a lot and get half of it, than to ask Him for a little and get all of it.

However, it is an unwise person who only thinks, dreams, and asks big but fails to realize that an enterprise is built by hard work and wise planning. Dreams for the future are possibilities, but they are not what I call *positivelies.* In other words, they are possible, but they will not positively occur unless we do our part. When we see a twenty-year-old athlete who is a gold medalist in the Olympics, we know he spent many years practicing while others were playing games. He may not have had all the "fun" his friends had, but he did develop his potential. Now he has something that will bring him joy for the rest of his life.

Far too many people take the quick fix method for everything. They only want what makes them feel good right now. They are not willing to invest in the future. Don't just enter the race for the fun of being in it— *run to win!* (SEE 1 CORINTHIANS 9:24-25). There is a gold mine hidden in every life, but we have to dig to get to it. We must be willing to dig deep and go beyond how we feel or what is convenient. If we will dig down deep into the Spirit, we will find strength we never knew we had.

The Lord Our God Is One

The Lord our God is one Lord [the only Lord]. —DEUTERONOMY 6:4

In the Old Testament, the Israelites often said, "The Lord our God is One." And I always wondered why they made such a big deal out of God being One.

Then I realized that the heathens were deceived into believing there was a god for everything. Can you imagine how complicated that must have been? To have a baby, they talked to the god of fertility. To grow crops, they talked to the god of the harvest. And all these different gods required different sacrifices for healing, peace, or whatever the people lacked.

They must have been busy just running around to false gods. That's why it was such good news when the one true God revealed Himself and said, "I've got it all. Anything you need, you can come to Me."

The Lord our God is One. The word *simple* means "one": "unmixed," "free of secondary complications." The word *pure* also means "one": "un-mixed with any other matter."

Whatever I need, I can go to the one pure God. If I need peace, if I need righteousness, if I need hope, if I need joy, if I need healing, if I need finances, if I need help—whatever I need—I simply go to the one true God. That is simple. That delivers me from complication. The Lord our God, He is One.

Blessing Your Enemies

Invoke blessings upon and pray for the happiness of those who curse you, implore God's blessing (favor) upon those who abuse you [who revile, reproach, disparage, and highhandedly misuse you]. To the one who strikes you on the jaw or cheek, offer the other jaw or cheek also; and from him who takes away your outer garment, do not withhold your undergarment as well.

—LUKE 6:28-29

Jesus was quite clear about what we are to do to those who hurt us: "But I tell you, Love your enemies and pray for those who persecute you." (MATTHEW 5:44) "Invoke blessings upon and pray for the happiness of those who curse you." (LUKE 6:28)

As I began to minister to people, I noticed that quite often they would express a genuine desire to forgive their enemies but would admit that they were unable to do so. I went to God in prayer seeking answers for them, and He gave me this message: "My people want to forgive, but they are not obeying the Scriptures concerning forgiveness." The Lord led me to several passages about praying for and blessing our enemies. Many people claim to forgive their enemies, but they do not or will not pray for those who have hurt them.

Ask God to show mercy, not judgment, to your abusers. Remember, if you sow mercy, you will reap mercy (SEE GALATIANS 6:7). Praying for those who have wronged us can also bring them to a place of repentance and a true realization of the harm they are causing others. Without such prayer, they may remain in deception. Blessing and not cursing your enemies is a very important part of the process of forgiveness. If you are willing to bless and pray for your enemies, you will activate Romans 12:21: "Do not let yourself be overcome by evil, but overcome (master) evil with good."

What's the Rush?

*To everything there is a season, and a time for
every matter or purpose under heaven.*

—ECCLESIASTES 3:1

Much of the world is in a hurry, always rushing, yet very few people even know where they are going in life. If we want to be at peace with ourselves and enjoy life, we must stop rushing all the time. People rush to get to yet another event that has no real meaning for them or that they really don't even want to attend. *Hurry* is the pace of the twenty-first century. Rushing has become a disease of epidemic proportions. We hurry so much, we finally come to the place where we cannot slow down.

I can remember the days when I worked so hard and hurried so much that even if I took a vacation, it was almost over by the time I geared down enough to rest. Hurry was definitely one of the "peace stealers" in my life and still can be, if I do not stay alert to its pressure. Life is too precious to rush through it. I find at times that a day has gone by in a blur. At the conclusion of it, I know I was very busy all day, yet I cannot really remember enjoying much, if any, of it. I have committed to learn to do things in God's rhythm, not the world's pace.

Jesus was never in a hurry when He was here on earth, and God is absolutely not in a hurry now. Ecclesiastes 3:1 states, "there is a season, and a time for every matter or purpose under heaven." We should let each thing in our lives have its season and realize we can enjoy that season without rushing into the next one.

Get Addicted to Peace

Peace I leave with you; My [own] peace I now give and bequeath to you. Not as the world gives do I give to you.

—JOHN 14:27

Many people cannot hear from God because they have too much turmoil in their lives. Their insides are like a freeway during rush-hour traffic. They literally don't know how to be peaceful; it is as if they are addicted to turmoil. They keep things agitated and stirred up, seemingly on purpose. In fact, they get comfortable living in a state of chaos. It has become their normal state, even though in God's economy it is not normal at all.

It sounds strange, but when I started learning to be peaceful, I was *bored* at first! I was so accustomed to having something major going on in my life all the time that I wondered, *What am I supposed to do with myself?* Romans 3:17 says, "And they have no experience of the way of peace [they know nothing about peace, for a peaceful way they do not even recognize]."

That describes how my life used to be. I had no experience at all in enjoying a peaceful life; I did not even know how to begin. I had grown up in an atmosphere of strife, and it was all I ever knew. I had to learn an entirely new way of living.

But now I'm addicted to peace. As soon as my peace disappears, I ask myself how I lost it and start looking for ways to get it back. I am believing that as you read this you will become so hungry for peace with God, peace with yourself, and peace with others that you will be willing to make whatever adjustments you need to make in order to have it. I am also believing that you will begin to follow peace at all times, because peace will lead you into the perfect will of God.

Jesus said that if we follow Him, He will give us peace (free of charge). In fact, He said He will bequeath His own peace to us (SEE JOHN 14:27).

The Gift of God's Favor

> *And Joseph's master took him and put him in the prison, a place where the state prisoners were confined; so he was there in the prison. But the Lord was with Joseph, and showed him mercy and loving-kindness and gave him favor in the sight of the warden of the prison. And the warden of the prison committed to Joseph's care all the prisoners who were in the prison; and whatsoever was done there, he was in charge of it. The prison warden paid no attention to anything that was in [Joseph's] charge, for the Lord was with him and made whatever he did to prosper.*
>
> —GENESIS 39:20-23

Although Joseph was being punished unfairly because he was jailed for something he didn't do, the Lord was still with him and took care of him. A person is really not in too much bad shape, even if he ends up in prison, if God gives him favor and places him in charge of everything that goes on there. God wants to give you favor, just as He gave favor to Joseph, but in order to receive that favor, you must do what Joseph did and believe for it. Joseph maintained a good attitude in a bad situation. He had a "faith attitude," and God gave him favor. When God's favor is upon you, people like you for no particular reason, and they want to bless you.

Natural vs. Supernatural Favor

So shall you find favor, good understanding, and
high esteem in the sight [or judgment] of God and man.

—PROVERBS 3:4

There is an important difference between natural favor and supernatural favor. Natural favor can be earned; supernatural favor can't. If you and I work at it hard enough and long enough, we can get people to like and accept us most of the time. But God doesn't want us to spend our time and energy trying to earn favor with Him or with others. He wants us to devote our time and energy to doing His will, whether it is popular or not.

Supernatural favor cannot be earned—it is a gift. That is the kind of favor God wants us to have, and the way we get it is simply by believing for it and receiving it from God. If you and I try to get people to like and accept us by saying and doing all the right things, we will have to keep on saying and doing all those things in order to keep their friendship and approval. And that is a form of bondage. We are no longer free to be led by God, but we must please the people or they might reject us. But supernatural favor does not depend upon pleasing people all the time. It depends upon God's grace to give acceptance and maintain it. That is why I pray daily for favor—supernatural favor.

I cannot tell you how many times I have seen God move supernaturally in my life and give me favor. He is getting me into areas of ministry that, based on my own knowledge and ability, I have no business being. Sometimes it amazes me when I see the things God is allowing me to do and the places He is allowing me to go—not to mention all the precious people He is drawing to my meetings. All I can do is say, "Thank You, Lord."

Whenever we quit trying to do it ourselves and start allowing the Lord to give us His favor, it creates within us a thankful and grateful heart.

He Will Never Leave Us

[I will] not in any degree leave you helpless nor forsake nor let [you] down (relax My hold on you)! [Assuredly not!]

—HEBREWS 13:5

I was born again when I was nine years old. The night I was saved, I had to sneak out of the house to go to church with some relatives who were visiting us because my dad wouldn't have permitted us to go if we had asked. I knew that I went to be saved that night, and I don't even know how I knew that I needed salvation. The pastor did not have an altar call that evening. I was really scared, but at the end of service I walked to the front of the church, taking two of my cousins with me. I looked at the pastor and said, "Can you save me?" He was sorry that he hadn't offered an altar call, but I had a glorious cleansing of my soul that night. I knew I was born again, but the next day I cheated in a game of hide-and-go-seek with my cousins by peeking to see where they were going, and I thought I lost my salvation! I was in my twenties before I realized that Jesus had promised not to abandon me. Hebrews 13:5 confirms this promise: "For He [God] Himself has said, I will not in any way fail you nor give you up nor leave you without support. [I will] not, [I will] not, [I will] not in any degree leave you helpless nor forsake nor let [you] down (relax My hold on you)! [Assuredly not!]"

A Friend of God

I will praise You, O Lord, with my whole heart; I will show forth (recount and tell aloud) all Your marvelous works and wonderful deeds!

—PSALM 9:1

Instead of talking to God only about our problems, we need to talk to Him about Him. We need to talk to Him about Who He is, about the power of His name, the power of the blood of His Son Jesus, and the great things we know that He can perform and has already performed. After we have praised and worshiped Him in this way, then we can begin to mention the problem. I would not like it if my children only came to talk to me when they had problems—I want them to fellowship with me. I can think of a few people right now who only call me when they have problems, and it hurts me. I feel that they care not about me but about what they want me to do for them. I am sure you have experienced this and feel the same way. These people may call themselves friends, but in reality they are not. Friends are for times of trouble, but that is not all they are for. As a friend, we need to show appreciation and spend time encouraging those we are in relationship with. We must avoid being the type of people who are what I call "takers." Those who always take but never give. I want to be the friend of God. He called Abraham His friend, and I want that also. The Lord is not just my problem solver; He is my everything, and I appreciate Him more than I know how to say.

Forgive Those Who Hurt You

> *Lord, fix not this sin upon them [lay it not to their charge]!*
> *And when he [Stephen] had said this, he fell asleep [in death].*
>
> —ACTS 7:60

In Acts 6 and 7 we read the story of Stephen who was called before the Jewish council and falsely accused of blaspheming God and Moses by preaching the gospel. After he had delivered a sermon that angered the council, he was taken out and stoned. But even as they were stoning him, Stephen prayed for his enemies, saying, "Lord Jesus, receive and accept and welcome my spirit! And falling on his knees, he cried out loudly, Lord, fix not this sin upon them [lay it not to their charge]!" (ACTS 7:59-60).

I am afraid that in that situation I would have been tempted to pick up a rock and throw it back. But that is not what Stephen did. He forgave his tormentors and prayed for them, saying in essence, "Forgive them, Lord, they don't understand what they are doing." A large majority of the time those who injure us don't understand what they are doing. They are just operating out of selfishness. Years ago someone told me something that helped me. He said that 95 percent of the time when people hurt our feelings, that was not what they intended to do.

God does not want us to have an offended heart. If we do, we will not be able to minister to others. You may think this doesn't relate to you because you don't have a pulpit ministry. But every believer has a ministry. You may not be on a platform teaching, but you have a ministry to your children, your spouse, your family, and God. How can we properly praise God with a wrong heart condition? It is easy for us to be offended. But according to the Bible love is not easily offended.

Keep the Devil on the Run

When he speaks a falsehood, he speaks what is natural to him, for he is a liar [himself] and the father of lies and of all that is false.

—JOHN 8:44

The devil lies to us, and if we aren't aggressive against him and don't stop listening to his lies, he will run our lives. He goes about *like* a roaring lion (SEE 1 PETER 5:8), but we have the Lion of Judah—Jesus, inside us. We are the ones who should be doing the roaring!

We should keep ourselves so spiritually attuned that when the devil makes one move toward us, we pick up exactly what he's trying to do and back him down immediately. It should take only a few seconds.

The devil is always trying to come against us. As long as we back down, he keeps on coming. If we make one move against him in the authority Jesus made available to us, the devil has to back down.

We need to continue standing in our authority against him. If we stop, he will start moving against us, backing us up. The devil is a liar, a bully, a bluff, a deceiver. He comes *like* a lion, but he is not the lion. We believers in Jesus Christ have the power of the Greater One inside of us. "Greater is he that is in you, than he that is in the world." (1 JOHN 4:4 KJV)

Know the Word well enough that the minute a thought comes into your head that doesn't line up with God's Word, you can say to the devil, "*Liar!* No, I'm not listening to you." You can spend your life backing up and hiding from the devil, or you can spend it forcing him to back up.

We Are God's Children

[And the Lord answered] Can a woman forget her nursing child, that she should not have compassion on the son of her womb? Yes, they may forget, yet I will not forget you.

—ISAIAH 49:15

Isaiah 49:15 reveals that our heavenly Father desires us to come to Him as children. In this verse, the Lord used the example of a nursing mother and how she tenderly cares for and has compassion on her child and his needs. Our heavenly Father wants us to know that we are His precious little ones—His children—and that when we come to Him as such, we show faith in Him which releases Him to care for us.

God is not like people. If people in your past have hurt you, don't let it affect your relationship with the Lord. You can trust Him. He will care for you as a loving Father. When we do not receive the care and love that we should in our childhood, it causes fears that were never in God's plan for us. Parents are to be a mirror image in the physical realm of what our relationship with God is to be like in the spiritual realm. Frequently, when individuals are reared in dysfunctional homes, it causes problems in their relationships with the Lord.

I pray that as you read these words and meditate on what I am sharing, God will set you free to be a responsible adult who can come to your heavenly Father in a childlike way.

God's Perfect Timing

But let endurance and steadfastness and patience have full play and
do a thorough work, so that you may be [people] perfectly and fully developed
[with no defects], lacking in nothing.

—JAMES 1:4

Due season" is God's season, not ours. We are in a hurry; God isn't. He takes time to do things right—He lays a solid foundation before He attempts to build a building. We are God's building under construction. He is the Master Builder, and He knows what He is doing. We may not know what He is doing, but He does, and that will have to be good enough. We may not always know, but we can be satisfied to know the One Who knows. God's timing seems to be His own little secret. The Bible promises us that He will never be late, but I have also discovered that He is usually not early. It seems that He takes every available opportunity to develop the fruit of patience in us.

Vine's dictionary of Greek words begins the definition of *patience* (IN JAMES 1:3), as "Patience, which grows only in trial." Patience is a fruit of the Spirit that grows under trial. My own particular natural temperament is filled with impatience. I have become much more patient over the years, but all the waiting required to teach me patience was hard on me. I wanted everything *now!*

Patience is vital to the development of our full potential. Actually, our potential is only developed as our patience is developed. It is God's way—there is no other, so why not settle down and enjoy the journey?

This Is a Test

> *And you shall [earnestly] remember all the way which the Lord your God*
> *led you these forty years in the wilderness, to humble you and to prove you, to*
> *know what was in your [mind and] heart, whether you would keep*
> *His commandments or not.*
>
> —DEUTERONOMY 8:2

The Bible says that God led the Israelites in the wilderness for forty years to humble them, to prove them, and to see if they would keep His commandments. Tests come in hard times, not good times, because not everything God asks us to do is going to be easy. That is why He tests us to see if we are ready and able before He promotes us to a higher level of responsibility. There are so many things that come our way every day that are just nothing more than a test.

For example, sometimes when we have to wait to be seated at a table in a restaurant and then get a bad meal, it's a test. Sometimes when our boss tells us to do something we don't want to do, it's a test. James 1:2-4 says that tests bring out what is in us. It is in times of trial that we become best acquainted with ourselves and what we are capable of doing. Peter didn't think he would ever deny Jesus, but when he was put to the test, that is exactly what he did. God is not impressed with what we say we will do; He is impressed with what we prove we will do under pressure.

We don't get promoted in ministry because we have our Bible underlined in two colors but because we have been tested and tried, and we dug in and we passed the tests even though it was hard. James writes, "Blessed (happy, to be envied) is the man who is patient under trial and stands up under temptation, for when he has stood the test and been approved, he will receive [the victor's] crown of life which God has promised to those who love Him." (JAMES 1:12)

Run to Him, Not Others

> *You [are like] unfaithful wives [having illicit love affairs with the*
> *world and breaking your marriage vow to God]! Do you not know that being*
> *the world's friend is being God's enemy? So whoever chooses to be a friend of*
> *the world takes his stand as an enemy of God.*
>
> —JAMES 4:4

In my kitchen there are some windows above the sink that are hard for me to reach. Now, when I go to open or close those windows, I can jump up on the counter and make a big ordeal out of it or I can save myself the struggle and strain by simply calling my husband, Dave, and asking him to come open or close them for me. Dave is much taller than I am, so with his long arms it is no problem for him to do what would be a really frustrating challenge for me.

That is the way we are with the Lord. We struggle and strain, wearing ourselves out trying to do something that the Lord could do for us with no effort at all—if we would just ask Him. But do you know what would insult my husband even more than refusing to let him help me? Running to the next-door neighbor and asking him to come over and open or close my windows for me. That is the kind of thing James is referring to here in this verse when he talks about our being "like unfaithful wives" who turn to other men for help rather than calling upon our own husbands, a symbol of the Lord.

I was frustrated in my life and ministry until I learned to stop either trying to do everything on my own or running to others with my problems rather than running to God.

Find a Happy Medium

Be well balanced (temperate, sober of mind), be vigilant and
cautious at all times; for that enemy of yours, the devil, roams around like a
lion roaring [in fierce hunger], seeking someone to seize upon and devour.

— I PETER 5:8

I remember sitting in my home looking up the word *gentle* in Strong's concordance and saying, "Lord, You've got to help me!" I thought I could never be gentle. Finally, the Lord began to do a work in me in the area of gentleness. The only problem was that, like so many other people in the body of Christ, I was such an extremist that I couldn't "strike a happy medium." Once I saw that I was overbalanced in one area, I thought I had to go totally in the other direction. I "adjusted" and "adapted" far too much. I became so "gentle" and "kind" and "patient" that I wouldn't exercise any discipline over my youngest son, who was born after my other children were grown. I also went overboard in my relationship with others. I let things get out of hand in my marriage, my home, and my ministry. I learned from my experiences that one extreme is just as bad as the other. What we must learn in all this is *balance*.

On one hand, we must not be harsh and hard. But on the other hand, we must not be weak and excessively soft. We must not be irritable and impatient, flying off the handle and acting out of emotion. On the other hand, we must not be so mild mannered that we become doormats and whipping posts for those who will take advantage of us if we give them a chance. There is a time to be patient and forbearing, and there is a time to be firm and decisive. There is a time to "not be angry," and there is a time to display righteous indignation. It is wisdom to know when to do which.

Let Your Actions Reveal Your Heart

*For as the human body apart from the spirit is
lifeless, so faith apart from [its] works of obedience is also dead.*

—JAMES 2:26

As Christians, it is important to make a declaration of faith with our actions and not just with what we say we believe in our hearts. People often say, "My heart is right," but people cannot read our heart; they can only see our actions. That is just as foolish as a man telling his wife, "You should know I love you; I married you, didn't I?" yet he never shows her any affection or gives her any reason in her emotions or mind to believe him.

It is important that we show, with our actions, what we believe in our hearts.

God's Grace Will See You Through

Not by might, nor by power, but by My Spirit . . . says the Lord of hosts.
—ZECHARIAH 4:6

Some time ago just before a meeting in which I was teaching on the subject of grace, someone handed my husband a written word from the Lord and asked him to give it to me. I am sure that person had no idea what direction I would be taking in that meeting, but the message certainly fit in with it.

I believe the following message is divinely anointed. I encourage you to read it carefully and receive what the Lord wants to speak to you today.

> I want you to face the mountain
>> so that you can see,
>> when the mountain is out of the way
>> all there is left is Me.
> Only I can move the mountain,
>> only I can push it away,
>> only I can conquer the problems
>> that you face today.
> Your only job is to believe, to listen
>> to My voice,
> and when you hear what I command,
>> obedience is your choice.
> But I will not make it too difficult for the vic-
>> tory is already Mine,
> and I will fill you with My Spirit and through
>> you My grace will shine.
> Not when you are perfect,
> like you think you need to be,
> but when your heart is willing to become more
>> and more like Me.

Focus Forward

Not that I have now attained [this ideal], or have already been made perfect, but I press on to lay hold of (grasp) and make my own, that for which Christ Jesus (the Messiah) has laid hold of me and made me His own. I do not consider, brethren, that I have captured and made it my own [yet]; but one thing I do [it is my one aspiration]: forgetting what lies behind and straining forward to what lies ahead, I press on toward the goal to win the [supreme and heavenly] prize to which God in Christ Jesus is calling us upward.

—PHILIPPIANS 3:12-14

If you have been miserable because of the things that have happened in your past, I encourage you to do as I did and set your focus in a new direction. Determine to be what God wants you to be, to have what God wants you to have, and to receive what Jesus died to give you.

When you feel discouraged, say, "I am not going to live in bondage anymore. I cannot do anything about what I have done in the past, but I can do something about my future. I am going to enjoy my life and have what Jesus died for me to have. I am going to let go of the past and go on pursuing God from this day forth!"

First Things First

> *But seek (aim at and strive after) first of all His kingdom and His*
> *righteousness (His way of doing and being right), and then all these things*
> *taken together will be given you besides.*
>
> —MATTHEW 6:33

Too often we spend all of our time seeking God for answers to our problems when what we should be doing is just seeking God.

As long as we are seeking God, we are staying in the secret place, under the shadow of His wing. Psalm 91:4 says, "Under His wings shall you trust and find refuge." But when we start seeking answers to all the problems and situations that confront us, trying to fulfill our desires rather than God's will, we get out from under the shadow of His wing.

For many years I sought God about how I could get my ministry to grow. The result was that it stayed just the same as it was. It never grew. Sometimes it even went backward. What I didn't realize was that all I needed to do was to seek the kingdom of God, and He would add the growth.

Do you realize that you don't even have to worry about your own spiritual growth? All you need to do is seek the Kingdom, and you will grow. Seek God, abide in Him, and He will cause increase and growth.

A baby just drinks milk and grows. All you and I have to do is desire the sincere milk of the Word, and we will grow (SEE 1 PETER 2:2). We can never experience any real measure of success by our own human effort. Instead, we must seek first the kingdom of God and His righteousness; then all these other things we need will be *added* to us.

God Meant It for Good

Then his brothers went and fell down before him, saying, See, we are
your servants (your slaves)! And Joseph said to them, Fear not; for am I in
the place of God? [Vengeance is His, not mine.] As for you, you thought evil
against me, but God meant it for good, to bring about that many people should
be kept alive, as they are this day.

—GENESIS 50:18-20

Whatever may have happened to us in the past, it does not have to dictate our future. Regardless of what people may have tried to do to us,
God can take it and turn it around for good. "We are assured and know
that [God being a partner in their labor] all things work together and are
[fitting into a plan] for good to and for those who love God and are called
according to [His] design and purpose." (ROMANS 8:28) Sometimes we
forget how big our God is.

Through everything that happened to him, Joseph kept his eyes on
God. He didn't sit around and gripe and complain and hold a "pity party."
Despite what others—even his own brothers—did to him, he didn't
allow himself to be filled with bitterness, resentment, and unforgiveness.
He knew it didn't matter who was against him, because God was for him
and would eventually work out everything for the best for all concerned.
Joseph knew that whatever happened, God was on his side. He let God
build his life, his reputation, and his career.

That is what you and I need to do. We need to put no confidence in
the arm of the flesh, but rather trust ourselves entirely to the arm of the
Lord.

Decide to Be Second

> *Love one another with brotherly affection [as members of*
> *one family], giving precedence and showing honor to one another.*
>
> —ROMANS 12:10

Giving preference to others requires a willingness to adapt and adjust. It means to allow another to go first or to have the best of something. We show preference when we give someone else the best cut of meat on the platter instead of keeping it back for ourselves. We show preference when we allow someone with fewer groceries in his cart than we have in ours to go in front of us at the supermarket checkout counter, or when we are waiting in line to use a public restroom and someone behind us in line is pregnant or elderly and we choose to let that individual go ahead of us. Each time we show preference we have to make a mental adjustment. We were planning to be first, but we decide to be second. We are in a hurry, but we decide to wait on someone else who seems to have a greater need.

A person is not yet rooted and grounded in love until they have learned to show preference to others (SEE EPHESIANS 3:17). Don't just learn to adjust, but learn to do it with a good attitude. Learning to do these things is learning to walk in love.

Keeping Our Priorities Straight

> *And He Himself existed before all things, and in Him all things consist*
> *(cohere, are held together). He also is the Head of [His] body, the church;*
> *seeing He is the Beginning, the Firstborn from among the dead, so that He*
> *alone in everything and in every respect might occupy the chief place*
> *[stand first and be preeminent].*
>
> —COLOSSIANS 1:17-18

I believe that one of the reasons people lose their peace and fail to have the things they want is because they get their priorities out of line. There are so many projects to which people can give their time and attention. Some of the choices we have are bad options and are easy to recognize as something to avoid, but many of our options are good. Yet even good things can get our priorities all messed up. What is a top priority for somebody else could be a problem for us. So we have to be careful that we don't just do what everybody else is doing. We need to do what God is leading us individually to do.

When setting our priorities, it's important to understand that Jesus is the holding power of all that is good in our lives. That is why He should always be our first priority. Jesus holds everything together. A couple can't have a good marriage if Jesus isn't holding it together. In fact, people won't have good personal relationships with *anybody* if Jesus is not leading and influencing individuals to love one another. Finances are a mess without Jesus. Our thoughts are clouded and confused without Jesus. Our emotions are out of control without Him.

Jesus is the head of the church body; therefore, He alone, in every respect, should occupy the chief place, stand first, and be preeminent in each of our lives. That means if Jesus is not first in our lives, then we need to rearrange our priorities.

The Greatest Commandment

> *You shall love the Lord your God with all your heart and with all your soul and with all your mind (intellect). This is the great (most important, principal) and first commandment. And a second is like it: You shall love your neighbor as [you do] yourself.*
>
> —MATTHEW 22:37-39

This was how Jesus responded when He was asked which was the greatest commandment and law. In Matthew 7:12, Jesus said, "Whatever you desire that others would do to and for you, even so do also to and for them, for this (sums up) the Law and the Prophets." So, to experience God and His plan for our lives, we are to look for the needs of others and do what we can to serve them.

Our religion is not pure if it is polluted with "self." Our self-centeredness keeps us from noticing what other people are going through. We don't have to totally forget about our desires. But we must chase selfishness away by not *always* thinking about them. Psalm 37:4 plainly tells us that when we delight in the Lord, He gives us the desires and secret petitions of our hearts.

Love Is Impartial

*And Peter opened his mouth and said: Most certainly and
thoroughly I now perceive and understand that God shows no partiality
and is no respecter of persons.*

—ACTS 10:34

If love is unconditional, then it must not show partiality. I remember an incident in which God taught me a lesson in this area. I had taken our son to the doctor to have a cast removed from his arm, which he had broken. While I was waiting, an elderly man came and sat down next to me. He wanted to talk, but I wanted to read. He kept telling me how he had fallen on the ice and hurt his leg and how much this doctor had helped him.

I must admit, I just wanted him to be quiet. I really paid no attention to him nor showed him any respect. I was somewhat aware that he was lonely and probably had very few people to talk with, but I was not willing to be his blessing for that day.

The Holy Spirit spoke in my heart and said, "How would you treat this man if he were a famous preacher you would like to get to know?" I was cut to my heart at those words. I immediately knew that I would hang on to every word, smile, make compliments, and do all kinds of things to help me establish a relationship—in short, all the things I was *not* doing for this man who meant nothing to me.

This kind of behavior is not acceptable for anyone who desires to have a strong love walk. The Word of God tells us that He does not show partiality, that He is no respecter of persons. To be honest, to remain impartial takes some soul-searching. The flesh has tendencies toward prejudice and partiality, but God condemns such things; therefore, we must condemn them also.

Guard Your Mind, Watch Your Mouth

> *This Book of the Law shall not depart out of your mouth, but you*
> *shall meditate on it day and night, that you may observe and do according*
> *to all that is written in it. For then you shall make your way prosperous, and*
> *then you shall deal wisely and have good success.*
>
> —JOSHUA 1:8

Joshua had plenty of enemies to confront on his journey. As a matter of fact, it seemed there was a never-ending parade of them. But please notice that Joshua was instructed by the Lord to keep the *Word*, not the *problem*, in his mouth and in his mind.

Like Joshua, if you and I are to make our way prosperous and have good success in this life, we will definitely need to put our thoughts and words on something other than the problem that faces us. We need to stop thinking about the problem, talking about the problem, and sometimes, we even need to stop praying about the problem. If we have prayed, God has heard. I am not saying there is not a time for importunity; but often we say we are fellowshipping with God, when in reality we are fellowshipping with our problem.

In Mark 11:23 Jesus instructed His disciples to *speak to* the mountain. He did not say, "*Talk about* the mountain." If there is a purpose in talking about it, then do so. Otherwise, it is best to keep quiet about it. Words stir up emotions that often cause upset because of excessive focus on the circumstance. It is valuable to go out and do something enjoyable while you are waiting for God to solve your problem. You may not feel like it, but do it anyway. It will help you! *Get your mind—and your mouth—off the problem!*

It Costs Nothing to Believe

*Where there is no vision [no redemptive revelation of God],
the people perish; but he who keeps the law [of God, which includes that of
man]—blessed (happy, fortunate, and enviable) is he.*

—PROVERBS 29:18

Those with a sad past need to be able to believe in a bright future. The writer of Proverbs says that where there is no vision, people perish. A vision is something we see in our minds, "a mental sight" as one definition puts it. It may be something God plants in us supernaturally or something we see on purpose. It involves the way we think about ourselves, our past, and our future. It does not cost *anything* to believe.

Some people are afraid to believe. They think they may be setting themselves up for disappointment. They have not realized they will be perpetually disappointed if they don't believe. I feel that if I believe for a lot and even get half of it, I am better off than I would be to believe for nothing and get all of it. I am challenging you to start believing good things. Believe you can do whatever you need to do in life through Christ.

Don't have a "give up easy" attitude. Let your faith soar. Be creative with your thoughts. Take an inventory. What have you been believing lately? An honest answer may help you understand why you have not been receiving what you have wanted to receive.

Why Does God Wait So Long?

All things are possible with God. —MATTHEW 19:26

When God came to Abraham and told him that He was going to bless him, Abraham said to God, "That's fine, but what I really want is a son." God said, "I am going to give you what you ask for," but He didn't give it to Abraham right away. The Word says, "Abraham was a hundred years old when Isaac was born." (GENESIS 21:5) Actually, twenty years went by from the time God promised Abraham that he would have a child to the time that child was born. In fact, Abraham was already old when God first gave him the promise of a son.

By the time Abraham fathered that child, his wife had already gone through the change of life. She had a barren womb. So Abraham and Sarah not only had a prayer request, but also needed a miracle.

Isn't it interesting that sometimes when you ask God for something, He lets it go so long, the only thing that can possibly produce what you asked for is a miracle? Why does God do that? Because He likes "to show Himself strong in behalf of those whose hearts are blameless toward Him." (2 CHRONICLES 16:9)

When Martha and Mary sent for Jesus to come and minister to their brother, Lazarus, who was gravely ill, why did Jesus wait two days longer, until Lazarus had actually died and was buried, before He went and raised Lazarus from the dead? It was because Jesus already knew what He was going to do for Lazarus.

If something is dead—a dream, a desire, a want, a need—it doesn't matter to God how dead it is. God can still bring it back to life in His timing because our God is an awesome God. Nothing is too hard for Him. That is why He is never in a hurry and why it seems as if He often waits until nothing will work but a miracle.

Run to God, Not Away from Him

For by the death He died, He died to sin [ending His relation to it] once for all;
and the life that He lives, He is living to God [in unbroken fellowship with Him].
Even so consider yourselves also dead to sin and your relation to it broken, but
alive to God [living in unbroken fellowship with Him] in Christ Jesus.

—ROMANS 6:10-11

Meditating on all of our faults and failures weakens us, but meditating on God's grace and willingness to forgive strengthens us. Our relationship and fellowship are to be with God, not with our sins. How much do you fellowship with your sins, failures, mistakes, and weaknesses? Whatever amount of time it is, it is wasted. When you sin, admit it, ask for forgiveness, and then continue your fellowship with God. The scripture above says we are alive to God, living in *unbroken* fellowship with Him. Don't let your sins come between you and the Lord. Even when you sin, God still wants to spend time with you, hear and answer your prayers, and help you with all of your needs. He wants you to run *to* Him, not *away* from Him!

You Are Everywhere You Go!

> *For our sake He made Christ [virtually] to be sin Who knew no sin,*
> *so that in and through Him we might become [endued with, viewed as being in,*
> *and examples of] the righteousness of God [what we ought to be, approved and*
> *acceptable and in right relationship with Him, by His goodness].*

—2 CORINTHIANS 5:21

What if everywhere you went, you ran into someone you didn't like? Wouldn't that be terrible? You attend a party, and you have to endure her conversation and views. You go to church, and she's sitting right beside you. *What a bummer to have to spend so much time with this person,* you think. Then it gets worse. There she is at the dinner table with you! She's lounging by the pool; she's even in your bed! She's everywhere! That sounds pretty awful, but it is the exact situation you find yourself in if you don't like yourself, because you are everywhere you go. You can't get away from yourself, even for a second, so you are in for a sad life if you dread your own company.

But believe it or not, even though we can all agree that it makes no sense to live your life this way, I find that *most* people don't like themselves. They may not even realize it, but some genuine soul-searching reveals the sad fact that they have rejected themselves and in some cases even hate themselves. I've come across a lot of people over the years, through my ministry and in day-to-day life, and I'm amazed at how few are truly at peace with themselves. Instead, they have declared war on themselves.

God wants you to love yourself, not in some wrong selfish or prideful way, but in a healthy way that truly understands how special you are to Him. As you begin to see yourself as God sees you, then not only will you love yourself, but you will have the confidence and faith to be a powerful force for good in the world.

Be Positive

It shall be done for you as you have believed. —MATTHEW 8:13

Many years ago, I was extremely negative. I always say that if I thought two positive thoughts in a row my mind would cramp up. My whole philosophy was: "If you don't expect anything good to happen, then you won't be disappointed when it doesn't." I had encountered so many disappointments in life—so many devastating things had happened to me—that I was afraid to believe anything good might happen. I had a terribly negative outlook on everything. Since my thoughts were all negative, so was my mouth; therefore, so was my life.

When I really began to study the Word and to trust God to restore me, one of the first things I realized was that the negativism had to go. In Matthew 8:13 Jesus tells us that it will be done for us as we have believed. The *King James Version* says, "As thou hast believed, so be it done unto thee." Everything I believed was negative, so naturally many negative things happened to me. This doesn't mean that you and I can get anything we want by just thinking about it. God has a perfect plan for each of us, and we can't control Him with our thoughts and words. But, we must think and speak in agreement with His will and plan for us.

If you don't have any idea what God's will is for you at this point, at least begin by thinking, *Well, I don't know God's plan, but I know He loves me. Whatever He does will be good, and I'll be blessed.* Begin to think positively about your life. Practice being positive in each situation that arises. Even if whatever is taking place in your life at the moment is not so good, expect God to bring good out of it as He has promised in His Word.

All Things Work for Good

> *We are assured and know that [God being a partner in their labor]*
> *all things work together and are [fitting into a plan] for good to and for those*
> *who love God and are called according to [His] design and purpose.*
>
> —ROMANS 8:28

This scripture does not say that all things are good, but it does say that all things *work together for good.* Let's say you're planning to go shopping. You get in the car, and it won't start. There are two ways you can look at this situation. You can say, "I knew it! It never fails. Every time I want to do something, it gets all messed up. I figured this shopping trip would end up a flop; my plans always do."

Or you can say, "Well, I wanted to go shopping, but it looks like I can't go right now. I'll go later when the car is fixed. In the meantime, I believe this change in plans is going to work out for my good. There is probably some reason I need to be at home today, so I'm going to enjoy my time here."

In Romans 12:16 the apostle Paul tells us to readily adjust ourselves to people and things. The idea is that we must learn to become the kind of person who plans things but who doesn't fall apart if that plan doesn't work out. Even a person who is really positive won't have everything work out the way he would like it to all the time. But the positive person can go ahead and decide to enjoy himself no matter what happens.

A Double Mind Is Double Trouble

[For being as he is] a man of two minds (hesitating, dubious, irresolute),
[he is] unstable and unreliable and uncertain about
everything [he thinks, feels, decides].

—JAMES 1:8

A person who is of two minds is hesitating, dubious, irresolute, unstable, unreliable, and uncertain about everything he thinks, feels, or decides. The *King James Version* of the above passage says, "A double minded man is unstable in all his ways." I don't think we should have a double heart. Instead, we should be decisive people. Leaders should be able to make decisions and then stick to them. If we make a decision and then continue to go back and forth in our mind about whether we did the right thing or not, we are being unstable in our ways.

We need to do the best we can to hear from God, then make a decision based on what He has said to us. Once we have decided something, we need to do it with all our heart. Whatever we decide to do, we need to do it wholeheartedly, putting our whole selves into it. In Romans 12, the apostle Paul talks about the different gifts of grace that have been given to the individual members of the body of Christ. In that chapter he tells us that if we are a teacher, we should give ourselves to our teaching. If we are a giver, we should give ourselves to our giving. If we are an exhorter, we should give ourselves to our exhortation.

In other words, don't get sucked up into everybody else's call that really is not the call on your life. Fight to stay centered on what God is calling you to do. Don't be double-minded. If you believe you have a call on your life, then believe it—consistently. Don't believe it on Monday, doubt it on Tuesday, believe it again on Wednesday, and then by Friday be ready to give it up because your circumstances are not good. Whatever your call may be, do it the best you know how, believing that you have heard from God.

Whom God Loves, He Chastens

For the Lord corrects and disciplines everyone whom He loves,
and He punishes, even scourges, every son whom He accepts and
welcomes to His heart and cherishes.

—HEBREWS 12:6

When we need correction—and there are times when we all need it—I believe it is the Lord's first desire to correct us Himself. Whom the Lord loves, He chastens. God's correction or chastisement is not a bad thing; it is always and ultimately only for our good.

The fact that it works toward our good does not mean it always feels good or that it is something we enjoy immediately: "For the time being no discipline brings joy, but seems grievous and painful; but afterwards it yields a peaceable fruit of righteousness to those who have been trained by it [a harvest of fruit which consists in righteousness—in conformity to God's will in purpose, thought, and action, resulting in right living and right standing with God]." (HEBREWS 12:11)

Correction is probably one of the most difficult things for most of us to receive, especially when it comes through another person. Even if we have problems, we don't want others to know we have them. I believe God prefers to correct us privately; but if we won't accept His correction or if we don't know how to allow Him to correct us privately, He will correct us publicly, using whatever source He needs to use. We may not always like the source God chooses to use, but it is wisdom to accept correction in order to avoid "going around the mountain one more time" (SEE DEUTERONOMY 2:3).

Persistence: The Vital Link to Victory

And Jesus, replying, said to them, Have faith in God [constantly].
Truly I tell you, whoever says to this mountain, Be lifted up and thrown into
the sea! and does not doubt at all in his heart but believes that what he says
will take place, it will be done for him.

—MARK 11:22-23

When Jesus said that we are to speak to our mountain in faith, commanding it to be lifted up and thrown into the sea, this is a radical statement and one that deserves some study. First of all, what do we say to the mountains in our lives? It is obvious that we are not to hurl our will at them, but the will of God, and His will is His Word.

In Luke 4 when Jesus was being tempted by Satan in the wilderness, He answered every trial with the Word of God. He repeatedly said, "It is written," and quoted scriptures that met the lies and deceptions of the devil head on. We have a tendency to "try" this for a while, and then when we do not see quick results, we stop speaking the Word to our problems and begin once again speaking our feelings, which are probably what got us into trouble to begin with.

A stonecutter may strike a rock ninety-nine times with a hammer, and there may be no evidence at all that the rock is cracking. Then on the one hundredth time, it may split in half. Each blow was weakening the stone even though there were no signs to indicate it. Persistence is a vital link to victory. We must know what we believe and be determined to stick with it until we see results.

We Have Not Because We Ask Not

Up to this time you have not asked a [single] thing in My Name [as presenting all that I AM]; but now ask and keep on asking and you will receive, so that your joy (gladness, delight) may be full and complete.

—JOHN 16:24

One day I woke up with a throbbing headache. I thought maybe I was catching a cold. I walked around with that miserable headache almost all day, telling everybody I met how terrible I felt—until finally the Lord said to me, "Did it ever occur to you to ask Me to heal you?" I believed in Jesus as my Healer, but I spent the day complaining and never once asked for healing.

That happens so often in our lives. We go around complaining about our problems and spending half our time trying to figure out what we can do to solve them. We do everything under the sun except the one thing we are told to do in the Word of God: ask, that we may receive that our joy may be full (SEE JOHN 16:24). Why are we like that? Because the flesh, our carnal human nature, wants to do things itself. That is the nature of the flesh. It wants to conquer. It wants to overcome its own problems in its own way. Why? So it can get the glory. The flesh wants to do it itself, because it wants the credit.

That is one reason we are not more successful than we are in our walk of faith. We are trying to obtain by our efforts what God wants to give us by His grace. But in order for Him to give us what we need, we must be humble enough to quit trying and start trusting. We must be willing to stop doing and start asking.

Calm Down and Lighten Up!

Do not worry or be anxious about tomorrow, for tomorrow will have worries
and anxieties of its own. Sufficient for each day is its own trouble.

—MATTHEW 6:34

My personal definition of *anxiety* is mentally leaving where you are and getting into an area of the past or the future. One of the things we need to understand is that God wants us to learn to be "now people." Too often we spend our time in the past or the future. We need to learn to live now—mentally as well as physically and spiritually. There is an anointing on today. In John 8:58, Jesus referred to Himself as *I AM*. If you and I, as His disciples, try to live in the past or the future, we are going to find life hard for us because Jesus is always in the present. That's what He meant when He said in Matthew 6:34, "Do not worry or be anxious about tomorrow, for tomorrow will have worries and anxieties of its own. Sufficient for each day is its own trouble."

Jesus has plainly told us we don't need to worry about anything. All we need to do is seek the kingdom of God, and He will add to us whatever we need, whether it is food or clothing or shelter or spiritual growth (SEE MATTHEW 6:25-33). We don't need to be concerned about tomorrow, because tomorrow will have problems of its own. We need to concentrate our full attention on today and stop being so intense and stirred up.

Calm down and lighten up! Laugh more and worry less. Stop ruining today worrying about yesterday or tomorrow—neither of which we can do anything about. We need to stop wasting our precious "now," because it will never come again. The next time you are tempted to get anxious or upset about something—especially something in the past or the future—think about what you are doing and turn your mind to what is going on today. Learn from the past and prepare for the future, but *live in the present.*

He Cares

> *I called upon the Lord and cried to my God; He heard my voice*
> *out of His temple (heavenly dwelling place), and my cry came*
> *before Him, into His [very] ears.*
>
> —PSALM 18:6

God loves you very much and wants to help you, but you need to ask Him to. A man told me recently that when he feels overwhelmed, he lifts up one hand toward heaven and says, "Come get me, Jesus." God hears the faintest cry of your heart, so stop trying to do everything on your own and ask Him for help. You may not think that God cares about something as simple as your health, but He does. He cares about everything that concerns you—the big as well as the small.

He wants you healthy and whole, and He is willing to help, if you'll just let Him. Pray to Him to help you find the spiritual strength you need to make any necessary changes in your life. God's grace is always available. As we choose to do what is right and lean on Him to give us strength, His power enables us to follow through and experience victory.

Simple Obedience

> *Oh, that they had such a [mind and] heart in them always*
> *[reverently] to fear Me and keep all My commandments, that it might*
> *go well with them and with their children forever!*
>
> —DEUTERONOMY 5:29

If we will simply listen to the Lord and do what He says, things will go well for us. Most people have no idea how simple it is sometimes to relieve stress, and Satan works to keep it that way! He works to complicate people's lives in every imaginable way because he knows the power and joy simplicity brings.

Satan wants to exhaust the energies God has given us by keeping us too busy and stressed out trying to handle all the things complicating our lives. He knows that if we learn to simply obey God, we will turn that power and energy against him by hearing and doing the work God directs!

The transformations many people desire in different areas of their lives come through forming a pattern of obeying God in the little things. He may ask you to come away and visit with Him for half an hour or an evening instead of watching television, going to a party, or talking on the phone. The more consistent you are in keeping yourself still enough to hear His voice and then obey His promptings, the sooner the needed work will be done in you for the transformation to be complete. God uses our obedience in the little things to transform our lives.

No matter what the situation, listen to the Lord and obey. Proverbs 3:6 states, "In all your ways know, recognize, and acknowledge Him, and He will direct and make straight and plain your paths." You may not understand the reasons the Lord asks you to do certain things or see any changes or results immediately, but keep obeying the Lord and things will go well with you and your children.

Come as You Are

And all of us, as with unveiled face, [because we] continued to behold [in the Word of God] as in a mirror the glory of the Lord, are constantly being transfigured into His very own image in ever increasing splendor and from one degree of glory to another; [for this comes] from the Lord [Who is] the Spirit.

—2 CORINTHIANS 3:18

There is a big emphasis today on spending personal time with the Lord, and rightly so. Unfortunately, many people have been frustrated by this emphasis in teaching. They want to spend time with God, but feel uncomfortable. Some express that they never sense God's presence. Or, they don't know what to do during those times. We must learn to "be" and not always feel that we must "do."

In the verse above we read that we must come with unveiled faces in order to receive the benefit God wants us to have from the New Covenant. To me, this means that when I stop being religious and legalistic and just come to Jesus, when I lay aside all "my" works and begin to see Him, when I allow Him to remove the veil from my eyes, then He and I can enter into a personal relationship that will ultimately change me into His image. More than anything else, we need His presence. He is the only One Who can do anything for us that will be permanent.

Common People with Uncommon Goals

*Now to Him Who, by (in consequence of) the [action of His] power
that is at work within us, is able to [carry out His purpose and] do
superabundantly, far over and above all that we [dare] ask or think
[infinitely beyond our highest prayers, desires, thoughts, hopes, or dreams].*

—EPHESIANS 3:20

God uses common, ordinary, everyday people who have uncommon goals and visions. That is what I am—just a common, ordinary person with a goal and a vision. But just because I am common and ordinary does not mean that I am content to be average. I don't like that word. I don't want to be average. I don't intend to be average. I don't serve an average God, therefore, I don't believe I have to be average—and neither do you.

Average is basically okay. It is not bad, but it is also not excellent. It is just good enough to get by, and I don't think that is what God wants us to be. I believe that any common, ordinary, everyday person can be *mightily* used by God. I believe that we can do great and mighty things—things that will amaze even us—if we believe that God can use us and if we will be daring enough to have an uncommon goal and vision. And what I mean by uncommon is something that doesn't make sense to the mind. We have to believe God for it.

In Ephesians 3:20 we are told that God is able to do exceedingly, abundantly, above and beyond all that we could *dare* to hope, ask, or think, according to His great power that is at work in us. God does it through us according to His power, but it is done through us, so we have to cooperate. That means we need to be daring in our faith and in our prayers. Some of us are not believing for enough. We need to stretch our faith into new realms. We need to be uncommon people with uncommon goals.

Dwelling in the Secret Place

He who dwells in the secret place of the Most High shall remain stable and fixed under the shadow of the Almighty [Whose power no foe can withstand].

—PSALM 91:1

God has a secret place where we can dwell in peace and safety. The secret place is the place of rest in God, a place of peace and comfort in Him. This secret place is a "spiritual place" where worry vanishes and peace reigns. It is the place of God's presence. When we spend time praying, seeking God, and dwelling in His presence, we are in the secret place.

The word *dwell* means "to make one's home; reside; live." When you and I *dwell in Christ—in the secret place*—we do not just visit there occasionally; we take up permanent residence there.

In the New Testament, one of the Greek words translated *dwell* is the same Greek word translated *abide* in John 15:7 (NKJV) where Jesus says, "If you abide in Me, and My words abide in you, you will ask what you desire, and it shall be done for you."

If you and I abide in God, it is the same thing as dwelling in God. As a matter of fact, the *Amplified Bible* translates John 15:7, "If you live in Me [abide vitally united to Me] and My words remain in you and continue to live in your hearts, ask whatever *you* will, and it shall be done for you."

In other words, we need to be firmly planted in God. We need to know the Source of our help in every situation and in every circumstance. We need to have our own secret place of peace and security. We need to rely on God and trust Him completely.

The Holy Spirit as Strengthener and Standby

And I will ask the Father, and He will give you another Comforter
(Counselor, Helper, Intercessor, Advocate, Strengthener, and Standby),
that He may remain with you forever.

—JOHN 14:16

Standby" has a special meaning and application to us in this modern age. We are all aware of airline passengers who travel "standby," meaning that they stand by the airline ticket counter waiting to step up and claim a seat on the first available flight. The Lord used this scene to teach me about the Holy Spirit as our Standby, One Who stands by us at all times waiting for the first available opportunity to jump in and give us the help and strength we need—which is why He is also called our Helper, our Strengthener.

I have learned that one of the most spiritual prayers we can offer is the one-word prayer, "Help!" I can't tell you how many times a week I stop and cry out to God, "Help me, Lord, strengthen me. I know You are here because the Bible promises me that You are always standing by to help me and strengthen me in every situation of life." Sometimes when I am preaching and teaching day after day, night after night, I get so worn out I just have to pray, "Lord, help me, I need Your strength."

There have been times when I have led seven meetings in four days. Often I get so tired that I have to remind myself that my help comes from the Lord and cry out to Him, claiming His promise that those who wait upon Him will renew their strength (SEE PSALM 121:2 AND ISAIAH 40:31). In such moments, I always receive the help and strength I need to finish the work that God has given me to do.

The Power of a Surrendered Will

And the word of the Lord came to Jonah the second time,
saying, Arise, go to Nineveh, that great city, and preach and cry out
to it the preaching that I tell you.

—JONAH 3:1-2

We read in the book of Jonah how God told Jonah to go to Nineveh and preach repentance to the people there. But Jonah did not want to, so he went to Tarshish, which is geographically opposite to Nineveh. Running from God does not help us to be at peace with Him.

What happens when we go in the opposite direction from where God has directed us? What happened to Jonah? When he boarded a ship and headed in his own direction, a storm arose. Many of the storms we face in life are the result of our own stubbornness. In many instances, we have been disobedient to the voice and leadership of God.

The violent storm that came upon Jonah frightened the men on the ship. They cast lots to see who was causing the trouble, and the lot fell on Jonah. He knew he had disobeyed God, so he told the men to throw him overboard in order to deliver them from danger.

They did as he requested, the storm stopped, and a great fish swallowed Jonah. From the fish's belly (not a pleasant place), he cried out to God for deliverance and repented of his stubborn ways. The fish vomited Jonah upon the dry land; and in Jonah 3:1, we see that the word of the Lord came to Jonah a second time. God told him again to go to Nineveh and preach to the people there. No matter how long we avoid God's instruction, it is still there for us to deal with when we stop running.

God's will makes us uncomfortable only as long as we are not pursuing it. In other words, we always know when something is just not right in our lives. Eventually we see that being *in* God's will, not *out* of His will, is what brings peace and joy to us. We have to surrender our own wills, because walking in our self-centered ways is what keeps us unhappy.

Succeed at Being Yourself

He renews my strength. He guides me along
right paths, bringing honor to his name.

—PSALM 23:3 (NLT)

At my age now I feel really great—which shows that things like energy, health, and happiness don't need to decline as we age. But part of my contentment comes because I've become comfortable with who I am. I've succeeded at being myself. I don't pine away for my twenties, partly because I didn't like my twenties anyway, and partly because it wouldn't matter if I did! Here I am now, and I have chosen to live today!

People who long for their youth are never content, because every day that youth gets a little farther away. Don't despise getting old, because if you stay alive you can't avoid it. It's much better to enjoy who you are now and try to live and look appropriate for someone like you. It helps to find role models. We don't think of fifty- or sixty-year-olds as needing role models, but they do! Everyone does.

Billy Graham is a good role model for me, and I can honestly say that I have never worried about how much he weighs or how many wrinkles he has. I admire him for his spirit, commitment, accomplishments, and dedication to God and his life's calling. Discontentment is one of the big giants we must conquer if we ever hope to enjoy life fully. Discontentment with looks, age, position, possessions, and anything else that makes us ungrateful for what we currently have.

We may not have all we would like to have, but we certainly have more than some people. No matter how you think you look, there is somebody who would love to look like you. No matter how old you are, there is someone older who would love to be as young as you. Cheer up and make the best of things. Love yourself and love your life; it is the only one you have!

Simple, Believing Prayer

And when you pray, do not heap up phrases (multiply words, repeating the same ones over and over) as the Gentiles do, for they think they will be heard for their much speaking.

—MATTHEW 6:7

We must develop confidence in simple, believing prayer. We need the confidence that even if we simply say, "God, help me," He hears and will answer. We can depend on God to be faithful to do what we have asked Him to do, as long as our request is in accordance with His will. Too often we get caught up in our own works concerning prayer.

Sometimes we lose sight of the fact that prayer is simply conversation with God. The length or volume or eloquence of our prayer is not the issue; it is the sincerity of our heart and the confidence we have that God hears and will answer us that are important. Sometimes we try to sound so devout and elegant that we get lost. If we could ever get delivered from trying to impress God, we would be a lot better off.

First Thessalonians 5:17 says, "Be unceasing in prayer [praying perseveringly]" or as the *King James Version* puts it, "Pray without ceasing." If we don't understand simple, believing prayer, that instruction can come down upon us like a very heavy burden. We may feel that we are doing well to pray thirty minutes a day, so how can we possibly pray without ever stopping? We need to have such confidence about our prayer life that prayer becomes just like breathing, an effortless thing that we do every moment we are alive.

We don't work and struggle at breathing, unless we have a lung disorder, and neither should we work and struggle at praying. I don't believe we will struggle in this area if we really understand the power of simple, believing prayer. We should remember that prayer is made powerful by the sincerity of it and the faith behind it.

Let God Pay You Back

And forgive us our sins, just as we have forgiven
those who have sinned against us.

—MATTHEW 6:12 (NLT)

Any time you are hurt by another person, there is always the feeling that he owes you something. Likewise, when you hurt someone else, you may have a sense that you need to make it up to him or pay him back in some way. Unjust treatment, abuse of any kind, leaves an "unpaid debt" in the spirit realm. Such debts are felt in the mind and the emotions. If revengeful feelings from what others owe you, or from what you owe them, become too heavy or linger in your heart too long, you may even see unhealthy results in your body.

Jesus taught His disciples to pray, "And forgive us our debts, as we also have forgiven (left, remitted, and let go of the debts, and have given up resentment against) our debtors." (MATTHEW 6:12) He was speaking about asking God to forgive our sins, and He referred to them as "debts." A debt is something that is owed by one person to another. Jesus said that God will forgive us our debts—release them and let them go, and act toward us as if we had never owed Him anything. He also commanded us to behave the same way toward those who are in debt to us. Once again, let me say that this may sound difficult, but it is much more difficult to hate someone and spend your entire life trying to collect a debt that the person can never pay.

The Bible says that God will give us our recompense (SEE ISAIAH 61:7-8). I never paid much attention to that scripture until some years ago while studying in the area of forgiveness and releasing debts. *Recompense* is a key word for anyone who has been hurt. When the Bible says that God will give us our recompense, it basically means that God Himself will pay us back what is owed us!

Avoid Strife to Maintain Peace

> *Then Abram talked it over with Lot. "This arguing between our herdsmen has got to stop," he said. "After all, we are close relatives! I'll tell you what we'll do. Take your choice of any section of the land you want, and we will separate. If you want that area over there, then I'll stay here. If you want to stay in this area, then I'll move on to another place."*
>
> —GENESIS 13:8-9 (NLT)

The relationship between Abram (later Abraham) and Lot illustrates the importance of maintaining peace in our relationships with others. Genesis 12 records the covenant of peace that God made with Abraham and his heirs. Abraham became extremely rich and powerful because God blessed him. God chose him to be the man through whom He would bless all the nations on the face of the earth.

I find it interesting that in the very next chapter, Genesis 13, strife came between Lot and Abraham's herdsmen (SEE V. 7). Strife is the exact opposite of peace. God gave Abraham peace, and Satan went immediately to stir up strife. God wanted to bless Abraham, and Satan wanted to steal his blessing. The Bible says that Abraham went to Lot and said, "Let there be no strife, I beg of you, between you and me, or between your herdsmen and my herdsmen." (GENESIS 13:8) He told Lot that they were going to have to separate, so Lot should choose the land he wanted, and Abraham would take what was left.

Lot, who would have had nothing if Abraham hadn't given it to him, chose the best part: the Jordan Valley. Abraham didn't say a thing; he just took the leftovers. He knew God would bless him if he stayed in peace. People who walk in peace in order to honor God cannot lose in life. But then God took Abraham up on a hill and said, "Now, you look to the north, to the south, to the east, and the west—and everything you see, I'll give to you" (SEE VV. 14-15). What a great deal! Abraham gave up one valley, and God gave him everything he could see.

Enter His Rest

So then, there is still awaiting a full and complete Sabbath-rest reserved for the [true] people of God; For he who has once entered [God's] rest also has ceased from [the weariness and pain] of human labors, just as God rested from those labors peculiarly His own.

—HEBREWS 4:9-10

If you are troubled and upset, worried and worn out about all the changes that need to be made in you, why not enter the rest of God? Struggling won't change you—neither will frustration or worry. The more you rest in God, the faster you will see change. If the canvas struggled under the artist's paint brush, the painting would never get finished. The canvas is perfectly still, totally submitted to the artist's wisdom and creativity. That is exactly the way we must be with God. He knows what He is doing and how to do it. We should believe in Him and enter His rest.

God Is Looking for Experienced Help

Although He was a Son, He learned [active, special]
obedience through what He suffered and, [His completed experience] making
Him perfectly [equipped], He became the Author and Source of eternal
salvation to all those who give heed and obey Him.

—HEBREWS 5:8-9

Have you ever needed a job, but every employment ad you read asked for someone with experience you didn't have? You wanted a job but did not have any experience, and it frustrated you. I have been in that situation, and I remember thinking, *How can I get experience if nobody will give me a job?* God also wants experienced help. When we go to work for God in His kingdom, He will use everything in our past, no matter how painful it was. He considers it experience. We have gone through some difficult things, and those things qualify us to help take someone else through them too. Even Jesus gained experience through the things He suffered.

I encourage you to look at your pain from a different viewpoint. A right perspective can make all the difference in the world. Take a look at how you can use your pain for someone else's gain. Can your mess become your ministry? Maybe you have gone through so much that you feel you have enough experience to be a specialist in some area.

I am a specialist in overcoming shame, guilt, poor self-image, lack of confidence, fear, anger, bitterness, self-pity, etc. Press past your pain and get your "master's degree" so you can work in the Kingdom for the One who is the master of restoring hurting people.

Become a Student of the Word

*Welcome the Word which implanted and rooted
[in your hearts] contains the power to save your souls.*

—JAMES 1:21

Sometimes God transcends the laws of nature and speaks to us through supernatural revelation. There is nothing more supernatural than the Word of God, which is given to us by divine inspiration of the Holy Spirit speaking through His prophets and disciples. The Bible has an answer for every question we might ever have. Anyone who wants to hear God's voice must be a student of the Word. Of all the other ways that God may speak to us, He will never contradict the written Word.

If we think we can hear clearly from God without spending time in the Word, we are mistaken. Listening for God's voice without being dedicated to spending time in the Word on a regular basis opens us up to hearing voices that are not from God. Knowing the written Word protects us from deception. Some people only come to God when they are in trouble and need help. But if they are not used to hearing from God, they will find it difficult to recognize His voice when they really need Him.

Even Jesus resisted Satan's lies by answering, "It is written" (SEE LUKE 4). Any idea, or prompting, or thought that comes to us needs to be compared to the Word of God. All vain imaginations are to be cast down and ignored (SEE 2 CORINTHIANS 10:5), but knowledge of the Word is of vital importance in discerning the voice of God.

Get Reappointed

We are hedged in (pressed) on every side [troubled and oppressed in every way],
but not cramped or crushed; we suffer embarrassments and are perplexed and
unable to find a way out, but not driven to despair; we are pursued
(persecuted and hard driven), but not deserted [to stand alone]; we are
struck down to the ground, but never struck out and destroyed.

—2 CORINTHIANS 4:8-9

All of us become disappointed when we have a plan that fails, a hope that does not materialize, a goal that is unreached. When things like that happen, for a certain period of time we experience a letdown, one that can lead to depression if it is not handled properly.

That's when we have to make the decision to adapt and adjust, to take a new approach, to just keep going despite our feelings. That's when we must remember that we have the Greater One residing within us, so that no matter what may happen to frustrate us, or how long it may take for our dreams and goals to become reality, we are not going to give up and quit just because of our emotions. That is when we must remember what God once told me in just such a moment: "When you get disappointed, you can always make the decision to get reappointed!"

Disappointment often leads to discouragement, which is even more of a "downer." How disappointing and discouraging it is to see the things we love senselessly destroyed by others or, even worse, by our own neglect or failure.

Regardless of how it may happen or who may be responsible, it is hard to go on when everything we have counted on falls down around us. That's when those of us who have the creative power of the Holy Spirit on the inside can get a new vision, a new direction, and a new goal to help us overcome the downward pull of disappointment, discouragement, and destruction.

The Unchanging Love of God

For I am the Lord, I do not change. —MALACHI 3:6

Real love, God's love, is the same all the time; it never changes. It just is! No wonder when Moses asked God what he should say to the Israelites when they asked him who had sent him to Pharaoh on their behalf, God answered, "I AM . . ." (EXODUS 3:13-14) I am more than willing to admit that I have not yet arrived in this area of unconditional love; but I certainly want to learn it, and I believe you do too. As human beings it seems we are ever changing, and we must learn to be more stable.

Stability was a trait I began to notice in Dave after we got married. I had never really been in the presence of stable people. Dave was just the same everywhere, all the time. He was not one way when he left for work in the morning and another way when he came home from work in the evening. His circumstances did not change his behavior. God had worked with Dave for years prior to our marriage and had developed stability in his character.

Stability must be worked in us. As we go around and around the same mountains in life, we finally learn not to let them upset us. Then and only then are we candidates for showing God's love to a needy world.

Express Your Faith

Because if you acknowledge and confess with your lips that Jesus is Lord and
in your heart believe (adhere to, trust in, and rely on the truth) that God
raised Him from the dead, you will be saved. For with the heart a person
believes (adheres to, trusts in, and relies on Christ) and so is justified (declared
righteous, acceptable to God), and with the mouth he confesses (declares openly
and speaks out freely his faith) and confirms [his] salvation.

—ROMANS 10:9-10

This is a very important principle that we are in danger of missing. We are saved by faith, but James said that faith without works is dead. I can believe in my heart that God is worthy of worship; but if I don't take action to worship Him, it doesn't do much good. I can say I believe in tithing; but if I don't tithe, it won't help me financially. Be bold—take some action and be expressive in your praise and worship. A lot of people even refuse to talk about God. They say, "Religion is a private thing." I cannot find anyone in the Bible who met Jesus and kept it private. When we are excited about praising and worshiping Him, it is difficult to have no outward expression. When He fills our hearts, the good news about Him comes out of our mouths.

The Wounded Healer

*Blessed be the God and Father of our Lord Jesus Christ, the Father of sympathy
(pity and mercy) and the God [Who is the Source] of every comfort
(consolation and encouragement), Who comforts (consoles and encourages) us
in every trouble (calamity and affliction), so that we may also be able to comfort (console and encourage) those who are in any kind of trouble or distress,
with the comfort (consolation and encouragement) with which we ourselves are
comforted (consoled and encouraged) by God.*

—2 CORINTHIANS 1:3-4

The best healer is often the wounded healer, because he knows what he is dealing with since he has suffered it himself. That's what Paul was saying in this passage from his letter to the church in Corinth. If you have suffered through some hard times in your life, you are going to be even more successful in ministering to those who are going through the same kind of suffering in their lives.

Though you may have had a rough time in your life, God can use what you have been through for His glory—if you will allow Him to do so! If I were still back where I started out, feeling sorry for myself, I would be no good to myself or anyone else. But because the Lord gave me the grace to lay down my self-pity and take up the challenge of living for Him, now I am able to help hundreds of thousands of people all over the nation and beyond.

To me the greatest testimony in the world is to be able to say, "God took what Satan tried to use to destroy me, and He turned it around for His glory and used it for the betterment of other people in the Kingdom." It takes God to do that! No matter where you may be today or what you may be going through, God can turn your situation around and use it to further His kingdom and bring blessings to you and to many others.

Patience Pleases God

> *For one is regarded favorably (is approved, acceptable, and thankworthy) if, as in the sight of God, he endures the pain of unjust suffering. [After all] what kind of glory [is there in it] if, when you do wrong and are punished for it, you take it patiently? But if you bear patiently with suffering [which results] when you do right and that is undeserved, it is acceptable and pleasing to God.*

—I PETER 2:19-20

If you and I are going to receive from these verses what God wants us to have, we will have to read them slowly and digest each phrase and sentence thoroughly. I will admit that I studied them for years trying to understand why it pleased God so much to see me suffer when the Bible plainly states that Jesus bore my suffering and pains of punishment (SEE ISAIAH 53:3-6). It was many years before I realized that the focal point of these verses in 1 Peter is not the suffering but the attitude one should have in suffering. Notice the word "patiently" being used in this passage, which says that if someone treats us wrong and we handle it patiently, it is pleasing to God. To encourage us in our suffering, we are exhorted to look at how Jesus handled the unjust attacks made on Him. The thing that pleases God is our patient attitude—not our suffering.

Are We Seeking God's Presence or His Presents?

You will show me the path of life; in Your presence is fullness of joy, at Your right hand there are pleasures forevermore.

—PSALM 16:11

Seeking God for who He is, not just for what He can do for us, is vital to our victory as believers. This was a major lesson for me. I had to learn to rejoice in God, not in what He was doing or not doing for me. The joy of the Lord is our strength (SEE NEHEMIAH 8:10), not the joy of circumstances. We will have little or no strength against the devil if we are unstable and allow our circumstances to determine our joy. It took a while for me to make this transition, but what an awesome difference it made in my spiritual life. Previously, I had always felt that I needed something, that something was missing in my walk with the Lord. I found it all in His presence, not in His presents. What we are looking for is not God's gifts, but God Himself. His presence is what sustains us and gives us life—abundant and everlasting life. We must decide that we will serve God even if we never get what we want. Like Job, we must say, "Though he slay me, yet will I trust in him." (JOB 13:15 KJV)

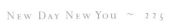

A Perfect Heart

For the eyes of the Lord run to and fro throughout the whole earth to show Himself strong in behalf of those whose hearts are blameless toward Him.

—2 CHRONICLES 16:9

The *King James Version* of this verse says that God looks for those "whose heart is perfect toward him." What does it mean to have a perfect heart? It means to have a heartfelt desire to do right and to please God. A person who has a perfect heart truly loves God, though he himself is not perfect. He may still have things in the flesh to deal with. His mouth may still get him into trouble. He may make mistakes or lose his temper. But when he does, he is quick to repent and make it right with God again. If he has offended someone else, he will humble himself and apologize.

When God looks for someone to use, He doesn't look for somebody with a perfect performance but a terrible heart attitude. He looks for someone who may not have a perfect performance but who has a right heart toward Him. God has all kinds of positions open in His kingdom. To fill those positions, He is always bringing one person down and lifting another person up. If we don't behave ourselves and keep a right attitude, we won't be in a position for God to use us in the way He wants to use us. He can promote us, but He can also demote us.

In our organization when we get ready to promote people, we don't look for those who are the most talented. We look for those who have a right heart attitude, those who are willing to do a little extra when called upon to do so. That is the way God is. And, one of the main things He looks for when He is ready to promote a person is a perfect heart.

His Sheep Know His Voice

And the sheep follow him because they know his voice.
They will never [on any account] follow a stranger.

—JOHN 10:4-5

There are many different ways that God speaks to us. Many people think they don't hear from God because they are looking for some supernatural manifestation that simply won't happen. Most of the time, God speaks through a still, small voice within that sounds quite natural. God says that we are His sheep and that He is our Shepherd, and that His sheep know His voice (SEE JOHN 10:1-5).

He may speak to us through nature, as He did with me a few days after I had received the baptism of the Holy Spirit. I drove past a field full of weeds, and in the middle of those weeds there were two or three patches of pretty flowers. I received an entire message from God about how flowers can grow in the middle of the weeds, and how good things are in our lives even in the midst of struggles and trials.

In all the years I have been listening for God's voice, I have had one open vision, and maybe four or five prophetic dreams. I am not making light of the fact that God speaks to some people through many dreams and visions; but most of the time, He just fills my thoughts with His thoughts and confirms them with His written Word. He gives me peace, and I try to follow His wisdom.

We need to discern the Lord's voice carefully, but we needn't over-spiritualize hearing from God. It is not as difficult as some may think. If God has something to say, He knows how to get His point across. It is our responsibility just to listen with expectancy and test what we hear against internal peace.

Are You Led by Your Emotions?

So then those who are living the life of the flesh [catering to the appetites and impulses of their carnal nature] cannot please or satisfy God, or be acceptable to Him. But you are not living the life of the flesh, you are living the life of the Spirit, if the [Holy] Spirit of God [really] dwells within you [directs and controls you].

—ROMANS 8:8-9

There are several definitions of the word *emotion*. According to Webster's dictionary, the root source of this term is the Latin *emovere,* meaning to move away. I find that definition very interesting because that is what carnal, uncrucified emotions try to do—to move us to follow them away from or out of the will of God.

In fact, that is Satan's plan for our lives—to get us to live by our carnal feelings so we never walk in the Spirit. The dictionary also says that *emotions* are "a complex, usually strong subjective response . . . involving physiological changes as a preparation for action." That is true. Because of their complexity, emotions are not easy to explain, which sometimes makes dealing with them difficult.

For example, there are times when the Holy Spirit is leading us to do something, and our emotions become involved, so we get all excited about doing it. The emotional support helps us feel that God really does want us to do the thing. At other times, the Lord will move us to do a certain thing, and our emotions will not want anything to do with what God is revealing to us and asking us to do. They give no support at all. At those times it is harder to obey God.

We are very dependent upon emotional support. If we lack understanding about the fickle nature of emotions, Satan can use them—or the lack of them—to keep us out of God's will. I firmly believe that no person will ever walk in God's will—and ultimately in victory—if he takes counsel with his emotions.

Trying Times Are Learning Times

For You, Who try the hearts and emotions and
thinking powers, are a righteous God.

—PSALM 7:9

God is a God Who tries emotions. What does the word "try" mean in this context? It means to test until purified. A few years ago, as I was praying, God said to me, "Joyce, I am going to test your emotions." I had never heard of anything like that. About six months later I suddenly seemed to become an emotional wreck. I cried for no reason. Everything hurt my feelings. I thought, *What is the problem here? What's going on?*

Then the Lord reminded me of what He had said to me earlier: "I am going to test your emotions." He led me to Psalm 7:9 and Revelation 2:23 and caused me to understand what He was doing for my own good. No matter who you are, there will be periods of time in which you feel more emotional than usual. You may wake up one morning and feel like breaking down and crying for no reason. During those times you have to be careful because your feelings will get hurt very easily.

There were times in my life when I would go to bed praying, feeling as sweet as could be, then wake up the next morning like I had stayed up all night eating nails! What should we do when we start feeling that way? First of all, we shouldn't start getting under condemnation. Secondly, we shouldn't even try to figure out what is happening. What we should do is simply say, "This is one of those times when my emotions are being tried. I'm going to trust God and learn to control them."

How are you and I ever going to learn to control ourselves emotionally unless God allows us to go through some trying times? If the Lord does not allow such testing times to come upon us, we will never learn how to deal with Satan when he brings them upon us—which he will sooner or later. Trying times are learning times.

Shrug Therapy

Casting the whole of your care [all your anxieties, all your worries, all your concerns, once and for all] on Him, for He cares for you affectionately and cares about you watchfully.

—I PETER 5:7

There are some things you can control in life—your choice of job, who your friends are, what you do for fun. There are others you can't—what other people say and do, the fluctuations of the stock market, the flat tire you got this morning. How you react to things you can't control helps determine your stress level and quality of health. People who regularly get upset over small things suffer in many ways. People who shrug them off do a lot better. The Bible calls it "casting your care."

Shrugging doesn't mean indifference; it simply means acknowledging there is nothing you can do to change things at that particular moment. The flat tire has already happened; dealing with it by calling AAA makes sense; throwing a tantrum and kicking it doesn't. The low-stress approach is to shrug things off. Life happens. God works in mysterious ways.

If you trust Him to work things out, you'll navigate the dips of life with barely a blip. I spend time ministering in India and Africa, and I'm confronted with the terrible poverty and hunger I see there. I care very deeply for these people and do everything I can to alleviate it, but I realize I am only one person and can only make my contribution. I can let it burn me up and shake my fist at the unfairness of it all, but what does that accomplish, other than make me sick and possibly render me unable to do anything? I do what I can, but I don't get upset about what is beyond my control. Do your best, pray, and God will do the rest!

Not Self-Confidence, God-Confidence!

*Put no confidence or dependence [on what we are] in the flesh and on outward
privileges and physical advantages and external appearances.*

—PHILIPPIANS 3:3

Everyone talks about self-confidence. All kinds of seminars are available
on confidence, both in the secular world and the church world. Confidence is generally referred to as "self-confidence," because we all know
that we need to feel good about ourselves if we are ever to accomplish
anything in life. We have been taught that all people have a basic need to
believe in themselves. However, that is a misconception. Actually, we do
not need to believe in ourselves—we need to believe in Jesus in us. We
do not dare feel good about ourselves apart from Him. When the apostle
Paul instructs us to "put no confidence . . . in the flesh," he means just
what he says—do not put confidence in yourself or in anything you can
do apart from Jesus.

We do not need self-confidence; we need God-confidence! Many people spend
their whole lives climbing the ladder of success only to find that when
they get to the top, their ladder was leaning against the wrong building.
Others struggle, trying to behave well enough to develop a measure of
confidence in themselves, only to endure repeated failures. Both of these
activities produce the same results: emptiness and misery.

I have found that most people fall into one of two categories: (1) they
never accomplish anything, no matter how hard they try, and end up hating
themselves because of their lack of achievement; or (2) they have enough
natural talent to accomplish great things, but take all the credit for their
achievements, which fills them with pride. Either way, they are a failure—
in the eyes of God. The only truly successful person in God's eyes is the individual who knows he is nothing in himself, but everything in Christ. Our
pride and boasting are to be in Jesus alone, and He is to have all the glory
(credit due) for whatever accomplishments we may achieve.

Choosing the Right Church

But [as for] you, teach what is fitting and becoming to sound (wholesome)
doctrine [the character and right living that identify true Christians].

—TITUS 2:1

I went to church for years and years and never heard a message about the power my words had on my life. I may have heard something about my thoughts; but if so, it wasn't enough to make any impact on my life because it did not change my thinking. I heard about grace and salvation and other good things. But it wasn't everything I needed to know in order to live in the righteousness, peace, and joy God offers to all who believe (SEE ROMANS 14:17). There are many wonderful churches that teach God's Word in its entirety; and I encourage you to make sure that wherever you choose to go to church, it is a place where you are learning and growing spiritually. We should not go to church just to fulfill an obligation we may think we have to God. We should go to church to fellowship with other believers in Jesus Christ, to worship God, and to learn how to live the life Jesus died for us to have and enjoy.

Rooted and Grounded in God

> *Be well balanced (temperate, sober of mind), be vigilant and cautious at all*
> *times; for that enemy of yours, the devil, roams around like a lion roaring [in*
> *fierce hunger], seeking someone to seize upon and devour. Withstand him; be*
> *firm in faith [against his onset—rooted, established, strong, immovable, and*
> *determined], knowing that the same (identical) sufferings are appointed to*
> *your brotherhood (the whole body of Christians) throughout the world.*
>
> —1 PETER 5:8-9

To be temperate is to be self-controlled. And to be sober of mind is to be level-headed. So here you and I are told to be well-balanced, self-controlled, level-headed, rooted, established, strong, immovable, and determined. According to this passage, how are we going to defeat the devil and withstand his physical and emotional onsets upon us? By being rooted and grounded in Christ. Satan may come against us with feelings, but we don't have to submit to our emotions. We can stand firmly against them even while they rage against us and even within us.

When problems arise—and they will from time to time—we are not to assume that the Lord will intervene without an invitation and take care of all our problems for us. We are to pray and ask Him to change our circumstances. Then we are to remain constant and unchanging, which will be a sign to the enemy of his impending downfall and destruction. Do you know why our constancy and fearlessness are signs to Satan that he will fail? Because he knows that the only way he can overcome a believer is through deception and intimidation. How can he threaten someone who has no fear of him? How can he deceive someone who recognizes his lies and refuses to believe them? What good does it do him to try to stir up fear or anger or depression in someone who chooses to stand firmly on the Word of God? When the devil sees his tactics are not working, he realizes he is failing and will be utterly defeated.

Honor God

> But as for you, the anointing (the sacred appointment, the unction) which
> you received from Him abides [permanently] in you; [so] then you have no
> need that anyone should instruct you. But just as His anointing teaches you
> concerning everything and is true and is no falsehood, so you must abide in
> (live in, never depart from) Him [being rooted in Him, knit to Him],
> just as [His anointing] has taught you [to do].
>
> —I JOHN 2:27

Sometimes we give more consideration to what people tell us than to what God has said to us. If we pray diligently, hear from God, but then start asking everybody else what they think, we are honoring people's opinions above the Word of God. This attitude will prevent us from developing a relationship in which we consistently hear from God.

The verse above confirms that we can trust God to instruct us without needing constant reassurance from others. It isn't saying that we don't need anybody to teach us the Word. Otherwise, God wouldn't appoint some to teach in the body of Christ. But it does say that if we are in Christ, we have an anointing that abides on the inside of us to guide and direct our lives. We might occasionally ask somebody for their wisdom, but we need not go to other people constantly to ask them about decisions we need to make for our lives.

Say NO to the Negative!

So whoever cleanses himself [from what is ignoble and unclean, who separates himself from contact with contaminating and corrupting influences] will [then himself] be a vessel set apart and useful for honorable and noble purposes, consecrated and profitable to the Master, fit and ready for any good work.

—2 TIMOTHY 2:21

You and I have two responsibilities in regard to "evil reports." One is not to give them, and the second is not to receive them. Each of us has a responsibility not to talk to others negatively and not to let others talk to us that way. It is our responsibility to help one another in a godly way to get out of the mode of thinking and speaking negatively about others, about ourselves, or about the situations we all have to face and deal with in this life. At one time when people would come to me to gossip about others, I thought I was obligated to listen to what they had to say. That's not what the apostle Paul tells us in Ephesians 4. He says that we are not to be involved in polluting our own minds or the minds of those around us. According to what Paul wrote to his young disciple Timothy in the above scripture, you and I are supposed to be clean vessels. We are to keep ourselves pure, and to help others to keep themselves pure as well.

The Laugh of Faith

The kings of the earth take their places; the rulers take counsel together
against the Lord and His Anointed One (the Messiah, the Christ).
They say, Let us break Their bands [of restraint] asunder and cast
Their cords [of control] from us. He Who sits in the heavens laughs;
the Lord has them in derision [and in supreme contempt He mocks them].

—PSALM 2:2-4

When God's enemies gather together against Him, He sits in the heavens and laughs. He is the Alpha and Omega, the Beginning and the End (SEE REVELATION 1:8), so He already knows how things are going to turn out. Since He is the beginning and the end, He must also be everything in between. If we are being led by God's Spirit, we can laugh also during those times. We laugh *the laugh of faith* as Abraham did. God told Him that even though he was too old to have a child in the natural, He would give him one anyway. Abraham laughed (SEE GENESIS 17:17)! Years passed before Abraham saw the fulfillment of God's promise. I am sure as he looked forward to the day he saw in his heart, he laughed.

We spend too much time in our thoughts looking at what is taking place now instead of looking at the finish line. Think of all the other things God has done for you. You had to wait for them also. He is faithful; He will do what He has promised. You may have to wait for a season, but if you decide to enjoy the trip, it will not seem nearly as long. You may be familiar with the old saying, "A watched pot never boils." When you stand and stare at a pot of water, it seems to take forever to come to the boiling point; but if you go about your business and do other things, keeping your mind off the water, it seems to take only a few seconds.

Watching your problem is like watching the pot of water. If you want to do your part, then get your mind off of your problem. It will be resolved a lot faster and you will be able to say, "I enjoyed the journey."

Dread Drains, Faith Energizes

Cast your burden on the Lord [releasing the weight of it]
and He will sustain you; He will never allow the [consistently] righteous to be
moved (made to slip, fall, or fail).

—PSALM 55:22

Dread is closely related to fear. We might say it is the forerunner to fear. I believe a lot of people dread many things and yet don't realize what a problem it is. We dread everything from getting out of bed to going to work, doing dishes, driving in traffic, and paying our bills.

How we approach any situation makes all the difference as to whether we will enjoy it. We will, of course, be miserable if we approach driving to work in traffic with a negative, complaining attitude. It won't do any good, because we must drive to work anyway. It is actually extremely foolish to dread things we must do and know we will do. The main thing dread does is steal the peace and joy of life. It also drains us of energy and strength we need for the day. Dread drains, faith energizes.

Being negative drains us, while being positive energizes us. Millions of people in the world today are tired. They see doctors who cannot find any real reason for their condition, so they tell them it is stress. Often we take medication for conditions that would be totally solved if we would eliminate worry, fear, and dread from our lives. If we will make a decision to approach every aspect of life, no matter what it is, with a pleasant, thankful attitude, we will see major changes for the better, even in our health.

The future is coming, no matter how much we fear or dread it. God gives us what we need for each day, but He does not give us tomorrow's grace or wisdom today. If we use today trying to figure out tomorrow, we feel pressure because we are using what we have been allotted for today. Probably one of the greatest ways we show our trust in God is by living life one day at a time. We prove our confidence in Him by enjoying today and not letting the concern of tomorrow interfere.

Meditating on the Right Things

I will meditate also upon all Your works and consider all Your [mighty] deeds.

—PSALM 77:12

The psalmist David spoke frequently about meditating on God, His goodness, His works, and His ways. It is tremendously uplifting to think on the goodness of God and all the marvelous works of His hands. I enjoy watching television shows about nature, animals, ocean life, etc., because they depict the greatness, the awesomeness of God, His infinite creativity and how He is upholding all things by the might of His power (SEE HEBREWS 1:3). Meditating on God and His ways and works will need to become a regular part of your thought life if you want to experience victory.

One of my favorite verses of Scripture is Psalm 17:15 in which the psalmist says of the Lord, "I shall be fully satisfied, when I awake [to find myself] beholding Your form [and having sweet communion with You]." I spent a lot of unhappy days because I started thinking about all the wrong things the minute I awoke each morning. In contrast, I've found that choosing to think about the Lord and fellowshiping with Him early in the morning is one sure way to start my day right and enjoy my life. I can truly say that I have been fully satisfied since the Holy Spirit has helped me operate out of the mind of Christ (the mind of the Spirit) that is within me.

Consider Your Ways

Is it time for you yourselves to dwell in your paneled houses while this house
[of the Lord] lies in ruins? Now therefore thus says the Lord of hosts: Consider
your ways and set your mind on what has come to you. You have sown much,
but you have reaped little; you eat, but you do not have enough; you drink, but
you do not have your fill; you clothe yourselves, but no one is warm; and he who
earns wages has earned them to put them in a bag with holes in it.

—HAGGAI 1:4-6

Beginning in Haggai 1:2, we see a group of people whom God had told eighteen years previously to rebuild His house. They still had not been obedient to what He had told them to do; yet they didn't understand why their lives were in a mess. They wondered where the blessing of God was. After reminding them of their disobedience to His instruction, the Lord spoke to them the verses above.

Does this sound like anybody you know? How often have you heard someone say, "I just don't understand what's going on, God. I just don't understand"? Now look at the answer in Haggai 1:7: "Thus says the Lord of hosts: Consider your ways (your previous and present conduct) and how you have fared."

In other words, if we are not satisfied with what is going on in our lives right now, maybe we should look back and let God show us how the way we have conducted ourselves has affected what is happening to us now. We must be willing to change our ways if we want to receive His blessing. If we are willing to change from the previous and present conduct that is holding back God's blessings, we can have greater victories than what we have ever had before.

Say Grace

O give thanks to the Lord, for He is good; for His mercy and
loving-kindness endure forever!

—PSALM 118:1

Thanking God for the bounty on your table is the best way I know to immediately bring yourself into a healthier relationship with your food. If you have a tendency to overeat, ask God to help you at this meal to stay in His perfect will. God wants you to enjoy what you eat, and true enjoyment does not mean eating so much that you spend the next few hours feeling sick and guilty. Realize that this meal is not the last one you will ever eat. There will be plenty of other meals in your life, so thank God, enjoy your food, make good choices, and stop as soon as you feel full.

Another great trick for reminding yourself that food is about more than taste is to tell yourself that you are eating for two. Many women switch to healthier diets once they get pregnant. They may have been willing to shortchange themselves nutritionally, but not their babies! Well, you are also eating for two. Since your body is the temple of the Holy Spirit, you can see how important it is to keep God's "vessel" healthy. You should keep yourself healthy so God can act through you in the world. Don't shortchange Him!

Spiritual Food for Spiritual Hunger

*Make no provision for [indulging] the flesh [put a stop to thinking about the
evil cravings of your physical nature] to [gratify its] desires (lusts).*

—ROMANS 13:14

Food addiction is easy, because food doesn't come with the same stigmas
as cigarettes or drugs. Unlike these vices, food has a legitimate—even
essential—role in health. Only when it slips into overuse does it become
a problem. But it's so easy to get to that point! Food is reliable. Unlike
spouses, friends, or great weather, it is always there. But that's the problem. Any time we feel spiritually empty, whether through sadness, depression, or boredom, it's easy to reach for food to fill that void. Soon,
we mistake spiritual hunger for physical hunger, and food becomes the
immediate answer to any drop in well-being. You know where this leads.
The more you try to treat your spiritual longing with food or other feel-
good stimuli, the greater your soul's cry for spiritual nourishment will be
and the greater your disease will become.

Fortunately, there is another source of comfort that is always there
when you need it. Unlike bad food or drugs, it doesn't leave you over-
weight, sick, or lethargic. It's even free. That something is God. He is
called the "Father of sympathy" the God of every comfort . . . Who consoles us in every trouble" (SEE 2 CORINTHIANS 1:3-4). When I hurt, I have
learned to run to God first, instead of another person or substance. I'm
not saying this is automatic. It took me years to get this straight, and I
still sometimes have to remind myself that what I truly need is *spiritual*
nourishment. But learning this habit will do more to keep your mind and
body sound and your life on an even keel than anything I know. Your spirit
needs nourishment just like your body does. Don't wait until you have a
crisis in your life to start feeding it.

Set Your Mind and Keep It Set

*And set your minds and keep them set on what is above
(the higher things), not on the things that are on the earth.*

—COLOSSIANS 3:2

The Bible says we are to set our minds on things above, not on things on the earth. Having been addicted to approval, I know how difficult it is not to think about it when we feel someone is not pleased with us. Thoughts of that person's anger and rejection seem to fill our every waking moment. Instead of trying not to think wrong thoughts, choose right ones. Fill your mind with positive thoughts. Meditate on God's Word and His will for you. Then wrong thoughts will find no place of entry.

We have all had the experience of being terribly worried about something, of having our minds rotating around and around a problem endlessly. If we get involved in something else that interests us, we stop worrying for a period of time. When it is quiet and we are alone, or when we have nothing else to do, we begin to worry again.

I have found that one of the best allies against wrong thinking is to stay busy doing something for someone else. I don't have time to think about "me" when I am occupied with someone else's need. In this way I set my mind on what is above, not on earthly things. I set my mind on God's instruction to me to walk in love (SEE EPHESIANS 5:2).

God Loves You Perfectly

> *For I am persuaded beyond doubt (am sure) that neither death nor life, nor angels nor principalities, nor things impending and threatening nor things to come, nor powers, nor height nor depth, nor anything else in all creation will be able to separate us from the love of God which is in Christ Jesus our Lord.*
>
> —ROMANS 8:38-39

I can talk about the love of God throughout an entire weekend conference, I can demonstrate all the different ways God has proven His love for us, but I cannot force anyone to receive His love. It is a personal choice that each person has to make. Even when we make mistakes and know that we do not deserve the love of God, we must still receive His love in order to enjoy the fullness of what He wants us to have.

The love of God will carry you through to victory when all of the powers and principalities of hell seem to be against you. The love of God will carry you through the storms of life and into a place of calm peace. But you will never be more than a conqueror (SEE ROMANS 8:37) if you do not have a revelation of how much you are loved by God.

We have to know that God loves us even during the times when we make mistakes and fail. His love is not restricted to the days when we think we have performed well. We need to be confident of His love, especially when we have trials and when the devil is mocking us with accusations, such as, "Well, you must have done something wrong."

When the accuser comes, we must know that God loves us. Even if we did do something wrong, even if we did open a door for the devil to enter in, even if we did act in ignorance, God still loves us. God is on our side (SEE ROMANS 8:28), and He is going to show us what we need to do to get out of the messes we got ourselves into.

Knowledge Can Be Dangerous

For I determined not to know any thing among you,
save Jesus Christ, and him crucified.

—1 CORINTHIANS 2:2 (KJV)

This is such a glorious scripture. You and I try to know everything, and here Paul is telling us that he did just the opposite. Unlike us, who worry about all the things we don't know, Paul was trying to get rid of some of the things he did know. Why? Because he had discovered that, as the Bible teaches, sometimes knowledge can be aggravating (SEE ECCLESIASTES 12:12). He had also discovered that knowledge can create pride: "[Yet mere] knowledge causes people to be puffed up (to bear themselves loftily and be proud)." (1 CORINTHIANS 8:1)

Sometimes the more knowledge we accumulate, the more problems we create. Often we plot and scheme and finagle to discover things that would be better left alone. Have you ever schemed to find out something that was going on and then when you did discover it, you sincerely wished you had stayed out of it? That is why Paul said that he had determined to know nothing but Jesus Christ, and Him crucified. Sometimes the more I think I know, the harder it is to follow God.

Believe in the Favor of God

But the Lord was with Joseph, and showed him mercy and loving-kindness
and gave him favor in the sight of the warden of the prison.

—GENESIS 39:21

There are many people spoken of in the Bible who received favor. Since God is no respecter of persons (SEE ACTS 10:34), we can believe for and receive favor in our daily lives.

Favor is available to us but like many other good things in life, just because something is available to us does not mean that we will ever partake of it. The Lord makes many things available to us that we never receive and enjoy because we never activate our faith in that area. I am a very bold, straightforward, tell-it-like-I-see-it woman. Many people don't handle that type of personality very well, so I knew I needed favor. I needed God to show people my heart and help them believe that I wanted to help them. I think we all have some personality quirks that can turn people off, so praying for favor is a wise thing to do.

When God gives us favor, people favor us—and often for no reason they can even explain. If three people applied for the same position and were all equally qualified, the one living under the favor of God would get it.

Favor is actually a part of grace. In the *English New Testament* the word *grace* and the word *favor* are both translated from the same Greek word *charis.* So the grace of God is the favor of God. And the favor of God is the grace of God—that which causes things to happen in our lives that need to happen, through the channel of our faith—the power of God doing something for us that we can neither earn nor deserve.

I know you have had times of receiving favor, and I am sure you enjoyed it very much. I am encouraging you to release your faith in this area in a greater way than ever before. Don't be afraid to ask God to give you favor.

Listen to the Promptings of the Spirit

But now we are discharged from the Law and have terminated all intercourse
with it, having died to what once restrained and held us captive. So now
we serve not under [obedience to] the old code of written regulations, but
[under obedience to the promptings] of the Spirit in newness [of life].

—ROMANS 7:6

According to this passage, we are no longer under the restraints of the law but now serve the Lord under obedience to the promptings of the Holy Spirit. A prompting is a "knowing" down on the inside of you telling you what to do. First Kings 19:11-12 describes the "still, small voice" the Lord used with Elijah: "And behold, the Lord passed by, and a great and strong wind rent the mountains and broke in pieces the rocks before the Lord, but the Lord was not in the wind; and after the wind an earthquake, but the Lord was not in the earthquake; and after the earthquake a fire, but the Lord was not in the fire; and after the fire [a sound of gentle still-ness and] a still, small voice."

A prompting from the Lord is not like hitting someone over the head with a hammer to prompt them to do something! The Lord did not use the great and strong wind, the earthquake, or the fire as a prompting but instead came as "a sound of gentle stillness" and "a still, small voice."

The prompting of "a still, small voice" is not necessarily a voice; it can be God's wisdom giving you direction in that moment. First Corinthians 1:30 tells us, "But it is from Him that you have your life in Christ Jesus, Whom God made our Wisdom from God." If we are born again, Jesus is living inside us. If He is inside us, we have God's wisdom in us to draw on at any moment! But unless we listen to wisdom, it won't do us any good.

Take a Praise Pause

Seven times a day and all day long do I praise You
because of Your righteous decrees.

—PSALM 119:164

I don't think anything blesses God more than when we stop right in the middle of what we're doing sometimes and lift our hands to worship Him or take a moment to bow down before Him and say, "I love You, Lord." In the scripture quoted above, the psalmist says he took time seven times a day and all day long to praise God.

Think about a businessman, for example, maybe the president of a large company. Wouldn't it be wonderful if two or three times a day, he would close the door to his office, turn the lock, kneel, and say, "God, I just want to take some time to worship You. Father, all these things You are giving me—the business, the money, the success—are great, but I just want to worship You. I magnify You. You are so wonderful. I love You. You are all I need. Father, I worship You. Jesus, I worship You. Holy Spirit, I worship You"? I believe that if the businessman did that, he would never need to be concerned about his business, his finances, or success. All of those things would be taken care of.

Matthew 6:33 (KJV) says, "But seek ye first the kingdom of God, and his righteousness; and all these things shall be added unto you."

A Personal Relationship

Jesus answered him, I assure you, most solemnly I tell you, that
unless a person is born again (anew, from above), he cannot ever see
(know, be acquainted with, and experience) the kingdom of God.

—JOHN 3:3

When the Bible says that we must be born again—it doesn't say that we must be religious. We must let Jesus come into our lives and sit on the throne of our hearts to rule and reign over every step we take. When He tells us to go a certain direction, He will also issue to us the power we need to do what He has told us to do. Jesus will never say, "Just do it!" He always gives us the power to do whatever He tells us.

The greatest hindrance to hearing from God is trying to get to Him through works instead of through a personal relationship with Him by being born again and fellowshiping with Him regularly. People can go to church for years and do religious things all their lives without ever knowing Jesus as the Lord of their lives.

It is frightening to realize that there are probably thousands of people sitting in churches every week who won't go to heaven. As I often say, "Sitting in a church won't make a person a Christian any more than sitting in a garage will make him a car." In Matthew 7:20-23, the Bible states that there are people who will say in the judgment, "Lord, Lord, have we not done many mighty works in Your name . . . ?" and He will say to them, "I never knew you; depart from Me, you who act wickedly [disregarding My commands]." People can be doing good works and yet disregarding God's commands if they are not taking the time to be with Him and hear His instructions.

Spending Time with God

Be strong in the Lord [be empowered through your union with Him]; draw your strength from Him [that strength which His boundless might provides].

—EPHESIANS 6:10

When I first started trying to spend time with God, it was hard for me. I felt silly and self-conscious. I was bored. I would sit and yawn and try not to fall asleep. Like anything worthwhile, sitting quietly in the presence of the Lord takes time to master. You have to keep at it. And it is not something you can learn from someone else. I don't think it is possible to teach another human being to fellowship with God. Why? Because each person is different and has to learn for himself how to communicate with his Creator.

My fellowship time includes prayer of all kinds (petition, intercession, praise, etc.), reading books that God is using to help me, Bible study, waiting on God, repentance, crying, laughing, receiving revelation. My time with Him is different almost every day.

God has an individual plan for each person. If you will go to Him and submit to Him, He will come into your heart and commune with you. He will teach and guide you in the way you should go. Don't try to do what someone else does or to be what someone else is. Just allow the Lord to show you how you are to fellowship with Him. Then follow as He directs your life, step by step.

Are You Trusting or Worrying?

> *Lean on, trust in, and be confident in the Lord with all your*
> *heart and mind and do not rely on your own insight or understanding.*
> *In all your ways know, recognize, and acknowledge Him, and He will direct*
> *and make straight and plain your paths.*

—PROVERBS 3:5-6

What do you let your mind do when you have problems? Do you try to figure things out instead of leaving them in God's capable hands?

There is the mind of the flesh, which is wrong thinking based on your thoughts and reasoning. And there is the mind of the Spirit, which is right thinking based on the Word of God and the inner promptings of the Holy Spirit. Confusion, frustration, and anxiety are the products of operating in the mind of the flesh. Joy is the product of the Spirit and of following the leading of the Spirit in prayer and fellowship with God.

If you operate in the mind of the Spirit, you can have "the peace of God, which passeth all understanding," and you can have "joy unspeakable" and be "full of glory" right in the middle of terrible trials and tribulations (SEE PHILIPPIANS 4:7; 1 PETER 1:8 KJV). The peace "which passeth all understanding" and "joy unspeakable" are types of peace and joy that don't make any sense. In other words, when you have these types of peace and joy within, you are happy just because you know that God is. He is able to "direct and make straight and plain your paths" in an exceedingly, abundantly above all-you-can-ask-or-think way. You don't have to try to change yourself or anyone else—and that makes you happy.

You don't have to worry about tomorrow—and that makes you happy. You don't have to worry about yesterday—and that makes you happy. You don't have to know how to do everything—and that makes you happy. All you need to do is know the One who knows. Trying to figure things out will only wear you out. But if you trust God for the answers, you can enter His rest.

Take Time to Be Still

In the morning You hear my voice, O Lord; in the morning I prepare [a prayer, a sacrifice] for You and watch and wait [for You to speak to my heart].

—PSALM 5:3

While learning to recognize the voice of God, you must find times just to be still in order to hear God's leading in your life. A busy, hurried, frantic, stressful lifestyle makes it very challenging to hear God.

Find a place to get quiet before God. Get alone with Him and tell Him that you need Him and want Him to teach you how to hear His voice. Ask Him to tell you what He has for your life. Ask Him what He wants you to do. Ask Him to show you what you are doing that He doesn't want you to do.

Present yourself to God, and listen. Even if you don't hear from Him, you will honor Him by seeking Him. He promises that if you seek Him, you will find Him—you will get a Word from God. He will lead you by an inner knowing, by common sense, by wisdom, and by peace.

I've found that God doesn't always speak to us right away or necessarily during our prayer time. He may end up speaking to you two days later while you are in the middle of doing something completely unrelated. I honestly don't know why God sometimes waits to respond; but I do know if we will be diligent to seek God, if we show Him that we want His will, He will speak to us. "Your ears will hear a word behind you, saying, This is the way; walk in it." (ISAIAH 30:21) It may not be in our timing, but God will speak to us and let us know the way we should go.

As you wait for answers from God, concentrate on obeying Him in order to keep a clear conscience. You will not have joy if you know God has told you to do something and you haven't obeyed. But if you follow God's voice, you will be radically and outrageously blessed.

Make Love a Habit

> *And let us consider and give attentive, continuous care to*
> *watching over one another, studying how we may stir up (stimulate and*
> *incite) to love and helpful deeds and noble activities.*
>
> —HEBREWS 10:24

If we intend to make love a habit, then we must develop the habit of loving people with our words. The fleshly (lower, sensual) nature points out flaws, weaknesses, and failures. It seems to feed on the negatives in life. It sees and magnifies all that is wrong with people and things. But the Bible says in Romans 12:21 that we are to overcome evil with good.

Walking in the Spirit (continually following the prompting or leading, guiding, and working of the Holy Spirit through our own spirit instead of being led by our emotions) requires being positive. God is positive, and in order to walk with Him we must agree with Him (SEE AMOS 3:3).

It is easy to find something wrong with everyone, but love covers a multitude of sins: "Above all things have intense and unfailing love for one another, for love covers a multitude of sins [forgives and disregards the offenses of others]." (1 PETER 4:8) Love does not expose faults; it covers them.

Producing Patience, Character, and Hope

> *Moreover [let us also be full of joy now!] let us exult and triumph in our troubles and rejoice in our sufferings, knowing that pressure and affliction and hardship produce patient and unswerving endurance. And endurance (fortitude) develops maturity of character (approved faith and tried integrity). And character [of this sort] produces [the habit of] joyful and confident hope.*
>
> —ROMANS 5:3-4

It is easy to say, "Don't worry." But to actually do that requires experience with God. I don't think there is any way a person can fully overcome the habit of worry, anxiety, and fear and develop the habit of peace, rest, and hope without years of experience. That's why it is so important to continue to have faith and trust in God in the very midst of trials and tribulations. It is so important to resist the temptation to give up and quit when the going gets rough—and keeps on getting rougher over a long period of time. It is in those hard, trying times that the Lord is building in us the patience, endurance, and character that will eventually produce the habit of joyful and confident hope.

Pray at All Times

> *Pray at all times (on every occasion, in every season) in the*
> *Spirit, with all [manner of] prayer and entreaty. To that end keep alert and*
> *watch with strong purpose and perseverance, interceding in behalf of all the*
> *saints (God's consecrated people).*
>
> —EPHESIANS 6:18

In Ephesians 6:10-17, the apostle Paul talks about the armor of God and how we are to use it and the weapon of the Word to engage in spiritual warfare. After each piece has been listed, in verse eighteen Paul sums up his message by saying, "Pray at all times." How often are we to pray? At all times.

What does that mean? Does it mean that when we are out doing the grocery shopping and God puts it on our heart to pray we are to drop to our knees right there in the middle of the supermarket aisle? I often kneel by my bed and pray. There are other times when I feel led by God to lie down, face to the floor, before Him and pray. We have to be careful not to confuse physical posture with prayer. We can also pray silently in the supermarket as we are walking down the aisles.

In the different seasons of life we are able to pray in different ways. A young mother with three or four little children, for example, is going to have to structure her prayer life differently from that of a grandmother whose family is all grown up and out of the house.

If we become too "religious" about prayer, thinking we must do it one way or the other because that is how someone else does it, we will bring condemnation on ourselves. The important thing about prayer is not the posture or the time or place but learning to pray in faith—at all times, unceasingly. Anytime the desire or need arises—*pray!*

Wait on Him

Those who wait for the Lord [who expect, look for, and hope in Him] shall change and renew their strength and power; they shall lift their wings and mount up [close to God] as eagles [mount up to the sun]; they shall run and not be weary, they shall walk and not faint or become tired.

—ISAIAH 40:31

Isaiah teaches us to wait for the Lord when we know our strength needs to be renewed. Waiting for God means spending time with Him in His Word and His presence. There are certain people we can draw strength from just by being around them. Their very presence, the way they talk and approach life, seems to make us feel better when we are discouraged or feeling down in any way. Likewise, there are others who can always make us feel worse. They have a way of putting a negative edge on everything.

When you and I need to be strengthened, we should spend time with God and with people filled with His Spirit. Spending time in God's presence is like sitting in a room filled with sweet-smelling perfume. If we sit there long enough, we take the fragrance with us when we leave. It will be in our clothing, in our hair, and even in our very skin.

Moses was a man of prayer. He spent a great deal of time fellowshiping with and talking to God. He knew that if God did not help him, he would fail miserably. Because of Moses' faithfulness to seek God, he was given an assuring message: "And the Lord said, My Presence shall go with you, and I will give you rest." (EXODUS 33:14)

Believing Is a Win-Win Situation

May the God of your hope so fill you with all joy and peace in believing
[through the experience of your faith] that by the power of the Holy Spirit you
may abound and be overflowing (bubbling over) with hope.

—ROMANS 15:13

Romans 15:13 is one of my favorite scriptures. It says that joy and peace are found in believing. I remember when I was going through a period of time in which I had lost my joy and my peace. I didn't know what was wrong with me, but I knew something was wrong. One night I was pretty desperate, so I went over to the little "promise box" full of scriptures and began flipping through it. I pulled out one of the little cards in it, and immediately the Lord spoke to me through it. It simply said, "Romans 15:13: Joy and peace are found in belief."

As soon as I got back to believing, my joy and peace came back. And the same is true for you. As soon as you start doubting, you lose your joy and peace; but as soon as you start believing again, your joy and peace come back to you. God has given us a tool to keep ourselves radically happy and peaceful. All we have to do is believe. Of course, as soon as we start believing, the devil starts screaming in our ears, "That's stupid! What if you believe and you don't get what you are believing?" That's when we have to answer back, "No, it's not stupid. What if I believe and get what I am believing? But even if I never get it, I am still happier and more peaceful by believing than I am by doubting."

So it is a win-win situation. There is no way to lose when we believe; because if we believe, we are liable to get what we are believing for. But even if we don't, we will stay happy and peaceful. So it is vital that we keep a believing heart.

I Promise to Love You, But . . .

*But one thing I do [it is my one aspiration]: forgetting what lies
behind and straining forward to what lies ahead.*

—PHILIPPIANS 3:13

Forgiveness is the core ingredient to every successful relationship. So many people carry exceptions to their offer of love. "I love you, but you really hurt my feelings yesterday." Or "I love you, but I'm too tired, too busy, too distracted, too annoyed, too angry, too unhappy to be nice to you right now."

True love simply says, "I love you!" No exceptions! The apostle Paul points out in Philippians 3:11-14 that to attain the spiritual and moral resurrection that lifts us out from among the dead, even while we are here in body, we must continue to forget the past and press on for the goal to win the prize to which Jesus is calling us. We are to forget what lies behind and press on to what lies ahead.

Women seem more prone to carrying grudges and remembering offenses for days, and some even remain bitter for years. Jesus calls us to a higher prize that requires us to both receive forgiveness and give it to others. The Lord's Prayer calls us to pray for forgiveness as we forgive others: "And forgive us our debts, as we forgive our debtors." (MATTHEW 6:12 KJV)

There's nothing in my flesh that wants to forgive Dave when I think he is wrong. But God wants me to respond with love and say no to my flesh and yes to Him, even though I don't feel like it. Years ago, as I began doing what God said to do, I honestly came to the point where I wanted what God wanted. I don't even know how or when that happened. A supernatural change takes place in us as we obey God out of respect for His Word.

God's Tattoos

> *Where could I go from Your Spirit? Or where could I flee from*
> *Your presence? If I ascend up into heaven, You are there; if I make my bed in*
> *Sheol (the place of the dead), behold, You are there. If I take the wings of the*
> *morning or dwell in the uttermost parts of the sea, even there shall Your hand*
> *lead me, and Your right hand shall hold me.*

—PSALM 139:7-10

Sometimes we try so hard to get into the presence of God, but the truth is that it is impossible to get away from Him. He is in constant pursuit of us. You may sometimes feel that the Lord is not near, but that is why knowing the Word is so important. The prophet Isaiah brought a complaint before the Lord, reporting that His people were saying: "The Lord has forsaken me, and my Lord has forgotten me. [And the Lord answered] Can a woman forget her nursing child, that she should not have compassion on the son of her womb? Yes, they may forget, yet I will not forget you. Behold, I have indelibly imprinted (tattooed a picture of) you on the palm of each of My hands." (ISAIAH 49:14-16)

Parents did not originate the idea of keeping pictures of their children handy—God carries a picture of His children everywhere He goes. The next time you question your self-worth, remember that God has your picture tattooed on the palms of His hands.

Be Content

*Let your conduct be without covetousness; be content
with such things as you have.*

—HEBREWS 13:5 (NKJV)

Contentment is a decision to be happy with what you already have. But I am convinced most people are not truly content. Unbelievers certainly aren't content, whether they realize it or not, but it is very sad how many believers have not learned to be truly content in their circumstances. I wonder how many people can truthfully say, "I'm happy with my life. I love my spouse and my family. I like my job. I'm satisfied with my house and my car. There are things I want God to do for me, but I am content to wait until He does them in His timing. I do not covet anything that belongs to my neighbor. I am not jealous of anyone else or envious of what others have. If God gave it to them, then I want them to enjoy it."

I believe God actually tests us in this way. Until we can pass His "I-am-happy-for-you-because-you-are-blessed" test, we are never going to have any more than what we have right now. Yes, God wants us to prosper in every way. He wants people to see His goodness and how well He takes care of us. But we must desire God more than we desire His blessings. So He tests us to make sure this is the case before He releases greater material blessings into our lives.

Finish What You Start

For we have become fellows with Christ (the Messiah) and share in all He has for us, if only we hold our first newborn confidence and original assured expectation [in virtue of which we are believers] firm and unshaken to the end.

—HEBREWS 3:14

Do not, therefore, fling away your fearless confidence, for it carries a great and glorious compensation of reward.

—HEBREWS 10:35

But we do [strongly and earnestly] desire for each of you to show the same diligence and sincerity [all the way through] in realizing and enjoying the full assurance and development of [your] hope until the end.

—HEBREWS 6:11

All of the scriptures above should be meditated upon and taken very seriously. God is not interested in our starting things that we never finish. It is easy to begin, but it takes great courage to finish. In the beginning of a new thing we get all excited. We have a lot of emotions (ours and everyone else's) to support us. When the emotions wear off and all that is left is a lot of hard work and the need for extreme patience, we find out who really has what it takes to truly succeed.

In God's mind we are never successful if we stop somewhere along the way. He wants us to finish our course and do it with joy! If you have been tempted recently to give up—don't! If you don't finish the thing you are currently involved in, you will face the same challenges in the next thing you start. Some people spend all their lives starting new things and never finishing anything. Let us make a decision that we will be more than people who never reached their full potential.

Stay Supernaturally Relaxed

Come to Me, all you who labor and are heavy-laden and overburdened, and I
will cause you to rest. [I will ease and relieve and refresh your souls.]

—MATTHEW 11:28

The longer we know the Lord, the more relaxed we should become when we face situations that try to steal our peace. Previous experience with God is valuable because we learn that somehow He always comes through. Each time we face a new crisis, we can remember that even though He may not have done exactly what we wanted Him to do, He always did something that worked out. Relaxing in the face of trials helps us to maintain our peace with God.

New believers who do not have personal examples on which to build their confidence in God must be more dependent on examples in the Bible of God's faithfulness. The testimonies of other believers can also greatly encourage them. Remember, Jesus said that we are to come to Him when we have problems, and He will give us rest.

Jesus wants us to live in a relaxed state, not tense, uptight, worried, or anxious about yesterday, today, or tomorrow. We can stop reasoning and trying to figure out what we need to do. And the Lord doesn't want us to be upset with other people who aren't doing what we want them to either.

Jesus wants us to trust Him and relax. I call this being *supernaturally relaxed,* because in the natural we may have difficulty learning how or finding time to relax. But when God adds His *super* to our *natural,* we end up with *supernatural.* We can have supernatural relaxation! Jesus was saying, "Come to Me about anything, because I always want to help you with everything." There's nothing too little and nothing too big to take to Him. You can't take too much. You can't have too many requests.

Making Healthy Choices

And out of the ground the Lord God made to grow every tree that is pleasant to the sight or to be desired—good (suitable, pleasant) for food.

—GENESIS 2:9

Learn to do everything you do for God's glory, including eating. Look at your dinner plate and ask if what you are about to eat is mostly what God created for you. Don't view eating as a secular event that has nothing to do with your relationship with God. Don't forget that God put Adam and Eve in the Garden of Eden and told them what they could eat. If eating had nothing to do with their walk with Him, He probably would not have mentioned food. Make good choices! Each time you choose good healthy foods, you are choosing life, which is God's gift to you. He wants you to look great and feel great, and you can, if you keep in mind that your body is the temple of God and the fuel you put into it determines how it will operate and for how long.

Be God-Loves-Me Minded

*But God shows and clearly proves His [own] love for us by the fact that while
we were still sinners, Christ (the Messiah, the Anointed One) died for us.*

—ROMANS 5:8

Paul prayed in Ephesians 3 that the people would experience the love
of God for themselves. The Bible says that He loves us. But how many of
God's children still lack a revelation concerning God's love? I remember
when I began Joyce Meyer Ministries. The first week I was to conduct a
meeting, I asked the Lord what He wanted me to teach and He responded,
"Tell My people that I love them."

"They know that," I said. "I want to teach them something really powerful, not a Sunday school lesson out of John 3:16." The Lord said to me,
"Very few of My people really know how much I love them. If they did,
they would act differently." As I began to study the subject of receiving
God's love, I realized I was in desperate need myself. The Lord led me
in my study to 1 John 4:16, which states that we should be conscious of
God's love. That means it should be something we are actively aware of.

I had an unconscious, vague sort of understanding that God loved me,
but the love of God is meant to be a powerful force in our lives, one that
will take us through even the most difficult trials into victory.

Keep Saying to Yourself

And there was a woman who had had a flow of blood for twelve years. And who had endured much suffering under [the hands of] many physicians and had spent all that she had, and was no better but instead grew worse. She had heard the reports concerning Jesus, and she came up behind Him in the throng and touched His garment. For she kept saying, If I only touch His garments, I shall be restored to health.

—MARK 5:25-28

What about the woman with the issue of blood? She had been having the same problem for twelve years. She had suffered greatly, and no one had been able to help her. Surely this woman was being attacked with thoughts of hopelessness. When she thought about going to Jesus, surely she must have heard, "What's the use?" But she pressed on past the crowd that was so thick on all sides that it was suffocating. She touched the hem of Jesus' garment, healing virtue flowed to her, and she was made well (SEE vv. 29-34). But there is a part we don't want to miss: "For she kept saying, If I only touch His garments, I shall be restored to health." (MARK 5:28)

She kept *saying!* She kept *saying!* Do you get it? She kept *saying!* No matter what she felt like, no matter how much others tried to discourage her, even though the problem was twelve years old, and the crowd looked impossible to get through, this woman got her miracle. Jesus told her that it was her faith that had made her whole (v. 34). Her faith was released through her words. Faith has to be activated if it is to work, and one of the ways we activate it is through our words. *Keep saying—and don't give up hope!*

Back on Track

For we are God's [own] handiwork (His workmanship), recreated in Christ Jesus, [born anew] that we may do those good works which God predestined (planned beforehand) for us [taking paths which He prepared ahead of time], that we should walk in them [living the good life which He prearranged and made ready for us to live].

—EPHESIANS 2:10

We are God's own handiwork. He created us with His own hands. We got messed up, so we had to be re-created in Christ Jesus. We had to be born again so that we could go ahead and do those good works that God had preplanned and predestined for us before Satan tried to ruin us. Just because you and I have had trouble in our lives or just because we have made mistakes does not mean that God's plan has been changed. It is still there. All we have to do is get back on track.

Unbroken Fellowship

If we [freely] admit that we have sinned and confess our sins, He is faithful and just (true to His own nature and promises) and will forgive our sins [dismiss our lawlessness] and [continuously] cleanse us from all unrighteousness [everything not in conformity to His will in purpose, thought, and action].

—1 JOHN 1:9

I often wonder how any human being can get through one day without God. If I feel that I am missing God's intimate presence for a day, I can hardly stand it. I'm like a little kid who has lost his mother in a store; all I can do is spend my time trying to get back to my parent. I don't want to be out of fellowship with the Lord. I must have Him to get through every single day of my life.

Through my conscience the Holy Spirit lets me know if I'm doing something wrong that grieves Him or that interferes with our fellowship. He shows me if I've done something wrong and helps me get back to the place I need to be. He convicts and convinces me, but He never, never condemns me.

If condemnation is filling our conscience, it is not from God. He sent Jesus to die for us, to pay the price for our sins. Jesus bore our sin and condemnation (SEE ISAIAH 53). We should get rid of the sin, and not keep the guilt. Once God breaks the yoke of sin from us, He removes the guilt too. He is faithful and just to forgive all of our sins and to continuously cleanse us from all unrighteousness.

Every single day of our lives we need forgiveness. The Holy Spirit sets off the alarm in our conscience to recognize sin, and He gives us the power of the blood of Jesus to continuously cleanse us from sin and keep us right before Him.

Be Faithful

*So then . . . consider Jesus . . . [See how] faithful He was to
Him Who appointed Him [Apostle and High Priest], as Moses was
also faithful in the whole house [of God].*

—HEBREWS 3:1-2

In Hebrews 3, we are told that both Moses and Jesus were faithful. In the New Testament, the Greek word translated *faithful* means "to be trusted, reliable," in other words, to be dependable. Do you know what it means for us to be dependable? It means we have to keep our word. If we tell somebody we are going to do something, then we need to do it. If we say we are going to be somewhere at a certain time, we need to be there and on time. It is amazing how many people are just not dependable. They can't be counted on to do what they say they will do or be where they say they will be when they say they will be there. Again, it doesn't matter how gifted a person is; if he is not faithful, God cannot use him.

And we must understand that God tests faithfulness. It is not enough to say, "Oh, yes, I'm faithful," because God will say, "Well, let's see." Do you know how God tests our faithfulness? He assigns us to do something for a period of time that we don't want to do, something that is not fun or exciting, something that may require us to submit to someone else's authority for a while, and He'll tell us in our heart, "Just be faithful." Faithfulness is not just showing up day after day—it is showing up day after day with a good attitude. God will reward that kind of faithfulness. Luke 16:12 tells us that if we are faithful over what belongs to someone else, God will give us our own.

Check Your Motives

> *Now am I trying to win the favor of men, or of God? Do I seek to please men? If I were still seeking popularity with men, I should not be a bond servant of Christ (the Messiah).*
>
> —GALATIANS 1:10

Our reason or motive for doing the things we do is very important. God wants us to have pure hearts. He wants us to do what we do because we believe He is leading us to do it or because it is the right thing to do. God wants us to be motivated by love. We should do what we do for the love of God and man. If we are motivated by fear, it does not please God.

God instructs us in His Word not to do good deeds to be seen of men. We are not to do things to be recognized and honored. When we pray, we are not to do it to be seen of men or to try and impress God by heaping up phrases and repeating them over and over. God is not impressed with the length and eloquence of our prayers. He is searching for sincerity and fervency. Any work of ours that is impure will be burned up on Judgment Day. We lose our reward for any work that is done with impure motives (SEE MATTHEW 6:1-7 AND 1 CORINTHIANS 3:13-15).

We should regularly take some time and ask ourselves why we are doing the things we do. It is not what we do that impresses God; it is the "why" behind what we do that He is concerned with.

The Joy of Salvation

And my soul shall be joyful in the Lord: it shall rejoice in his salvation.

—PSALM 35:9 (KJV)

David spoke of the joy that his soul found in the Lord and in His salvation, as we see in Psalm 51:12 (KJV) in which he prayed after falling into sin with Bathsheba, "Restore unto me the joy of thy salvation; and uphold me with thy free spirit." In Luke 10:17-20 we read what Jesus told the seventy He had sent out to minister in His name:

> *The seventy returned with joy, saying, Lord, even the demons are subject to us in Your name! And He said to them, I saw Satan falling like a lightning [flash] from heaven. Behold! I have given you authority and power to trample upon serpents and scorpions, and [physical and mental strength and ability] over all the power that the enemy [possesses]; and nothing shall in any way harm you. Nevertheless, do not rejoice at this, that the spirits are subject to you, but rejoice that your names are enrolled in heaven.*

If you and I had no other reason at all to rejoice, salvation is reason enough in itself for us to be exceedingly joyful. Just imagine how you would feel if everything in your life was perfect, but you did not know Jesus, or, even worse, if you had to face your current circumstances without knowing the Lord.

Sometimes we hear people say, "I feel as though I am between a rock and a hard place." When people who don't know Jesus say this, they are being honest; they *are* between a hard place and a hard place. But for those who are in relationship and fellowship with the Lord, they are between the Rock (Jesus) and a hard place. Standing on the Rock is a much better place to be than whatever is available to those without Christ.

The Spirit Guides, the Devil Shoves

I [the Lord] will instruct you and teach you in the way you should go; I will counsel you with My eye upon you.

—PSALM 32:8

When we are in trouble, the Lord promises in His Word to deliver us. Jesus sent His Holy Spirit to teach us what we need to know. He said to His disciples:

I have still many things to say to you, but you are not able to bear them or to take them upon you or to grasp them now. But when He, the Spirit of Truth (the Truth-giving Spirit) comes, He will guide you into all the Truth (the whole, full Truth). For He will not speak His own message [on His own authority]; but He will tell whatever He hears [from the Father; He will give the message that has been given to Him], and He will announce and declare to you the things that are to come [that will happen in the future]. He will honor and glorify Me, because He will take of (receive, draw upon) what is Mine and will reveal (declare, disclose, transmit) it to you. Everything that the Father has is Mine. That is what I meant when I said that He [the Spirit] will take the things that are Mine and will reveal (declare, disclose, transmit) it to you. (JOHN 16:12-15)

I am so glad Jesus promises that the Holy Spirit will *guide us*—not *push* and *shove* us, but guide us—to truth. The devil wants to pressure us and manipulate us, but the Holy Spirit wants to gently lead us. That is one of the ways we can recognize whether we are hearing from God or from the enemy. If you feel pressed, confused, controlled, or stressed about something, then it is not of God; that is not how He works. Instead, the Holy Spirit will gently "reveal, (declare, disclose, transmit)" the truth to you.

Don't Run from Facing the Truth

And the man said, The woman whom You gave to be with me—
she gave me [fruit] from the tree, and I ate. . . . And the woman said, The
serpent beguiled (cheated, outwitted, and deceived) me, and I ate.

—GENESIS 3:12-13

When confronted with their sin in the Garden of Eden, Adam and Eve blamed each other, God, and the devil, thus evading personal responsibility for their actions. In the past, I observed this same kind of scene countless times in my own home between Dave and me. It seemed that we were continually evading the real issues in life, never wanting to face reality. I vividly remember praying for Dave to change. I had been reading my Bible and was seeing more and more of his flaws, and how much he needed to be different! As I prayed, the Lord spoke to me and said, "Joyce, Dave is not the problem . . . you are."

It was a shocking blow to my pride, but it was also the beginning of my recovery in the Lord. Like most people, I blamed everything on someone else or some circumstance beyond my control. I thought I was acting badly because I had been abused, but God told me, "Abuse may be the reason you act this way, but don't let it become an excuse to stay this way!" I don't think there is anything more emotionally painful than facing the truth about ourselves and our behavior. Because it is painful, most people run from it. It is fairly easy to face truth about someone else—but when it comes to facing ourselves, we find it much harder to handle.

Manifesting Your Reality

> For the rest, brethren, whatever is true, whatever is worthy of reverence
> and is honorable and seemly, whatever is just, whatever is pure, whatever is
> lovely and lovable, whatever is kind and winsome and gracious, if there is any
> virtue and excellence, if there is anything worthy of praise, think on and weigh
> and take account of these things [fix your minds on them].
>
> —PHILIPPIANS 4:8

Manifesting your reality" sounds like something from a contemporary self-help course, but the concept comes straight out of the Bible: "As he thinks in his heart, so is he." (PROVERBS 23:7) I like to say it like this: "Where the mind goes, the man follows."

Positive thoughts are the precursors to a positive life. On the other hand, our lives can be made miserable by anxious thoughts and negative expectations. We usually think our problems are the thing ruining our life, but usually it is our attitude toward them that does the ruining.

We all encounter people who have a great attitude despite being in trying circumstances. We also encounter those who have money and privilege to burn, yet they murmur and complain, are negative and critical, and are filled with self-pity and resentment. We have more to do with how our lives turn out than we like to admit. Learning how to think right is mandatory for good health.

Thoughts affect emotions, and they both affect the body. In order for you to be whole, you must maintain a healthy mind. Make a decision right now that you are going to have a healthy mind. Renewing your mind will take some time and effort. You must learn new, positive ways to think, but reading God's Word can help you do just that.

Let It Drop

> *And whenever you stand praying, if you have anything against*
> *anyone, forgive him and let it drop (leave it, let it go), in order that your*
> *Father Who is in heaven may also forgive you your [own] failings*
> *and shortcomings and let them drop.*
>
> —MARK 11:25

According to the dictionary, *forgive* means "to renounce anger or resentment against, to absolve from payment of (e.g., a debt)." I like the phrase used by the *Amplified Bible* in this verse, "Let it drop." How many times have you had a problem with someone and think you have settled it between you, but the other person keeps bringing it back up?

My husband and I have had those kinds of experiences with each other many times in our shared life. I believe most men are more willing and able to let things go than women. The popular stereotype of the nagging wife is not entirely inaccurate. I know, because I used to be one of them.

Dave and I would have a disagreement or problem between us and he would say, "Oh, let's just forget about it." But I would keep dragging it up again and again. I can remember him saying to me in desperation, "Joyce, can't we just drop it?" That's what Jesus is telling us to do here in this verse. Drop it, leave it, let it go, stop talking about it.

Love Man, Trust God

> But when He was in Jerusalem during the Passover Feast, many believed in His
> name [identified themselves with His party] after seeing His signs (wonders,
> miracles) which He was doing. But Jesus [for His part] did not trust Himself to
> them, because He knew all [men]; And He did not need anyone to bear witness
> concerning man [needed no evidence from anyone about men], for He Himself
> knew what was in human nature. [He could read men's hearts.]
>
> —JOHN 2:23-25

Jesus loved people, especially His disciples. He had great fellowship with
them. He traveled with them, ate with them, and taught them. But He did
not put His trust in them, because He knew what was in human nature.
That is the way we should be. We should love people, but trust God. I
love my husband. He and I have a wonderful relationship together. I don't
think I could find a better man to be married to than Dave Meyer. He is
good to me. He respects me. He treats me the way a husband should treat
his wife. But, being human, he still sometimes says and does things that
hurt me, just as I sometimes say and do things that hurt him.

Why does that happen even in the best of human relationships? It happens because we are not perfect. Only God can be counted on never to
fail us, disappoint us, hurt us, or do us wrong. As much as we may love,
honor, cherish, and respect others—especially our spouse or our family
members—we must not place our trust in the weak arm of the flesh but
only in the strong arm of the Lord.

Complete in Christ

And ye are complete in him, which is the head of all principality and power.

—COLOSSIANS 2:10 (KJV)

And you are in Him, made full and having come to fullness of life [in Christ you too are filled with the Godhead—Father, Son and Holy Spirit—and reach full spiritual stature]. And He is the Head of all rule and authority [of every angelic principality and power].

—COLOSSIANS 2:10

Feeling that something is missing in our lives and not knowing what it is leaves us frustrated and continually searching. We become like the people God talked about in Jeremiah 2:13, those digging empty wells that have no water in them. We try first one thing and then another, but nothing quenches our thirst for whatever it is that is missing in our lives. We might describe our feelings as being incomplete; yet like the verse above says, we are complete in Jesus.

To be complete means to be satisfied, filled up, assured. Without Christ, people are always searching, looking for something. We all want to feel satisfied. We all want contentment. We all want to know we are loved and accepted for who we are. We may think acceptance and approval from people will make us feel complete. However, the Bible teaches us that when we trust in man to give us what only God can give, we live under a curse; but when we believe, trust in, and rely on the Lord, we are blessed (SEE JEREMIAH 17:5-8). The joy, peace, and fulfillment we seek come from being filled with God, and nothing else.

The Holy Spirit as a Lifter

And I will ask the Father, and He will give you another Comforter
(Counselor, Helper, Intercessor, Advocate, Strengthener, and Standby),
that He may remain with you forever.

—JOHN 14:16

Do you know that even the ministry of the Holy Spirit is one of lifting up? Before Jesus ascended into heaven, He said to His disciples, "I am going to ask the Father to send the Holy Spirit upon you to be your Comforter." The Greek word from which the word "Comforter" is translated in this verse is *parakletos,* meaning "called to one's side, i.e., to one's aid." In other words the Comforter is one who comes to stand alongside to encourage, edify, and exhort. Everything the Holy Spirit does is to keep us lifted up. He is our permanent "pick-me-up" to keep us from becoming depressed.

According to *Webster's II New College Dictionary* (1995), *depress* means: "1. To lower in spirits: SADDEN. 2. To press down: LOWER. 3. To lessen the activity or the force of: WEAKEN."

When Satan comes against you and me to depress us, he is trying to lower our spirits, sadden us, press us down, lessen our activity and force for God. He is trying to keep us from moving forward, because one of the synonyms of the word *depressed* is *backward.* Satan wants to use depression to "pull our power plug," to drive us backward, while God wants to empower us and propel us forward. The question is, are we pressing on or are we being pressed down?

Each one of us has to face and deal with disappointments and discouraging people and situations every day of our lives. However, we have been given the Holy Spirit to help lift us up and see us through.

A Glorious Freedom

A man can receive nothing [he can claim nothing, he can
take unto himself nothing] except as it has been granted to him from heaven.
[A man must be content to receive the gift which is given him from heaven;
there is no other source].

—JOHN 3:27

In the third chapter of John's Gospel, the disciples of John the Baptist came to him and reported that Jesus was beginning to baptize as John had been doing and that now more people were going to Jesus than were coming to John. This message was carried to John in a wrong spirit; it was intended to make him jealous. The disciples who brought the report were obviously insecure and being used by the devil in an attempt to stir up some wrong feelings in John toward Jesus.

In the verse above, what John was saying to his disciples was that whatever Jesus was doing, it was because heaven had gifted Him in that way. John knew what God had called him to do, and he knew what Jesus was called to do. He also knew that a person could not go beyond his call and gifting. John was saying to his followers, "Be content." He knew that God had called him to be a forerunner for Jesus, to prepare the way for Him, and that when it was time for Jesus to come to the forefront, he had to become less visible to the people.

Here are John's words to his disciples in response to their statement regarding the crowds who were flocking to Jesus: "He must increase, but I must decrease. [He must grow more prominent; I must grow less so]." (JOHN 3:30) What a glorious freedom that John enjoyed! It is wonderful to feel so secure in Christ that we do not have to be in competition with anyone.

Oh, Well

Cease from anger and forsake wrath; fret not
yourself—it tends only to evildoing.

—PSALM 37:8

Whenever I find myself in a situation I can't do anything about, I have found that a good way to cast my care upon the Lord is simply to say, "Oh, well."

Take, for example, the morning that Dave spilled his orange juice in the car and got a little of it on my sweater. Immediately he said, "Devil, I'm not impressed." And I said, "Oh, well." So that problem was solved, and we pressed forward with the rest of our day.

Some things just aren't worth getting upset about, yet many people do. Unfortunately a large majority of Christians are upset, fretful, and full of anxiety *most* of the time. It is not the big things that get to them; it is the little things that don't fit into their plans. Instead of casting their care and just saying, "Oh, well," they are always trying to do something about something they can't do anything about. On more than one occasion that simple phrase "Oh, well" has really helped me to make it through.

A Father's Love

As far as the east is from the west, so far has He removed our transgressions from us. As a father loves and pities his children, so the Lord loves and pities those who fear Him [with reverence, worship, and awe]. For He knows our frame, He [earnestly] remembers and imprints [on His heart] that we are dust.

—PSALM 103:12-14

God removes all that makes us unrighteous (our transgressions) and sends it as far away as the east is from the west. How far is the east from the west? A long way! God knows our weaknesses, and He remembers that we are but dust. We put a lot more pressure on ourselves than God would ever put on us.

When my son was small, he decided to do something nice for me. He got a bowl of water and went out on the porch. Soon he came to me and said, "Mommy, I washed the windows for you." The porch was wet. He was wet. The windows were smeared up. But he did it because he loved me. God reminded me of this one time. He said, "Do you remember what you did afterward? You sent your son off to get cleaned up and then you went and cleaned up his mess when he wasn't looking." God showed me that He does the same with us.

God is aware of our imperfections, and He receives what we do out of love for Him. He will cover our tracks, clean up our messes, and hide them so we won't even realize what a mess we made. He does this because we are in Christ, Christ is in Him, and He is in us.

The Courage to Say No

The thief comes only to steal and kill and destroy; I have
come that they may have life, and have it to the full.

—JOHN 10:10 (NIV)

My husband Dave once did one of the wisest things I've seen. Before we entered full-time ministry he worked as an engineer. He was offered a promotion that included a pay raise and a lot of prestige. But he turned it down. At first I was angry with him. I thought he was making a big mistake. Didn't he want to climb the corporate ladder? Wasn't he the best person for the job?

He explained that he had watched the other men in that position. They had to travel extensively, and they were constantly saddled with unreasonable deadlines that put them under tremendous stress. "That is not the way I want to live," Dave said. He chose the position that allowed him to stick to his core values—commitment to family, and comfort with self— rather than chasing corporate power so others would look up to him.

Besides, why choose a bigger paycheck if you just spend it on doctor bills to relieve your stress-induced illnesses? Job stress causes as much illness in this country as smoking and lack of exercise. Like those things, it kills. Do whatever you need to do to make sure you fully enjoy the life He has provided for you. Sometimes saying no takes more courage than saying yes.

You can take this concept beyond the work arena. Removing all the things from your schedule that aren't bearing good fruit will greatly reduce your stress level and enable you to truly enjoy the things you choose to concentrate on.

What the Devil Means for Harm, God Will Use for Good

As for you, you thought evil against me, but God meant it for good, to bring about that many people should be kept alive, as they are this day.

—GENESIS 50:20

After Joseph had risen to be second in command of all Egypt under Pharaoh, his brothers, who had sold him into slavery, came to Egypt to buy grain during the famine Joseph had predicted would come. Later, Joseph arranged for his father, Jacob, his brothers, and all of their families to move to Egypt to live out the rest of the famine in peace and prosperity. When their father, Jacob, died, Joseph's brothers were afraid that Joseph would try to take vengeance on them for what they had done to him in his youth. Here in this verse we see Joseph's assurance to them of his forgiveness of their wrongdoing toward him. Actually, we see his good attitude being displayed. Notice what he tells them: "You meant it for evil, but God meant it for good, to save many people from starvation."

It is amazing how many times Satan will set a trap for us, meaning it for our harm and destruction. But when God gets involved, He takes that thing that Satan meant to use to destroy us and turns it so that it actually works for our good instead.

My own situation bears this out. I was sexually, mentally, and emotionally abused for many years in my childhood. This was certainly a terrible thing to happen to a child and definitely a work of Satan, but God has worked it out for good.

My mess has become my message; my misery has become my ministry; and I am using the experience I gained from my pain to help multitudes of others who are hurting. I encourage you not to waste your pain. God will use it if you give it to Him.

The Spirit of Peace

But when they deliver you up, do not be anxious about how or what
you are to speak; for what you are to say will be given you in that very hour
and moment, for it is not you who are speaking, but the Spirit of your Father
speaking through you.

—MATTHEW 10:19-20

Do you realize how much peace can be ours if we will just stop trying to figure out in advance everything we need to say and do in every situation we face in life? If you are like me, you wear yourself out trying to prepare yourself for every situation you are likely to run into in the future. You try to plan and rehearse every word you are going to speak in every interview and conversation. Jesus is telling us here that we don't have to do that. He is telling us to trust all that to the Holy Spirit Who will guide us and direct us.

When we do have to make hard decisions or solve complicated problems or confront difficult people, the Holy Spirit will decide the proper time and the best approach. He will give us the right words to say. Until then, we don't need to bother ourselves with it. If we will listen to what the Lord is telling us here in this passage, not only will we have more peace, but we will also enjoy more success. Because when we do have to speak, what comes out of our mouth will be spiritual wisdom from God and not something that we have come up with out of our own carnal mind.

Worship Is Wisdom

The reverent fear and worship of the Lord is the beginning of Wisdom.

—PSALM 111:10

If you will read the book of Proverbs and look at all the radical promises that are made to the person who walks in wisdom, and then realize that reverence and worship are the beginning of wisdom, you will quickly see why reverence and worship are so important.

The Bible says that those who walk in wisdom will be wealthy. They will live a long life. They will be exceedingly happy. They will be blessed, so blessed that they will be envied (SEE PROVERBS 3:1-18). But there is no such thing as wisdom without worship.

Many people today are seeking knowledge, and knowledge is good, but wisdom is better. Wisdom is the right use of knowledge. Knowledge without wisdom can cause one to be puffed up, or filled with pride, which will ultimately ruin his life. A wise person will always be knowledgeable, but not all knowledgeable people are wise. I believe that in our society today, we exalt knowledge more than we should. Education seems to be most people's main goal, and yet our world today is rapidly declining morally.

Education is good, but it is not better than wisdom. God's Word tells us to cry out for wisdom; seek it as we would silver and gold; make it a vital necessity in life. There is nothing more important than wisdom, and the beginning of it is reverence and worship. The worshiper will be taught wisdom by God.

Speak as God Speaks

But avoid all empty (vain, useless, idle) talk,
for it will lead people into more and more ungodliness.

—2 TIMOTHY 2:16

Avoid all empty, idle, vain, and useless talk. Instead, learn to speak as God speaks. It is the Word of God, spoken in truth and love from your lips, that will return to Him after accomplishing His will and purpose. But in order to speak that Word in truth and love, your heart must be right before the Lord, for it is out of the abundance of the heart that the mouth speaks—for good or for evil. You are bound by your words, by your declarations.

You are also judged by them. Watchman Nee once said, "If you listen to a person, you can detect by their words the spirit that is coming forth from them." That is why it is so important to place a guard upon your lips so that what issues forth from them is not only truthful but also kind and positive and edifying and in line with the will of God.

You can change your action and behavior, but to do so you must first change your thoughts and words. And to do that, you need the help of the indwelling Spirit of God. If you truly want your life to be totally different, then submit yourself to the Lord and in humility ask Him to transform you into the image and nature of His Son Jesus Christ. He is doing that for me; and if He can do it for me, He can—and will—do it for you too.

Diversity and Variety

And out of the ground the Lord God formed every [wild] beast and living creature of the field and every bird of the air and brought them to Adam to see what he would call them; and whatever Adam called every living creature, that was its name. And Adam gave names to all the livestock and to the birds of the air and to every [wild] beast of the field.

—GENESIS 2:19-20

I am sure if you think about it a little, you will agree that our God is an awesome God. Simply take a walk and look around you. If it will help you, put the book down and do it now. Find out what is in the ocean, or how bees and flowers work together. Then realize that the same Holy Spirit present at Creation is living inside of you if you have truly accepted Jesus Christ as your Lord and Savior (SEE ACTS 2:38).

There is a lot of creativity inside each of us that we need to tap into without fear. I think we often get into ruts. We do the same thing all the time even though we are bored with it because we are afraid of change.

We would rather be safe and bored than excited and living on the edge. Some people stay in jobs or professions all their lives because what they are doing is safe. They may hate their jobs and feel completely unfulfilled, but the thought of doing anything else is frightening beyond words. Or maybe they do think and dream about a change, but their dreams will never manifest because they are afraid of failure. I do not advocate jumping out in the middle of every "whim" that comes along, but there is a definite time to step out of the ordinary and into new things.

God has created you and me to need and crave diversity and variety. There is nothing wrong with us if we feel sometimes that we just need a change. On the other hand, if we can never be satisfied for very long no matter what we are doing, then we have the reverse problem. The Word of God instructs us to be content and satisfied (SEE HEBREWS 13:5 AND I TIMOTHY 6:6). *Balance* is the key.

Exceedingly, Abundantly, Above and Beyond

> God . . . is able to [carry out His purpose and] do superabundantly,
> far over and above all that we [dare] ask or think [infinitely beyond our
> highest prayers, desires, thoughts, hopes, or dreams].
>
> —EPHESIANS 3:20

When I pray about or simply meditate on all the people who are hurting, I have a strong desire to help them all. I sometimes feel that my desire is bigger than my ability, and it is—but it is not bigger than God's ability! When the thing we are facing in our lives or ministries looms so big in our eyes that our mind goes "tilt," we need to *think in the spirit*.

In the natural, many things are impossible. But in the supernatural, spiritual realm, with God nothing is impossible. God wants us to believe for great things, make big plans, and expect Him to do things so great it leaves us with our mouths hanging open in awe. James 4:2 tells us we have not because we ask not! We can be bold in our asking.

Sometimes in my meetings people will approach the altar for prayer and sheepishly ask if they can request two things. I tell them they can ask God for all they want to, as long as they trust Him to do it His way, in His timing. It is untold what people can do—people who don't *appear* to be able to do anything.

God does not usually call people who are capable. If He did, He would not get the glory. He frequently chooses those who, in the natural, feel as if they are in completely over their heads but who are ready to stand up on the inside and take bold steps of faith as they get direction from God. We usually want to wait until we "feel ready" before we step out, but if we feel ready then we tend to lean on ourselves instead of on God.

Know your weaknesses and know God—know His strength and faithfulness. Above all else, don't be a quitter.

The Little Foxes That Steal Your Joy

All the days of the desponding and afflicted are made evil [by anxious thoughts and forebodings], but he who has a glad heart has a continual feast [regardless of circumstances].

—PROVERBS 15:15

I once went through a period in my life when I was plagued by anxiety. I was filled with fear and dread for no particular reason. I kept feeling something terrible was going to happen. Finally I went to the Lord and asked Him what was troubling me. He told me it was "evil forebodings." At the time I didn't even know what that phrase meant or where it came from. Sometime later I came across Proverbs 15:15 in the *Amplified Bible*. I immediately recognized the term the Lord had used when He told me what was bothering me—"evil forebodings."

In those days I was like so many other people. I was looking for some "monster problem" that was keeping me from enjoying life. I was so intense about everything, I was creating problems for myself where none really existed. Once in a meeting, the Lord told me to speak out something. Apparently someone needed to hear this: "Stop making a big deal out of nothing." I used to be the type of person who needed to hear direction like that. I could make mountains out of molehills. I had to learn to just let some things go—forget them and go on. Some of us become upset over things that just are not worth becoming upset over—those "little foxes, that spoil the vines." (SONG OF SOLOMON 2:15 KJV) If our lives consist of becoming upset over one little thing after another that really don't matter, we won't have much peace or joy.

Be an Example

Pattern yourselves after me [follow my example], as I
imitate and follow Christ (the Messiah).

—1 CORINTHIANS 11:1

What a bold, awesome statement! What exactly was Paul saying in this verse? He was saying the same thing he said in 1 Corinthians 4:16: "So I urge and implore you, be imitators of me."

He was telling the believers in Corinth, "Watch my life, and I will show you how Jesus wants you to live." That is what God wants us to do. He wants us to have the confidence to know that we are doing everything in our power to obey God to such a degree that we don't feel we have anything to hide from anybody. He wants us to be confident that anyone who models himself after us will turn out to be like Jesus both in attitude and behavior.

I love Romans 5:19: "For just as by one man's disobedience (failing to hear, heedlessness, and carelessness) the many were constituted sinners, so by one Man's obedience the many will be constituted righteous (made acceptable to God, brought into right standing with Him)."

This verse says that just one man or woman can affect the world. If that is so, then surely one of us can affect the neighborhood we live in, the place where we work, the circle of friends we do things with—if we make the right choices.

Fear Not

No man shall be able to stand before you all the days of your life. As I was with Moses, so I will be with you; I will not fail you or forsake you.

—JOSHUA 1:5

I have heard it said there are 365 references to "fear not" in the Bible. I know there are at least 355, according to *Dake's Annotated Reference Bible,* one "fear not" for almost every day of the year. Do you really want to obey the Scriptures and "fear not"? If so, you will be in good company because every person in the Bible who was ever used by God to any degree was told over and over by Him, "Fear not." One of those people was Joshua. Joshua, the man God chose to follow Moses, had a big job ahead of him: to lead the children of Israel into the Promised Land.

God wasn't telling Joshua to be like Moses; but that He would be to Joshua what He had been to Moses. God would not fail or forsake Joshua. He was saying, "Fear not, Joshua, I will be with you!" When God tells you He will be with you, that means no matter what the circumstances are like, everything will work out all right because God will never fail you or forsake you.

Do It Afraid!

Be strong, courageous, and firm; fear not . . . for it is the Lord your God Who goes with you; He will not fail you or forsake you.

—DEUTERONOMY 31:6

Fear is nothing but a feeling that causes certain manifestations. It causes us to tremble, sweat, turn red, shake, and have wobbly knees. The Bible doesn't say, "Tremble not." The Bible doesn't say, "Sweat not," or, "Shake not." The Bible says, "*Fear* not." And the word *fear* implies running away from something! In other words, God is saying when *fear* comes, which it will because fear is the enemy of confidence, don't let it stop us. We are to *do* it afraid!

When I received this revelation, I could hardly believe it. It seemed too good to be true. I realized there wasn't anything wrong with me when my knees knocked together in new situations or when I felt I was going to faint. Because I went ahead and did what I was supposed to do in spite of how I felt, I wasn't a coward. We are cowards only if we *run*. Maybe you have been allowing *a feeling* to control and determine your destiny. Maybe you think that some people have fear and others don't. But the truth is that fear comes to *everybody*. What we do in spite of that fear makes the difference between victory or defeat in our lives.

Out of the Spirit, Not the Head

*[For being as he is] a man of two minds (hesitating, dubious,
irresolute), [he is] unstable and unreliable and uncertain about everything
[he thinks, feels, decides].*

—JAMES 1:8

You and I have two huge vats of information within us. One is carnal information that comes off the top of our head. The other is spiritual information which wells up out of our hearts. One is muddy, polluted water, and the other is clean drinking water. It is up to us to decide which source we are going to drink from. Some people try to drink from both sources. That's what the Bible calls being double-minded.

Do you know what it means to be double-minded? It means that your mind is trying to tell you one thing, and your spirit is trying to tell you just the opposite. Instead of saying, "I'm not going to believe that because it's a lie," you get caught in a cross fire, going back and forth between the two thoughts.

If you and I are ever going to live the happy, victorious, and successful Christian life the Lord wills for us, we are going to have to decide which fountain of information we are going to drink from. We are going to have to learn to live out of our spirits and not out of our heads.

Shake It Off

> *Let us strip off and throw aside every encumbrance (unnecessary weight) . . . and let us run with patient endurance and steady and active persistence the appointed course of the race that is set before us.*
>
> —HEBREWS 12:1

One of my favorite stories is about a farmer's donkey that fell into a dry well. The animal cried pitifully for hours as the farmer tried to figure out what to do for his poor donkey. Finally, he concluded that the well was too deep, and it really needed to be covered up anyway. Besides, the donkey was old, and it would be a lot of trouble to get him out of the pit. The farmer decided that it was not worth trying to retrieve the animal, so he asked his neighbors to help him fill in the well and bury the donkey.

They all grabbed shovels and began to toss dirt into the well. The donkey immediately realized what was happening, and he began to bray horribly. Crying would be our normal response if somebody was mistreating us this badly, so this donkey was responding the same way we would at first, but then he got real quiet. A few shovel loads of dirt later, the farmer looked down the well and was astonished at what he saw. With every shovel of dirt that hit the donkey's back, the donkey would shake it off and step on top of it.

As the neighbors and the farmer continued to shovel dirt on top of the animal, he continued to shake it off and take a step up. Pretty soon the donkey shook off the last shovel full of dirt, took a step up, and walked right out of the well. We can learn from this story. When trouble comes, if we will get still and listen, God will tell us what to do.

By the grace and mercy of God, I was able to shake off a lot of things in my life, a lot of hurt feelings, a lot of mistreatment, a lot of abuse, a lot of unfair, unjust, unkind things. Just like the donkey, in order to keep pressing on and have victory in our lives, we are going to have to learn to shake off the troubles that come our way.

Two Kinds of Suffering

> *Moreover [let us also be full of joy now!] let us exult and triumph*
> *in our troubles and rejoice in our sufferings, knowing that pressure and*
> *affliction and hardship produce patient and unswerving endurance.*
>
> —ROMANS 5:3

At some point in your Christian life, you may have heard that Jesus wants to set you free from all your suffering, and that is true—He does. However, there is a transition involved, and transition is never easy. The pathway to freedom and enjoying your life may be difficult at times. However, pressing forward toward freedom is definitely easier than staying in bondage.

When I first realized that Jesus could and desired to set me free, I wanted to have that freedom. But my attitude was, "I will not suffer anymore; I have suffered enough." But as long as we are in bondage, we are suffering anyway; and it is the type of suffering that has no end. If we are willing to let Jesus lead us through whatever we must go through in order to be free, it may hurt for a while; but at least it will be suffering that leads to victory, to a new life of freedom.

Many people never experience the joy of freedom because of a wrong mind-set concerning suffering. The scripture above reveals that we should *choose* by faith to be joyful while we are going through difficult transitions, knowing that because God loves us, it will produce a good end, which is, in this case, mature character.

A Confident Heart

My heart is fixed, O God, my heart is steadfast and confident!

——PSALM 57:7

Notice that this passage says that not only must our heart be fixed and steadfast, it must also be confident. I have discovered that staying confident at all times is vital to successful ministry. I have found that even while I am busy ministering, even while I am up in front of an audience teaching, the devil will try to introduce thoughts into my head to make me lose confidence. For example, if two or three people look at their watches, the devil whispers to me, "They're so bored they can't wait to get out of here." If a couple of people get up and go to the restroom, the devil will say, "They're leaving because they don't like your preaching."

Whatever we do for the Lord, the devil will try to do something to cause us to lose confidence. He doesn't want us to have confidence in our prayers. He doesn't want us to believe we can hear from God. He doesn't want us to have any confidence concerning the call on our life. He wants us to go around feeling like a failure.

That is why we need to keep a confident heart within us all the time. We shouldn't drag ourselves out of bed each day in fear or discouragement. Instead, we should get up every morning prepared to keep Satan under our feet.

How do we do that? We do it by confidently declaring what the Word says about us, such as: "I am more than a conqueror through Jesus. I can do all things through Christ Who strengthens me. I am triumphant in every situation because God always causes me to triumph." As we will see, that not only causes the devil to leave us alone, but it also strengthens our confidence.

Putting on God's Armor

Be strong in the Lord [be empowered through your union with Him]; draw your strength from Him [that strength which His boundless might provides].

—EPHESIANS 6:10

Do you know what happens when you spend time with God? You begin to act like David when he faced the giant Goliath. You begin to take a stand and demand of the enemy, "Who do you think you are to defy the army of the living God?" (SEE 1 SAMUEL 17:26). As soldiers of the cross, you and I are not supposed to be afraid of our enemy, the devil.

When a spirit of fear comes along, rather than shaking like a leaf, we are to be as bold as a lion. The devil comes against those who are doing damage to his kingdom, those who are doing something for God. How do we withstand the devil? By putting on the full armor of God, taking up the shield of faith, by which we can quench all his fiery darts, and by wielding the sword of the Spirit, which is the Word of God (SEE EPHESIANS 6:13-17). But all of that armor and all of those weapons come from spending time in fellowship with the Lord. Ephesians 6:10 actually begins this discourse on the armor of God, saying, "Be strong in the Lord [be empowered through your union with Him]." To me, that says, "Be strong through your fellowship with God." Then verse 11 goes on to say, "Put on God's whole armor." Only after being strengthened in fellowship can we properly wear the armor.

Step Out and Find Out

No eye has seen, no ear has heard, no mind has conceived
what God has prepared for those who love him.

—I CORINTHIANS 2:9 (NIV)

Perhaps God has been speaking to you about some changes in your life and you want them, but you are afraid. I want to encourage you not to be afraid to step out. Even if you make a mistake, it won't be the end of the world.

Go through the doors He is opening. You may even have to take a few steps in some direction and see if a door previously closed will open as you approach it. Maybe you have a little direction from God, but you don't see the full picture. God leads step by step. He may never show you step two until you take step one. I am not advocating doing foolish things, but I do encourage you to find the balance between living in fear and living in wisdom.

God is progressive, and I have found that my faith is also. I may have a little faith, and so God shows me a little something to do. Then as I am faithful over the little thing, He shows me the next step, and by then, my faith has grown to be able to handle it.

Don't spend all of your life looking back and wishing you had tried different things or done things differently. Wondering what could have been is a lonely feeling. I can promise you that you will not enjoy everything you try. But at least you will have the personal experience of knowing. You won't have to live your whole life hearing about what everyone else is doing and wondering what it would be like. You are not going to be able to do everything, but step out in God's timing into the things you feel He is leading you into.

Stay Expectant Every Day

He [Jesus] said to them [the disciples], It is not for you to become acquainted with and know what time brings [the things and events of time and their definite periods] or fixed years and seasons (their critical niche in time), which the Father has appointed (fixed and reserved) by His own choice and authority and personal power.

—ACTS 1:7

Often we experience a lot of disappointment, which hinders joy and enjoyment, due to deciding for ourselves that something has to be done a certain way or by a certain time. When we want something very strongly, we can easily convince ourselves that it is God's will for us to have it.

I always believe for things. I am goal-oriented and always need something to look forward to. Many years ago, I was letting what I thought was faith frustrate me. I attempted to use my faith to get what I wanted. When it did not arrive on time, I felt I had failed in the faith department.

Now, after almost twenty years, I know that I can and should use my faith, but God has an appointed time. "In due time" (1 PETER 5:6), "at the appointed time" (GENESIS 18:14), "when the proper time" (GALATIANS 4:4)—these are things the Bible says about God's timing.

Jesus Himself made it clear that it is not for us to know what these times are. Remaining expectant every day, no matter how long it takes, is one of the things that will keep you and me flowing in joy.

I am sure most of us are expecting. I know I am. There are things God has spoken to me—things He has placed in my heart—that I have not seen manifested yet. Some of them have been there as long as fifteen or sixteen years. Other things He spoke around the same time have come to pass. I used to be confused. Now, I am no longer confused; I am expecting. My time can come at any moment, any day—maybe today—and so can yours.

Pray: Anywhere, Anytime

> *Pray at all times (on every occasion, in every season)*
> *in the Spirit, with all [manner of] prayer and entreaty.*
>
> —EPHESIANS 6:18

This important verse lets us know that we can pray anywhere at any time about anything and that we should be watchful to do so. If we believe and practice this scripture, it can be life-changing and certainly prayer-changing.

It seems even when we do think about some prayer concern, we almost always follow that thought with another type of wrong thinking: *I need to remember to pray about this during my prayer time.* Why don't we stop and pray right then? Because we have a mental stronghold in this area. We think we must be in a certain place, in a certain frame of mind, and in a certain position before we can pray.

It's no wonder we don't get much praying done. If the only time we can pray is when we are sitting still and doing absolutely nothing else, most of us certainly won't be praying without ceasing.

We should all set aside a time to spend with God when we are doing nothing else, and we should discipline ourselves to keep our appointments with Him. Yes, we should have these set-apart times, but in addition to that we should be exercising our privileges of prayer all day long. Our prayers can be verbal or silent, long or short, public or private—the important thing is that we pray!

Beware the "Flesh Days"

In all your ways know, recognize, and acknowledge Him, and
He will direct and make straight
and plain your paths.

—PROVERBS 3:6

I have found that the more obedient I am, the easier it is to be obedient again. And the more disobedient I am, the easier it is to be disobedient. Some days we can tell as soon as we wake up that we're going to have what I call a "flesh day." We start the day feeling stubborn and lazy.

Our first thoughts are: *I'm not cleaning this house, I'm going shopping. I'm not staying on this stupid diet either. I'm eating what I want to eat all day, and I don't want anybody in my face bugging me about it. If they do, I'm going to tell them what I think.*

If we *feel* that way when we wake up, we have a decision to make. We can follow those feelings or we can pray, "God, please help me, quick!" Our feelings can come under the lordship of Jesus Christ if we ask Him to help us straighten out our attitude.

I know all about flesh days; I know we can start out acting badly and it can go from bad to worse. It seems that once we give in to a selfish attitude and follow our flesh, it's downhill to a wasted day. But every time we obey our conscience, we widen the window that God can use to lead us by His Spirit. Every time we follow the leading of our conscience, it lets in more light the next time. Once we enjoy knowing that God will truly lead us to a better plan, it gets easier to obey Him promptly.

Getting Past Your Past

> *For I know the thoughts and plans that I have for you, says the Lord, thoughts and plans for welfare and peace and not for evil, to give you hope in your final outcome.*
>
> —JEREMIAH 29:11

A lot of people let the past dictate their future. Don't do that! Get past your past. We all have a past, but we all have a future. The Bible teaches us in Ephesians 2:10 that we are re-created in Christ Jesus so we might do the good works He planned beforehand for us and live the good life He prearranged and made ready for us. The word *re-created* indicates we were created, messed up, and in need of repair.

In Jeremiah 18:1-4 we read of the potter who had to remake his vessel because it had been marred. That is a picture of us in the hands of the Lord, the Master Potter. We are said to be new creatures when we enter into a relationship with Christ. Old things pass away. We have an opportunity for a new beginning. We become new spiritual clay for the Holy Spirit to work with. God makes arrangements for each of us to have a fresh start, but we must be willing to let go of the past and go on. We make a way for the new by believing what God says about it.

Don't let your past failures leave you hopeless about your future success. Your future has no room in it for the failures of the past. As I have stated, just because you have failed at some things does not make you a failure. Whatever Satan has stolen through deception, God will restore doubled, if you are willing to press forward, forgetting the past. You have to let go in order to go on!

Complain and Remain, Praise and Be Raised

Jesus therefore answered and said unto them, Murmur not among yourselves.

—JOHN 6:43 (KJV)

Complaining is a sin! It is a corrupt form of conversation that causes many people a great deal of problems in their lives. It also opens many doors for the enemy. Words are containers of power. Complaining, grumbling words carry destructive power. They destroy the joy of the one doing the complaining and can also affect other people who have to listen to them.

In Ephesians 4:29 the apostle Paul instructs us not to use any foul or polluting language. At one time I would not have known that included complaining, but now I have learned that it does. Murmuring and complaining pollute our lives and probably sound like cursing to the Lord. To Him it is verbal pollution. To pollute is to poison. Did you ever stop to think that you and I can poison our future by complaining about what is going on right now?

When we complain about our current situation, we remain in it; when we praise God in the midst of difficulty, He raises us out of it. The best way to start every day is with gratitude and thanksgiving. Get a jump on the devil. If you don't fill your thoughts and conversation with good things, he will definitely fill them with evil things. Truly thankful people do not complain. They are so busy being grateful for the good things they do have that they have no time to notice the things they could complain about. Praise and thanksgiving are good; complaining and grumbling are evil.

Fill Up Your Love Tank

May Christ through your faith [actually] dwell (settle down, abide, make His permanent home) in your hearts! May you be rooted deep in love and founded securely on love.

—EPHESIANS 3:17

Each one of us is born with a "love tank," and if our tank is empty, we are in trouble. We need to start receiving love from the moment we are born and continue receiving it—and giving it out—until the day we die. Sometimes Satan manages to arrange things so that instead of receiving love, we receive abuse. If that abuse continues, we become love starved and warped, so that we are unable to maintain healthy relationships.

Many people develop addictive behaviors of different types. If they can't get good feelings from within themselves, they look for them on the outside. One of the things we must understand is that people have to have a certain number of good feelings. We are all created to have good feelings about ourselves. We cannot go around hurting, being wounded, and feeling bad all the time. We are just not designed to live that way.

To find those good feelings, many people turn to sex, drugs, alcohol, tobacco, food, money, power, gambling, work, television, sports, and many other addictive things. They are simply trying to get those good feelings they are missing from within themselves and their relationships.

The good news is that whatever may have happened to us in the past, whatever we may have been deprived of, we can get it from the Lord. He is our Shepherd, so we shall not want (SEE PSALM 23:1). He has promised not to withhold any good thing from us (SEE PSALM 84:11).

If we did not get enough love when we were growing up, or if we are not getting enough love now, we don't have to go through the rest of our lives with an empty "love tank." Even if there is not one other human being on this earth who loves us, we are still loved by God, and we can become rooted and grounded in His love.

Shine On!

And the Lord said to Moses, Say to Aaron and his sons, This is the way you shall bless the Israelites. Say to them, The Lord bless you and watch, guard, and keep you; The Lord make His face to shine upon and enlighten you and be gracious (kind, merciful, and giving favor) to you; The Lord lift up His [approving] countenance upon you and give you peace (tranquility of heart and life continually).

—NUMBERS 6:22-26

Do you know what God's countenance is? It is His face, His appearance. When any man or woman of God says to us, "The Lord make his face shine upon thee, and be gracious unto thee: The Lord lift up his countenance upon thee, and give thee peace" (NUMBERS 6:25-26 KJV), what he or she is saying is, "May others see God's glory shining upon you and through you."

May I encourage you to do something? As you leave the house to go through your day, ask the Lord to make His face shine upon you. Ask Him to lift up His countenance upon you and give you peace. Ask Him to shine His glory upon you, as He did with Moses. Then let that light so shine before others that they may see it and glorify your Father Who is in heaven (SEE MATTHEW 5:16).

Letting your light shine can be as simple as putting a smile on your face. That is one way to "flip on the switch" of God's glory. The light of God's glory is in you, but if you never show it outwardly, people won't be blessed.

First Things First

> *But seek (aim at and strive after) first of all His kingdom and His*
> *righteousness (His way of doing and being right), and then all these*
> *things taken together will be given you besides.*
>
> —MATTHEW 6:33

Often we don't think about what our priorities are, but we still have them. Our priorities are whatever is first in our thoughts and in how we plan our time. Having real peace in our lives requires making God first above all other things that demand our attention.

If you put God first in your finances, first in your time, first in your conversation, first in your thoughts, first in your decisions, your life will be a success. I am living evidence of this truth. Before I learned to put God first, I was living in the worst messes that anybody could have. I had a bad attitude and couldn't think two positive thoughts in a row. I didn't like anybody, and nobody liked me. The abuse in my childhood had left me full of bitterness, resentment, and unforgiveness.

Our lives will not be blessed if we keep God in a little Sunday-morning box and let Him have our priority attention for only forty-five minutes, once a week during a church service. If Christians were putting Jesus first in everything, then the world would be in a better condition. There are, of course, sincere, God-fearing, dedicated believers in every church and in society, but not nearly as many as there should be.

I've trained myself to start each day by giving God the firstfruits of my time. I've realized that I'm not going to get through the day peacefully if I don't spend time with God and put Him first.

Freely Eat

You may freely eat of every tree in the garden. —GENESIS 2:16

After God created Adam and Eve, He gave them some very simple dining instructions. Did He say, "You may freely eat of every Krispy Kreme on the street"? No. Did He say, "You may freely eat of every chip in the bag"? No. He did not tell them to freely eat fast food, frozen pizza, or even low-fat cookies.

God told Adam and Eve to eat from the garden, and we'd do well to stick to His advice. We've been inundated with an overwhelming amount of bad diet information from past decades that has clouded the very simple truths of healthy eating: eat the foods that come from God, in as close a state as possible to how God made them, and you can't go wrong. Only when we get corrupted by the foods made by men in laboratories and factories do we get in trouble.

Develop a Lifestyle of Giving

For God so loved the world that He gave. —JOHN 3:16

God is working amazing financial miracles for us so that we can operate the world ministry that we now have. But even in the earlier years of our lives, when we went through hard times financially, we still sowed the tithe. We just had enough to pay our bills and then we had to believe God for everything else that came in.

When I look back, some of those leaner times hold my best memories and were the most fun times for us. I had a little prayer book that I kept, and one time I wrote down, "Dear Father, I need twelve new dishtowels and I don't have the money to buy them. Please provide those dishtowels." One day, a friend of mine rang the doorbell and said, "I hope you don't think I am totally insane, but I believe God told me to bring you a dozen dishtowels."

The excitement of God hit me, and I almost knocked her over as I screamed with delight and shouted, "That's God!" Who gets that excited over dishtowels these days? But excitement comes into your life when you begin to live God's way.

If you need financial miracles, don't be afraid to obey God concerning your finances. Begin proving God's power to bless you by tithing and then giving even beyond that. As a couple, Dave and I are both trying to live a lifestyle of giving, and we enjoy giving away more every year. As we obey God and give when He leads us to do so, somebody always gives back to us and keeps us in that realm of exciting miracles. We actually search for ways to give. We don't wait for some great feeling to come over us; we give on purpose and with purpose. As a result, our joy and prosperity are always increasing.

You Can Do What God Has Called You to Do

*I can do everything God asks me to with the help of Christ
who gives me the strength and power.*

—PHILIPPIANS 4:13 (TLB)

Recently I saw a sign on a church that said, "Trust in God, believe in yourself, and you can do anything." That is not correct.

There was a time in my life when I would have seen that sign and said, "Amen!" But not anymore. You and I really cannot do *anything* we want to do. We cannot do anything or everything that everyone else is doing. But we can do everything *God has called us to do.* And we can be anything *God says we can be.*

We must get balance in this area. We can go to motivational seminars and be told with a lot of emotional hype, "You can do anything. Think you can do it; believe you can do it; say you can do it—and you can do it!" That is true only to a degree. Carried too far, it gets off into humanism. We need to speak about ourselves what the *Word* says about us.

We can do what we are *called* to do, what we are gifted to do. There are ways we can learn to recognize the grace gifts that are on our lives.

I have learned this regarding myself: when I start getting frustrated, I know it is a sign that either I have gotten off into my own works and am no longer receiving God's grace, or I am trying to do something for which there was no grace to begin with.

Grace Is Not a License to Sin

Moreover the law entered, that the offence might abound. But where sin abounded, grace did much more abound. . . . What then? shall we sin, because we are not under the law, but under grace? God forbid. Know ye not, that to whom ye yield yourselves servants to obey, his servants ye are to whom ye obey; whether of sin unto death, or of obedience unto righteousness?

—ROMANS 5:20; 6:15-16 (KJV)

When Paul started teaching the people of his day about the law and grace—how the law produces sin, but where sin abounds, grace abounds even more—the early believers got a bit confused. They reasoned, "Well, then, if the more we sin, the more grace abounds, and if God takes such delight in giving us His grace, then we ought to sin as much as we can so we can get more grace" (SEE ROMANS 6:15).

So Paul had to write, "God forbid! Don't you know that when you sin you become a servant to sin? How can you go on living in sin when you have been declared dead to sin?" (SEE ROMANS 6:16).

Grace is not just an excuse to stay where we are, claiming that we don't have to do anything about ourselves and our lives because we are not under the law but under grace. That is the mistake the early believers were making.

Yes, God's grace will keep us from condemnation even though we sin. God's grace does keep our names written in the Lamb's Book of Life even though we aren't perfect. God's grace does save us, declare us righteous in His sight, assure us His blessings and a home in heaven, carry us through this life, and give us peace of mind and heart and many, many other wonderful things.

But God's grace does more than all of that; it also teaches us to live as God intends for us to live—which is in holiness. It not only gives us the power to live, but it is given to us to lift us out of sin.

Confusion Is Not from God

For God is not the author of confusion, but of peace.

—1 CORINTHIANS 14:33 (KJV)

I was holding a meeting in Kansas City, and it came to my heart to ask the audience how many of them were confused. There were about 300 people at that meeting, and from what I could tell, 298 of them raised their hands. And my husband was one of the two who didn't raise a hand. I can tell you that Dave has never been confused in his life because he doesn't worry. He doesn't try to figure out anything. He is not interested in having all the answers to everything, because he trusts God.

When you trust God, you can relax and enjoy life. You don't have to go through life worrying and trying to figure out how to solve all your problems. Think about all the things you have worried about in your life and how they have all worked out. That ought to help you realize that worry and reasoning are a waste of time and energy. Stop worrying. Stop complicating your life by trying to figure out everything. Just admit that you don't know, that you are not able, that you need God. Then go on living, and enjoy life while God is giving you the answers.

Never Go to Bed Angry

When angry, do not sin; do not ever let your wrath (your
exasperation, your fury or indignation) last until the sun goes down.

—EPHESIANS 4:26

Now, I don't know about you, but I'm glad this verse is in the Bible, because it helps us to build character by giving us a guideline to follow in handling our anger: let go of anger before bedtime. There is only one problem. What happens when we become good and mad just before bedtime? If we become mad in the morning, at least we have all day to get over it. But when we become mad close to bedtime, we have to make a quick decision.

Why is it so bad for us to go to bed angry? I think it is because while we sleep, what we are angry about has time to get a hold on us and take root in us. But the Word says, "Leave no [such] room or foothold for the devil [give no opportunity to him]." (EPHESIANS 4:27) This verse tells us what happens if we refuse to get over our anger by bedtime: It opens a door for the devil and gives Satan a foothold. Once Satan gets a foothold in our lives, then he can move on to a stronghold. You may wonder, *Well, if I am mad, what should I do about it?* Get over it! You may think, *That's easy for you to say, but you're not in my situation.* I may not be in your situation, but you are not in my situation either. We all have different situations. If you are going to live a joyful, victorious life, you have to do so by choice and not by feeling.

In Deuteronomy 30:19 the Lord tells us, "I have set before you life and death, the blessings and the curses; therefore choose life." Choose life by refusing to give in to anger. Take responsibility for your anger and learn to deal with it—process it and bring closure to it, and that will relieve the pressure.

Meditation Produces Success

This Book of the Law shall not depart out of your mouth,
but you shall meditate on it day and night, that you may observe and do
according to all that is written in it. For then you shall make your way
prosperous, and then you shall deal wisely and have good success.

—JOSHUA 1:8

Most people do not delve into the Word of God very deeply. As a result, they get confused about why they are not powerful Christians living victorious lives. The truth is that most of them really don't put much effort of their own into the study of the Word. They may go out and hear others teach and preach the Word. They may listen to sermon tapes or read the Bible occasionally, but they are not really dedicated to making the Word a major part of their lives, including spending time thinking about it.

The flesh is basically lazy, and many people want to get something for nothing (with no effort on their part); however, that really is not the way it works. *A person will get out of the Word what he is willing to put into it.*

If you want to be a success and prosper in all your dealings, the Bible says you must meditate on the Word of God day and night. How much time do you spend thinking about the Word of God? If you are having problems in any area of your life, an honest answer to this question may disclose the reason why.

You Are Responsible for Your Own Life

Be doers of the Word, and not hearers only. —JAMES 1:22 (KJV)

One of the biggest problems in society today is that people don't want to take responsibility for their lives. They want quick fixes. Society has trained them to believe that if they have problems, somebody else is responsible. Their parents are responsible. Their spouses are responsible. Their schools or employers are responsible. The company that made the cigarettes or vehicle or junk food is responsible.

I'm not saying you are responsible for the current state of your life. Lots of uncontrollable events occur in our lives. Sometimes we do get very bad messages in childhood. Sometimes we have bad people in our lives who hurt us. The situation you find yourself in may or may not be your fault. But it is your fault if you take it lying down! You do not have to stay in that bad situation. You get to make a choice. And that choice is 100 percent yours.

No matter how you got to where you find yourself today, don't let it be an excuse to stay there. I had many excuses and reasons for my poor health, bad attitude, and unbalanced life. As long as I offered excuses, I never made progress.

The time has come to be very honest with yourself and with God. When you have a moment of privacy, take a deep breath, clear your head, and repeat this phrase: "I am responsible for my own life. No one can take charge of it but me. If I am unhappy or unhealthy, I know I have the power to change that. I have all the help and knowledge I need; and with God's hand today, I start becoming the person of excellence I have always known I could be."

Do You Worship or Worry?

And the Lord said to Moses, Make a fiery serpent [of bronze] and set it on a
pole; and everyone who is bitten, when he looks at it, shall live.

—NUMBERS 21:8

In Numbers 21, we see that when the Israelites were out in the wilderness, they were dying in large numbers because of a plague of snakes that had come upon them as a result of their sin. Moses went and fell down before God and worshiped Him. He turned his attention immediately to God, not to himself or anyone else, to solve the problem.

I have discovered that throughout the Bible when people had a problem, they worshiped. At least the ones who were victorious did. They didn't worry—they worshiped. I would ask you today: *Do you worry or worship?* Moses sought God about how to handle the snakes. He didn't make his own plan and ask God to bless it; he didn't try to reason out an answer, nor did he worry—he worshiped. His action brought a response from God.

We know that the pole with the bronze serpent on it represented the cross and Jesus taking our sin upon Himself on it. The message is still the same today: "Look and live." Look at Jesus, at what He has done, not at yourself and what you have done or can do.

The answer to your problem, whatever it may be, is to not worry but worship. Begin to worship God because He is good, and His goodness will be released in your life.

Love Does Not Rejoice at Injustice

It does not rejoice at injustice and unrighteousness,
but rejoices when right and truth prevail.

—1 CORINTHIANS 13:6

Love is grieved at injustice. It always wants what is fair and right. It craves justice not only for itself but especially for others. I don't like to see people mistreated. I have been hurt a lot in my life, and I well remember how it feels.

We should care about others and their pain, pray for them, and do what we can to relieve their suffering. Love is not unfeeling; it cannot look at unjust situations and just simply not care or do nothing. The worldly mentality of "don't bother me with it, that is your problem" has no place in the lives of Christians.

Obviously, we cannot physically or financially fix everyone's problem, but we can care. We can work with the Holy Spirit to make sure we don't allow our hearts to become hardened by all the violence and injustice all around us.

God is love, and He loves righteousness (knowing you are right with God—acting right, talking right, etc.). Therefore, those who walk in love must also love righteousness. Psalm 97:10 states that if we love the Lord, we must hate evil. Those who love righteousness are often persecuted for it—Jesus was, and we are not above our Master (SEE MATTHEW 10:24). Don't hate evil people, just their evil ways. God hates sin, but He loves sinners.

Keep walking in love, hating injustice and unrighteousness, and the favor of God will come upon your life in an astounding way.

Let Go and Let God Be God

O our God, will You not exercise judgment upon them? For we
have no might to stand against this great company that is coming against us.
We do not know what to do, but our eyes are upon You.

—2 CHRONICLES 20:12

Here Jehoshaphat admits to God openly his total inability to deal with the problem. For years I tried very hard to change myself without success. I tried so hard and so long to break bad habits only to fail time and time again. I tried to alter different things in my life, to get prosperity, to make my ministry grow, and to be healed. I remember wanting to give up simply because I was so exhausted from trying to fight my own battles. I went through all that on a regular basis until one day I was being really kind of melodramatic about it, trying to impress God with how miserable I was. I said something like, "God, I've had it. This is it. I'm through. Nothing I'm doing is working. I give up. I'm not going to do this anymore."

Just then, deep inside me, I heard the Holy Spirit say, "Really?" There was real excitement in His voice. That happens because the only time He gets to work in us is when we become so exhausted that we finally decide, "Instead of trying to do this myself, I'm going to give up and let God be God." Trying to be God will wear you out fast. Why not give up your own effort and do what Jehoshaphat did in verse 12? Admit to God that you have no might to stand against your enemies and that you don't know what to do, but you are looking to Him for direction and deliverance.

The Blessing of Conviction

> *And when He comes, He will convict and convince the world and bring*
> *demonstration to it about sin and about righteousness (uprightness of heart*
> *and right standing with God) and about judgment.*
>
> —JOHN 16:8

Jesus told the disciples that when the Holy Spirit came, He would have an intimate, personal ministry to them. One of the things the Holy Spirit is responsible for is guiding believers into all truth, and He is the agent in the process of sanctification in believers' lives. This is partially accomplished by His convicting powers. In other words, every time we are getting off track or going in a wrong direction, the Holy Spirit convicts us that our behavior or decision is wrong.

This is accomplished by a "knowing" in our spirit that what we are doing is not right. When you and I feel convicted, we should repent and change our direction. If we know how to and are willing to cooperate with the Holy Spirit, we can move on to spiritual maturity and release all the planned blessings of God in our lives. If, however, we ignore this conviction and go our own way, we will find the way very hard and difficult.

Satan does not want us to receive conviction, nor does he even want us to understand it. He always has a counterfeit for all the good things God offers—something somewhat like what God offers, but which, if received, will bring destruction instead of blessing. I believe Satan's counterfeit for true godly conviction is condemnation. Condemnation always produces feelings of guilt. It makes us feel "down" in everyway. We feel "under" something heavy, which is where Satan wants us.

God, on the other hand, sent Jesus to set us free, to give us righteousness, peace, and joy (SEE ROMANS 14:17). Our spirits should be light and carefree, not oppressed and heavy with burdens that we are unable to bear. We cannot bear our sins; Jesus came to bear them. He alone is able to do so, and we must receive His ministry.

Spiritual Nourishment

I tell you, do not be anxious and troubled [with cares] about your life, as to what you will [have to] eat; or about your body, as to what you will [have to] wear. For life is more than food, and the body [more] than clothes.

—LUKE 12:22-23

If you have a rich spiritual life, you'll already be satisfied with the moment, the day, the year. We all have these moments at times. You wander through a summer field of fireflies and suddenly feel still and awed at the beauty of it all. You hold your new son or grandson on your lap and feel a great spiritual bond of love all around you. You're sitting in a pew Sunday morning and the light comes through the stained glass and fills your heart with joy. The moment is complete in itself. You don't think, *My heart is full of joy, and boy, do I wish I had a slice of chocolate cake in my hand!*

You can know the complete fulfillment of spiritual nourishment and know that if you can experience it regularly, you'll have no problem eating and drinking only what you need. In fact, we should all feel those transcendent moments more often than we do. I believe they are essential to physical, emotional, and spiritual health. And I think we spend too little time trying to achieve them and too much time meditating on our problems. Whether it's in therapy, at home, or with friends over coffee, if we stew in our own problems all the time, they are only going to be with us that much more.

Get your mind off the problems, and spend more time meditating on the one, true solution—God's love. Our problems in life—and there will be problems—should drive us to God, not away from Him. Jonah tried running from his duty to the Lord by sailing to a remote destination, and look what happened to him! Don't follow Jonah's path. Run to God! He won't just help you find the solutions to your spiritual hunger; He is the solution!

God's Ways Are Not Our Ways

My thoughts are not your thoughts, neither are your ways my ways.

—ISAIAH 55:8 (NIV)

I have discovered that God often seems unreasonable. What He chooses to do does not always make sense to us. It does not always fit into our balance of reason. We have a tendency to want things to make sense, but God wants us to learn to be led by our trust and not by our understanding. We should thank God that His ways are not our ways. My life would have turned out badly if God had given me my way in many situations. It is wise for us to pray, "Your will be done, Lord, not mine."

I often tell the Lord what I would like to have, but follow it up with, "However, if You know it is not right for me, please don't give it to me." His thoughts are above our thoughts. He sees the end from the beginning. All His ways are right and sure. In the natural we can think something makes sense, but it may not be what God wants at all.

Emptied and Filled

I have been crucified with Christ [in Him I have shared His crucifixion]; it is
no longer I who live, but Christ (the Messiah) lives in me; and the life I now
live in the body I live by faith in (by adherence to and reliance on and complete
trust in) the Son of God, Who loved me and gave Himself up for me.

—GALATIANS 2:20

When I first started ministering, I wanted to help people. The Lord
spoke to me then and said: "When you are empty of yourself so that all
you have left within you is the ability to depend on the Holy Spirit, when
you have learned that everything you are and have comes from Him, then
I'll send you around to your neighbors to fill their empty vessels with the
life I have poured into your empty vessel." Arriving at the place of being
empty of ourselves is not an easy task and is rarely ever a quick one.

I spent many years wondering if I would ever reach a place of manifesting humility instead of pride—of being dependent on God instead
of independent, of trusting in His arm instead of my own. If you feel the
same way, let me encourage you that as long as you don't give up, you are
making progress. It may seem as though reaching the place you desire is
taking forever, but "He who began a good work in you will continue until
the day of Jesus Christ [right up to the time of His return], developing
[that good work] and perfecting and bringing it to full completion in you."
(PHILIPPIANS 1:6)

It is only after we realize it is not us doing good works, but rather the
Lord, that we can even begin to serve Him as we should. Someone has
said, "It remains to be seen what God can do through a man or woman
who will give Him all the glory." If we press on and are sincere about
spiritual maturity, we will all eventually be empty of ourselves and ready
to be used by God to fill other empty people.

Hold Things Loosely

But God is the Rock and firm Strength of my heart and my portion forever.

—PSALM 73:26

One of the ways that we try to build our faith is to look at the nice things we have but realize how much of it we could live without. It pleases me to think about how pretty our home is, but I know that if we had to live in a two- or three-room apartment again, I would be just as happy because my joy is coming from the inside of me and not from things that I have.

We find balance in realizing that everything we have is on loan from God. He's given it to us to use, but we are neither to possess it nor let it possess us. The minute we start grasping at things that become too important to us, God will start shaking them from our hand. If we will let go when He shakes it, and say, "Okay, You're right, God, I am getting too attached to this, or I am starting to like this too much, or I am depending on this too much," then most of the time He lets us keep it. But if we grasp too tightly and it becomes too important to our sense of security and our joy depends on it, then God will take it away from us. God will give us all kinds of things to use and enjoy, but He will not let them possess us.

We're in a Hurry, but God's Not

To everything there is a season, and a time for
every matter or purpose under heaven.

—ECCLESIASTES 3:1

We never learn patience without something to be patient about. Patience is something that has to be worked in us—it doesn't just appear. The fruit of patience is in our spirits, because as children of God, the Holy Spirit is resident within us.

But for patience to be expressed through our souls (our mind, will, and emotions), a work must be done in us. Once the prescribed time of waiting for the birth of each of my children had passed, I tried everything imaginable to bring on labor. I walked, took castor oil, worked harder than usual, hoping it would help "speed things up." With one of them, I even went into the hospital so the doctor would induce labor. It didn't work; I was sent home. The doctor basically said, "Go home and let nature take its course."

My advice to you from the Word of God and from my experience in life is, "Don't be in such a big hurry." You may be full of dreams for your life, but you may also be trying to achieve your dreams out of season. We can make huge messes in our lives and sometimes get upset with God because things didn't work out the way we thought the Lord said they would. Things will happen as God said if we wait on His timing. We are the ones in a hurry. God is not in a hurry!

Stay busy delighting yourself in the Lord, and let Him give you what He wants you to have. If God has placed the desire in you, you can be assured that He will bring it to birth in the right season. Wait on God for direction and instruction on how to proceed, do what He tells you or shows you, but don't go beyond that.

What to Do When Trouble Comes

Fight the good fight of the faith.   —1 TIMOTHY 6:12

Sooner or later we all have some trouble in life. We all have some trials and some tribulations. Everybody goes through times of testing. And not every storm shows up in the forecast. Some days we can wake up and think everything is going to be great. Before that day is over, we may be tested by all kinds of trouble we were not expecting.

Trouble is part of life, so we simply have to be ready for it. We need to have a planned response to trouble, because it is more difficult to get strong after trouble comes. It is better to be prepared by staying strong.

The first thing you need to do when trouble comes is pray, "God, help me stay emotionally stable." Do not let your emotions overwhelm you. The next thing you need to do is trust God. The instant that fear rises up, pray.

Stay emotionally stable, trust God, and pray. Then while you are waiting for God to answer, simply keep doing good. Keep your commitments. Do not stop serving the Lord just because you have a problem. The greatest time in the world to keep your commitments to God is in the midst of difficulty and adversity. When the devil sees that trials and tribulations won't stop you, he will stop troubling you for a while.

To be prepared for the next time you find yourself in a difficult situation, practice saying, "I am going to be faithful to God, and God is going to give me double for my trouble. Satan, you thought you were going to hurt me, but I am going to get a double blessing, because I am one who diligently seeks the Lord."

Only Believe

Jesus asked, "Do you believe that I am able to do this?" ——MATTHEW 9:28

In Mark 5:36 (GNT), He said, "Don't be afraid, only believe." There have been many times in my life when I have been discouraged and not known what to do, or felt that nothing was working and that everybody was against me. Whether it was about unfilled financial needs or unrelenting pain in my body, I would say to God, "What do You want me to do?" The thing I have heard over and over again is, "Only believe." Hebrews 4:3 tells us that believing brings us into the rest of God. Once we enter that rest, it is wonderful because although we may still have a problem, we are not frustrated by it anymore.

In Mark 11:24 Jesus said that whatever you ask for in prayer, believe that you receive it, and you will get it. In Acts 16:31 we are told, "Believe in the Lord Jesus Christ, and you will be saved." Hebrews 11:6 tells us that those who come to God must believe that He exists and that He rewards those who seek Him. Can you see from these scriptures how important it is to believe? If you and I want to receive anything from God, we must first believe that He is, and then we must believe that He is good.

Eliminating Prejudice

God shows no partiality and is no respecter of persons. —ACTS 10:34

Jesus dealt with dividing walls in His day. The Jews felt contempt for the Gentiles, whom they called dogs. Many men saw women as inferior and, as a result of their wrong attitude, sometimes women were mistreated. As a woman I could look back and decide to hate all men because my female ancestors were treated unfairly. In the same way, Jews could spend their lives hating Germans because of a crazy, demon-possessed man named Adolf Hitler. Americans could hate the Japanese because they bombed Pearl Harbor and thrust the United States into World War II. African Americans could spend their lives hating white people because of slavery.

None of us can go back and undo the past. No matter how much we would like to, it is not possible. We cannot even pay people back for what they did to us or failed to do for us in the past. Only God can do that. Our only peaceful option is to forget what lies behind and press on to what lies ahead (see PHILIPPIANS 3:13-14).

Life is too short to spend it hating. Examine yourself in this area. Be honest with yourself concerning whether or not you are prejudiced. Even if you find only a little bit of prejudice, repent of it, and pray sincerely that it will be removed from your heart. Say to yourself, "I am no better than anyone else; we are all equal in God's eyes. Every person is God's creation, and He stated that everything He made was good."

Show Love to Strangers

*Do not forget or neglect or refuse to extend hospitality to strangers
[in the brotherhood—being friendly, cordial, and gracious, sharing the
comforts of your home and doing your part generously], for through it some
have entertained angels without knowing it.*

—HEBREWS 13:2

A clique is an exclusive group, one to which not everyone is welcome.
Being "in" makes us feel important, but being "out" can be very painful. I
find that even the church is full of cliques.

As believers in the Lord Jesus Christ, you and I are instructed in the
Word of God to make strangers feel welcome, to be hospitable toward
them, and not to mistreat them in any way. This is especially important in
church. I wonder how many people finally get up enough courage to visit
a church on Sunday morning but never go back because everyone there
ignored them.

Of course, not all churches are cold and uncaring. Many are warm,
friendly, and loving; and those are the ones that will flourish. Everyone
wants to be accepted, made to feel welcome, and loved. God gave the
Israelites specific instructions not to wrong or oppress strangers, telling
them to remember that they were once strangers in the land themselves
(SEE EXODUS 22:21).

We have all been the new person at work or at school, in a neighborhood or a church. We should remember how much we appreciated those
who took the initiative to be friendly with us. We must always remember
the golden rule: "Do to others as you would have them do to you" (LUKE
6:31 NIV).

The Freedom of Confession

I acknowledged my sin to You, and my iniquity I did not hide. I said, I will
confess my transgressions to the Lord [continually unfolding the past till all is
told]—then You [instantly] forgave me the guilt and iniquity of my sin.

—PSALM 32:5

In 1 John 1:9, the Bible teaches us that if we admit our sins and confess them, He will forgive us and cleanse us from all unrighteousness. Start by freely admitting all your faults. Hold nothing back. Admit them to God and to people. Don't make excuses or place blame elsewhere.

As you do this, you will experience a new freedom, and your relationship with Jesus and with people will improve greatly. I have found that if I tell people my faults before they find them on their own, neither one of us is as bothered by them.

Be open with people. Most people respect and admire honesty and openness. It is what we try to hide that comes back to haunt us. Invite Jesus into every area of your life. Don't feel you must hide your faults from Him. He knows all about them anyway. Actually, the Lord knows more about us than we can remember or will ever discover and He loves us anyway.

Give God not only what you are but especially give Him what you are not. It is easy to offer Him our strengths, but we should also offer Him our weaknesses because His strength is made perfect in our weaknesses. Don't hold anything back; give God everything! The Lord doesn't see only what we are right now, He sees what we can become because He is patient with us.

Faith or Fear?

For whatever does not originate and proceed from faith is sin [whatever is done without a conviction of its approval by God is sinful].

—ROMANS 14:23

Is it possible to allow someone to control and manipulate us, honestly saying we are doing so in faith? Of course not! We know this type of behavior is rooted in fear, not faith. Faith obeys God, but fear is easily intimidated and finds many excuses for disobedience.

A person who is a perfectionist, a workaholic, or involved in sexual perversion is just as dependent as someone who is addicted to a chemical substance like tobacco, alcohol, or drugs. If we try to meet the needs of that person at the expense of our own needs, we are co-dependent upon that individual.

It is good to help people who have been hurt; but when their emotional needs begin to control us, we are in danger of being led by them and their problems instead of being led by the Holy Spirit of God. Faith causes us to step out and say or do what God places in our hearts, but fear causes us to timidly stay under control and domination.

How many times have we heard manipulative people say things like, "I'm old, and you don't care anything about me now," or "I raised you all of your life. I sacrificed to house and clothe you and put you through school, and now you want to just leave me here all alone"?

There is a balance to be maintained in such situations. That balance is the Holy Spirit within us to guide us into the truth of each situation. He will provide us the wisdom to know when we are to be adaptable and adjustable and when we are to take a firm stand and be immovable. Always keep in mind *that faith obeys God; fear is easily moved by unbridled emotion!*

Discernment

> *But the spiritual man tries all things [he examines, investigates,*
> *inquires into, questions, and discerns all things].*
>
> —I CORINTHIANS 2:15

As long as we try to figure out our own problems, we will only get more and more frustrated and confused. The reason is because we are trying to operate without the grace of God.

In my ministry, the prayer request I receive most often is for guidance. Many people just do not seem to know what to do. They are frustrated and confused by the situations they face in their everyday lives. They need help, and they don't know where to look for it.

If I have a problem, I don't need to try to figure it out—I need discernment. I need to hear from the Lord. I need God's Word on my situation. I need for Him to show me what to do. Discernment is simply God's wisdom for any situation of life. It is a "spiritual knowing" about how to handle things.

One time as I was praying and asking God for discernment, the Lord spoke to me and said, "Joyce, you are never going to have discernment until you give up reasoning." Now, notice that the Lord didn't say "until I deliver you from reasoning," He said "until you give up reasoning."

If you are trying to figure out everything in life, you must realize that it is just a habit, a bad habit, one that you will have to break. Your mind may be like mine was. I was addicted to excessive reasoning. There's certainly nothing wrong with using our minds . . . God has blessed us with strong minds to accomplish many great things. But as soon as you begin to feel frustrated and confused, as soon as you start to lose your sense of inner peace, you need to say to yourself, "Uh-oh, I've gone too far." You must give up your efforts and entrust yourself totally to the Lord, leaving your situation entirely in His hands.

Familiarity Can Cause Disrespect

*Thank [God] in everything [no matter what the
circumstances may be, be thankful and give thanks], for this is the will of God
for you [who are] in Christ Jesus.*

—1 THESSALONIANS 5:18

Familiarity can breed contempt or disrespect. Think of how a person treats a new car. He admires it, thinks it is beautiful, washes it all the time, and expects everyone to be very careful when inside it.

But what happens when the car has been around for a few years? It is now dirty all the time, dented, full of empty soda cans and hamburger wrappers. What happened? The owner became familiar with it, took it for granted, and no longer showed it the same respect he did when it was new. He could have kept it looking and running as if it was new had he given it the attention he had in the beginning.

We find a great example of the dangers of familiarity in the Bible concerning the ark of God. When David was attempting to bring it home, a man called Uzza put out his hand to steady the ark on the cart that was carrying it, and God struck him dead because no one was supposed to touch it (SEE 1 CHRONICLES 13).

Uzza knew the strict guidelines concerning the ark, so why did he touch it? I believe it was because it had been stored in his father's home for quite some time, and he had become familiar with it. His respect level had lowered without his even knowing it, simply due to his being around the ark too much. In this case, familiarity cost him his life.

It is the same thing that happens in a marriage, or in a friendship, or with any privilege we are afforded. New things seem wonderful, but when we become familiar with them, we begin to have less respect for them, or even contempt. Don't let what is special become mundane. To keep from taking each other for granted, we can practice remembering how precious people are and focus on thankfulness for their presence in our lives.

Giving Thanks

Jesus lifted up His eyes and said, Father, I thank You that You have heard Me.

—JOHN 11:41

Here we see a good example of Jesus giving thanks to God. When you pray, I encourage you to end your prayer, as Jesus did here, by saying, "Father, I thank You that You have heard me." One reason I encourage you to do that is because, as John tells us, when we know that God has heard us, we know that He has granted us our requests (SEE 1 JOHN 5:14-15). The devil wants you and me to pray and then go off wondering whether God has heard us and is willing to grant us what we have asked. The way we overcome that doubt is by lifting up the voice of thanksgiving (SEE PSALM 26:7 AND JONAH 2:9).

You Can't "Catch" Holiness

Thus says the Lord of hosts: Ask now the priests to decide this question of law: If one carries in the skirt of his garment flesh that is holy [because it has been offered in sacrifice to God], and with his skirt or the flaps of his garment he touches bread, or pottage, or wine, or oil, or any kind of food, does what he touches become holy [dedicated to God's service exclusively]? And the priests answered, No! [Holiness is not infectious.] Then said Haggai, If one who is [ceremonially] unclean because he has come in contact with a dead body should touch any of these articles of food, shall it be [ceremonially] unclean? And the priests answered, It shall be unclean. [Unholiness is infectious.]

—HAGGAI 2:11-13

Holiness has been defined as "separation to God," a separation that should result in "conduct befitting those so separated." In the New Testament, the same Greek word translated *holiness* is also translated *sanctification,* which the Greek dictionary says "cannot be transferred or imputed." That means that holiness is an individual possession, one that is built up little by little. It can not be given to or taken from another person.

In other words, you and I cannot become holy by going through a prayer line or by having hands laid on us or by associating with someone else who is holy.

As we see in this passage from the Old Testament prophet Haggai, unholiness is infectious; holiness is not. What that means is that you and I can associate with someone who is living a sinful life, and that individual's sinfulness can rub off on us. We can catch it like a disease.

But holiness is not like that. It can't be picked up by contact or exposure; it has to be chosen on purpose.

Becoming God's Mouthpiece

She opens her mouth in skillful and godly Wisdom, and on her tongue is the law of kindness [giving counsel and instruction].

—PROVERBS 31:26

Regardless of our specific ministry within the body of Christ, each of us is a mouthpiece for God in some way. Whether you and I have been given a worldwide teaching gift or whether we have been given the ability to witness to our coworkers, God wants us to use our mouth for Him.

A wise man once said to me, "Joyce, God has given you the ear of many. Stay broken and only speak when spoken through." Obviously this requires intensive training by the Holy Spirit. If we desire the words of our mouth to carry God's power, then our mouth must belong to Him. Is your mouth God's mouth? Have you really given it to Him for His purpose?

A person's heart can become hardened as a result of making excuses for his behavior. For a long time, I excused my "mouth problems" by blaming them on my personality, or on abuse in my past, or on the fact that I felt bad or was so tired. Actually the list of excuses we make for our failure to conform to the will and Word of God is endless. Finally the Holy Spirit got my full attention so that I began to become accountable for my words. I still have a long way to go, but I feel I have made much progress because I have reached the stage of true repentance.

Those who desire to be used by God need to allow Him to deal with them concerning their mouth and what comes out of it.

A Thankful Heart

> *Do not fret or have any anxiety about anything, but in every circumstance*
> *and in everything, by prayer and petition (definite requests), with*
> *thanksgiving, continue to make your wants known to God.*
>
> —PHILIPPIANS 4:6

Years ago I taught a message saying that when you ask God for something, you should thank Him ahead of time that you are going to get it because that will help release your manifestation. I believe that. I took the scripture above to mean just that, that when I pray for something, I should start thanking God that it was on its way. But one day God revealed a broader scope of that verse to me. He said, "No, what I am really saying there is that when you pray and petition Me for anything, make sure you are doing it from a foundation of a thankful heart." Then He went on to say, "If you are not thankful for what you already have, why should I give you more to complain about?"

In those days, I had a complaining heart, a murmuring, grumbling, faultfinding heart. I could find a thousand things to grumble about, but God does not want us to have a grumbling heart. He wants us to get to the place that we are living epistles, read of all men. From our lifestyle, people should be able to tell that there is something different about us, asking us "Why are you so happy? Why are you so peaceful? Why are you so loving?" We are supposed to be salt and light to the world. Our lives are supposed to make people want what we have.

Defeating Doubt

And take the helmet of salvation and the sword
that the Spirit wields, which is the Word of God.

—EPHESIANS 6:17

There was a man who was sick and confessing the Word over his body, quoting healing scriptures, and believing for his healing to manifest. While doing so, he was intermittently attacked with thoughts of doubt. After he had gone through a hard time and was beginning to get discouraged, God opened his eyes to the spirit world. This is what he saw: a demon speaking lies to him, telling him that he was not going to get healed and that confessing the Word was not going to work. But he also saw that each time he confessed the Word, light would come out of his mouth like a sword, and the demon would cower and fall backward.

As God showed him this vision, the man then understood why it was so important to keep speaking the Word. He saw that he did have faith, which is why the demon was attacking him with doubt. Doubt is not something God puts in us. The Bible says that God gives every man a measure of faith (SEE ROMANS 12:3).

God has placed faith in our hearts, but the devil tries to negate our faith by attacking us with doubt. Doubt comes in the form of thoughts that are in opposition to the Word of God. This is why it is so important for us to know the Word of God. If we know the Word, then we can recognize when the devil is lying to us. Then we can speak the Word and get the upper hand over doubt.

You Are Precious to God

Now on the final and most important day of the Feast, Jesus stood, and He
cried in a loud voice, If any man is thirsty, let him come to Me and drink!

—JOHN 7:37

You are precious and valuable, and God has a plan to manifest His goodness and kindness through what He wants to do for you. It does not matter what you have done or what has been done to you—the past remains in the past. God has a great future for you. You can have a wonderful life, but you have to receive it. You have to agree and say, "That is for me."

Jesus *cried out* to tell us that He has what we need: "Now on the final and most important day of the Feast, Jesus stood, and He cried in a loud voice. If any man is thirsty, let him come to me and drink!" (JOHN 7:37). What you cannot do for yourself, God has already done for you. He invites you now to come and receive it, to drink it, to take it into yourself. You do that by believing it is for you.

To *drink* is defined as "to take in or receive avidly"; "to receive into one's consciousness." Remember that Jesus said, "Now ask and keep on asking and you will receive, so that your joy (gladness, delight) may be full and complete." (JOHN 16:24) If you ask and receive, then your joy will be full.

How are we going to impress a depressed world if we believers are as depressed as those who are without Christ? God wants His people to show forth the glory of His kindness upon them. As we receive God's provision, our joy will be complete, which is the way the church is supposed to be.

Act as a receptacle for God's blessings. Take in what Jesus has paid for with His own life to provide for you. Study the Word so that you will be sure of His promises. Pray to Him, saying, "Here I am, Lord. Pour it on. I receive the fullness of whatever your Holy Spirit has for me."

Bold Enough to Be Led by the Spirit

The wicked flee when no man pursues them, but the
[uncompromisingly] righteous are bold as a lion.

—PROVERBS 28:1

If we intend to succeed at being ourselves, we must reach a point where we can be led by the Holy Spirit. Only God, through His Spirit, will lead us to succeed and be all we can be. Other people usually won't, the devil certainly won't, and we are not able to do it ourselves without God.

Being led by the Spirit does not mean we never make mistakes. The Holy Spirit doesn't make mistakes, but we do. Following the Spirit's leading is a process which can only be learned by doing. We start by stepping out into things we believe God is putting on our hearts, and we learn by wisdom and experience how to hear more clearly and definitely.

I say that boldness is required to be led by the Spirit because: 1) only boldness steps out, and 2) only boldness can survive making mistakes. When insecure people make mistakes, they often will never try again. Bold people make many mistakes, but their attitude is, "I'm going to keep trying until I learn to do this right."

Those who suffer from condemnation usually don't believe they can hear from God. Even if they think they may have heard from God and do step out, a minor failure is a major setback to them. I am prepared mentally and emotionally not to be defeated by mistakes and problems when they do come.

Be bold. Be determined that you are going to be all God wants you to be. Don't hide behind fears and insecurities any longer. If you have already made major blunders in your life and have been living under condemnation because of them, this is the time to *press on!* You are reading this book for a reason, and I encourage you to take this message personally, just as though God were talking directly to you through it. Be determined to press on toward victory.

Our Standard Is Jesus

That you may walk (live and conduct yourselves) in a manner worthy of the
Lord, fully pleasing to Him and desiring to please Him in all things.

—COLOSSIANS 1:10

Obey God in every little thing, and you will enjoy an excellent life. Be diligent in your obedience. Learn to live your life before God and not before man. Go the extra mile and do all the little things that God tells you to do, even though nobody else may ever know. Put your grocery cart back in the stall where it belongs instead of leaving it out in the middle of the parking lot. Why? Because the owner of the property has put up a sign saying, "Please return carts here," and God has said to submit to authority (see TITUS 3:1).

The flesh says, "Well, everybody else leaves their carts everywhere; why should I put mine up?" Because our standard is not others—our standard is Jesus. When I compare myself to everybody else, I don't look too bad. But if I compare myself to Jesus, I am humbled and ask God to help me! Until Jesus comes to get us, we need to compare ourselves to Him and the standard of holiness that He holds up for our lives.

Knowing When to Speak

But avoid all empty (vain, useless, idle) talk, for it
will lead people into more and more ungodliness.

—2 TIMOTHY 2:16

One of the areas in which I have had to learn obedience to the Lord is in talking—or more precisely, when to *stop* talking.

If you are a big talker like me, you understand why I say there is anointed-by-the-Holy-Spirit talk, then there is vain, useless, idle talk—the kind the apostle Paul warns about in his letter to young Timothy, cited in the verse above.

There have been times when we have had guests in our home and I have finished saying what the Lord wanted me to say, but then continued talking. We can usually pinpoint the moment when what we are doing switches from being anointed by God to being *us* continuing on in the flesh—in our own strength. After that point I was rambling, really saying nothing, or repeating the same things over and over.

Sometimes when people left our house to go home, I was exhausted. If I had quit talking two hours earlier when the Lord told me, I wouldn't have been worn out! The special requirement the Lord had for me was to learn to say what He wanted me to say, then stop.

Have you ever been talking with someone about a tender subject when the discussion suddenly takes a turn and becomes a little heated? You can tell feelings are starting to get out of control, and that little prompting on the inside of you says, "That's enough. Don't say any more." That prompting, though small, is very strong, and you know saying one more thing would not be wise. But after thinking for a minute, you decide to plunge on in with the flesh! A few minutes later, you're in an all-out war! The minute the Spirit says, "That's enough," we need to stop. If we keep going, we are asking for frustration and defeat.

Serving One Another Is Serving God

*Whatever may be your task, work at it heartily (from the soul), as
[something done] for the Lord and not for men, Knowing [with all certainty]
that it is from the Lord [and not from men] that you will receive the
inheritance which is your [real] reward. [The One Whom] you are actually
serving [is] the Lord Christ (the Messiah).*

—COLOSSIANS 3:23-24

One morning as I got up and went downstairs to make coffee, I felt the
Lord tug at my heart to make Dave a fruit salad. Our housekeeper was
off that day, and Dave really enjoys his fruit salad in the morning. To be
honest, I did not want to make a fruit salad. I could have handled bringing Dave an apple and a banana, but I did not want to take the time to cut
them all up in a bowl and serve it to him. I wanted to go pray and read my
Bible!

Sometimes we make the mistake of thinking that spiritual activity re-
places obedience and makes us spiritual, but it doesn't. The Lord spoke to
my heart that serving Dave was actually serving Him. I obediently made
the fruit salad.

It seems that everyone today wants to be free, and Jesus has indeed set
us free, but He has not set us free to be selfish and to want to be served,
but rather to serve others.

Peace in the Midst of the Storm

A furious storm of wind [of hurricane proportions] arose,
and the waves kept beating into the boat, so that it was already
becoming filled. But He [Himself] was . . . asleep.

—MARK 4:37-38

In Mark 4:35-41 we read how a storm arose when Jesus and His disciples were in a ship crossing the Sea of Galilee. The disciples got all upset, but Jesus calmly rebuked the storm, speaking peace to it, and it quieted down. Do you know why He was able to speak peace to the storm? *Because He never let the storm get on the inside of Him.* The disciples could not calm the storm because they were as disturbed as the waves were. Remember, you can't give away something you don't have. Jesus gave them peace because He had peace to give them. He had a peaceful heart within Him. I tell you, I want to be the kind of person who has a soothing effect on people when I get around them. I want to be the kind of person who can spend a few minutes in a strife-filled room, and all of a sudden everyone starts to calm down.

When Jesus walked around on the earth, He had something going out of Him—the anointing or the virtue of God, which is the power of God. Something was constantly emanating from Him that brought healing and hope and salvation to people's lives. It wasn't just something God put on Him; there was a foundation there of how He was living His life. Yes, He was anointed, but that anointing was not going to be released if He didn't live His life right. And that's exactly why He never let the devil upset Him. He didn't let the storms of life get on the inside of Him. He kept His heart peaceful, calm, and loving. And we are to be like Him.

The Power of Private Praise

*But when you pray, go into your [most] private room, and, closing
the door, pray to your Father, Who is in secret; and your Father, Who sees
in secret, will reward you in the open.*

—MATTHEW 6:6

As Jesus has told us, there are some things we are to do in private. There are times when I go into my bedroom, lock the door, and dance and worship before the Lord, sometimes crying and sometimes laughing all by myself. If anybody saw me, they might think I needed to be locked up. In private, I express myself freely with no inhibitions; I don't need to be concerned about offending or confusing anyone. If you do these things openly, the world will tell you that you are crazy. They do not understand how you feel because they don't have the relationship with God that you have. However, you can do them in private, between you and God alone, and you will see good fruit develop in your life. The fruit comes from what God sees, not what people see.

I believe that all of us ought to get in a private place and rejoice before the Lord, bow down before Him, lift up our hands to Him in praise, and if we need to, even weep in His presence. Worship and praise should not be confined to the church service. I worship God publicly when I gather with other people who are worshiping, and I worship at home alone. Both private and public praise and worship are very important. I encourage you to frequently enter into both.

Determined People Succeed

> *[Urged on] by faith Abraham, when he was called, obeyed and went forth to a place which he was destined to receive as an inheritance; and he went, although he did not know or trouble his mind about where he was to go.*
>
> —HEBREWS 11:8

I enjoy watching or reading biographies of various people who have succeeded in ministry, entertainment, or business. Without fail, almost every one of them has "paid their dues," so to speak. What I mean is that in the early days of their quest they had to be very determined not to give up or quit. They endured many failures before having any success.

Occasionally, we see what I call "shooting stars," people who quickly rise to the top of their profession without going through all the difficult early days, but they normally don't last too long. They come out of nowhere and disappear just as quickly. Character is developed during difficult times. Our call and desires are tested when we are told no, time after time, and still remain determined.

I am told that Abraham Lincoln ran for several public offices and was defeated several times before he was elected to the office of president of the United States. Many people would have given up, but not him. Thomas Edison, who invented the electric light, had about a thousand experiments fail before he succeeded.

Only determined people succeed. Just because we take a step of faith does not mean we will avoid the rest of the process. God usually builds slow and solid, not fast and fragile.

There's Life in the Word

And He said to them, Be careful what you are hearing. The measure
[of thought and study] you give [to the truth you hear] will be the measure
[of virtue and knowledge] that comes back to you—and more [besides] will be
given to you who hear.

—MARK 4:24

This is like the principle of sowing and reaping. The more we sow, the more we will reap at harvest time. The Lord is saying in Mark 4:24 that the greater the amount of time you and I personally put into thinking about and studying the Word we hear, the more we will get out of it.

[Things are hidden temporarily only as a means to revelation.] For there
is nothing hidden except to be revealed, nor is anything [temporarily] kept
secret except in order that it may be made known (MARK 4:22).

This verse and the one above are surely telling us that the Word has hidden in it tremendous treasures, powerful life-giving secrets that God wants to reveal to us. They are manifested to those who meditate on, ponder, study, think about, practice mentally, and mutter the Word of God. I know personally, as a teacher of God's Word, the truth of this principle. It seems there is no end to what God can show me out of one verse of Scripture. I will study it one time and get one thing, and another time see something new that I did not even notice before.

The Lord keeps revealing His secrets to those who are diligent about the Word. Don't be the kind of person who always wants to live off of someone else's revelation. Study the Word yourself and allow the Holy Spirit to bless your life with truth.

God Is Watching

For the eyes of the Lord run to and fro throughout the whole earth to show Himself strong in behalf of those whose hearts are blameless toward Him.

—2 CHRONICLES 16:9

God is watching you, and He sees everything you do. The psalmist said of Him, "You know my down sitting and my uprising; You understand my thought afar off." (PSALM 139:2)

God is eagerly seeking opportunities to reward you for your faith in Him. Jesus said, "Behold, I am coming soon, and I shall bring My wages and rewards with Me, to repay and render to each one just what his own actions and his own work merit." (REVELATION 22:12) That means that people will receive pay for the actions they commit while on this earth. Now, that can be exciting in one way, and frightening in another way.

We need to realize that God is watching us, and that no one is really getting by with anything. God neither sleeps nor slumbers (SEE PSALM 121:4). He knows everything that goes on behind closed doors. So we need to live as if we really believe that God is watching our every move. When we sit and have a conversation, we need to remember that God is the unseen guest Who is listening to everything we have to say.

Do not become discouraged in doing good, for God sees everything you are doing for others on His behalf. Not one good work that you do with the right motive has gone unnoticed. God sees every person you help, every person you are kind to; He knows every time you show somebody a little bit of mercy, every time you show someone forgiveness, and He will reward you for it.

Spend Time in God's Presence

As for me, I will continue beholding Your face in righteousness (rightness, justice, and right standing with You); I shall be fully satisfied, when I awake [to find myself] beholding Your form [and having sweet communion with You].

—PSALM 17:15

There is a God-shaped hole inside every one of us, and we cannot buy something across the counter to fill that hole. The only thing that is going to fill that craving is God Himself. One prayer will not be enough. We have to have daily maintenance. The Bible says, "Ever be filled and stimulated with the [Holy] Spirit." (EPHESIANS 5:18)

I spent years trying to find a time to fit God into my day. God finally told me to stop trying to work Him into my schedule, but to work my schedule around Him.

Contentment is found in the Lord's presence. The Psalms proclaim that the fullness of joy is in God's presence: "You will show me the path of life; in Your presence is fullness of joy, at Your right hand there are pleasures forevermore." (16:11)

We will be fully satisfied when we awake to find ourselves beholding His form and having sweet communion with Him. When God is first in our lives to the point where He is the first thing on our minds when we wake up in the morning, we will have a depth of satisfaction that no devil can take away from us.

God's Way Is Best

For who has known the mind of the Lord and who has understood His thoughts, or who has [ever] been His counselor?

—ROMANS 11:34

We need to come to the realization that God is smarter than we are. His plan really is better. No matter what you or I may think, God's way is better than ours. I look back now at many of the frustrating times I went through trying to give birth to things in my timing and being frustrated about waiting, and I realize now that I really was not ready for them. God knew I wasn't ready, but I thought I was. I spent so much of my time asking, "Why, God, why?" and "When, God, when?" I asked questions only God had the answers to, and He had no intention of telling me. Remember, God wants our trust—not our questions.

I have discovered over the years that trust requires unanswered questions. When we face puzzling situations, we should say, "Well, Lord, this does not make any sense to me, but I trust You. I believe You love me and that You will do Your best for me at the right time." God does not need our counsel in order to work; He needs our faith.

In Exodus 33:13 Moses prayed for God to show him His ways: "Now therefore, I pray You, if I have found favor in Your sight, show me now Your way, that I may know You [progressively become more deeply and intimately acquainted with You, perceiving and recognizing and understanding more strongly and clearly] and that I may find favor in Your sight." We should pray that prayer regularly, remembering that God's ways include His timing.

Don't Be Afraid of Making Mistakes

We are assured and know that [God being a partner in their labor] all things work together and are [fitting into a plan] for good to and for those who love God and are called according to [His] design and purpose.

—ROMANS 8:28

I have discovered that if our hearts are right and we do the best we know to do when we hear from Him, God will redeem us and honor our steps of obedience. If we move in childlike trust to obey what we believe in our hearts He has told us to do, even if that decision is wrong, God will take that mistake and work it out for our good.

Many people are afraid to move because they think that if they make a mistake, God will be angry with them. But this is where trusting His character is so vital to walking in faith. People who are too afraid to obey are so miserable anyway that they couldn't get any worse off by stepping out and trying to do what God is telling them to do.

I loved my job serving as an associate pastor at a St. Louis church. I didn't leave there because I wanted to leave, but God's anointing lifted off of me, and I became miserable until I obeyed Him. I realized that I would only find peace if I tested out what I believed He had told me to do. It was the only way to find out if I was right or wrong about hearing His voice.

So now, I exhort you with this truth: don't spend all your life playing it safe! Safety is very comfortable, but it may be keeping you from God's perfect plan for your life.

Don't Despise Small Beginnings

Who [with reason] despises the day of small things?

—ZECHARIAH 4:10

Probably most of us who are believing God for something can find evidence of a small beginning: a little seed, a cloud the size of a man's hand (SEE I KINGS 18:44). Rejoice over that seed. It is a sign of greater things to come. Don't curse your seed by complaining over it. God gives us seed, something that causes us to hope—a little thing perhaps, but something is better than nothing. We should say, "Lord, this is only a little thing, but thank You for giving me some hope, something to hold on to. Thank You, Lord, for a beginning."

Take that seed and plant it by believing over it. The Holy Spirit showed me that I was throwing away a lot of my seed. When we despise something, we regard it lightly. We take no notice of it and count it as nothing. We do not take care of it. If we don't take care of what God gives us, we lose it. *If we lose the seed, we will never see the harvest.* Part of Hebrews 13:5 says, in essence, be content with what you have. That scripture goes on to say, "For He [God] Himself has said, I will not in any way . . . let [you] down." That is why we can be content—by faith—during the small beginning. We know that the Lord is the Author and the Finisher (SEE HEBREWS 12:2). What He begins, He completes (SEE PHILIPPIANS 1:6). He will do that for us—if we will hold our faith firm until the end (SEE HEBREWS 3:6).

The Lord Is Our Refuge

*I love You fervently and devotedly, O Lord, my Strength. The Lord is
my Rock, my Fortress, and my Deliverer; my God, my keen and firm Strength
in Whom I will trust and take refuge, my Shield, and the Horn of my salvation,
my High Tower. I will call upon the Lord, Who is to be praised; so shall I be
saved from my enemies.*

—PSALM 18:1-3

A rock is a type of a sure foundation. When the waters of trial threaten
to rise up and overwhelm us, we need to do as David did and climb up on
the rock that is higher than we are. David also called the Lord his Fortress.
A fortress is a castle, a fort, a defense, a place into which we go when we
are being hunted or attacked. It is not a hiding place in which our enemy
cannot find us. It is a place of protection in which we can see and be seen
but cannot be reached because we are safe in God's protection.

David also called the Lord his High Tower—another lofty and inacces-
sible place—and his Shield and Buckler—which are part of the protec-
tive armor that surrounds the believer (SEE EPHESIANS 6:10-17). God is
not just above us and around us, He is even underneath us, because the
psalmist tells us, "The Lord upholds the [consistently] righteous." (PSALM
37:17)

God is holding us up by His powerful right hand and is surrounding us
as the mountains surround the holy city of Jerusalem. The devil is against
us; but God is for us, and over us, and with us, and in us. Because He cares
for us, He watches over us and keeps us so we can find rest and peace
under the shadow of His wings as we cast all our care upon Him.

Facing Fear

The devil, as a roaring lion, walketh about, seeking whom he may devour.

—1 PETER 5:8 (KJV)

Notice the scripture says "may" and not "will." In other words, you have something to do with whether he is able to devour you. And if you know anything about Satan, he doesn't have any power. The only power he has is the power you give him.

Fear, of course, is one of his favorite tactics, so he will try to use fear to stop you. But don't give in to him. Go ahead and do it afraid. When God tells you to give somebody a tract or witness to a person, say, "Yes, Lord, I want to do what You're telling me to do. I feel kind of afraid, Lord, but I believe You're with me, so I'm just going to do it." When God tells you to give an extra-big offering in church because He wants you to plant it as a seed (SEE LUKE 6:38) so that you can come up higher in your finances, say, "Okay, Lord, I'll do it. I know that means I will have to really trust You for some provision, but because I believe I'm hearing from You, I'll do it."

Don't let the devil rob you of the destiny God has for you. Step out and face your fears; face your pain. You can be a victorious Christian, or you can be one who is never quite able to enjoy the fullness of God. The only difference between the two is that one is stopped by fear and the other does it afraid. Determine today to *do it afraid!*

Christlike Communication

Let your speech at all times be gracious (pleasant and winsome), seasoned [as it were] with salt, [so that you may never be at a loss] to know how you ought to answer anyone [who puts a question to you].

—COLOSSIANS 4:6

Throughout the New Testament, we see Jesus acting in two contrasting ways. He confronted the moneychangers in the temple, overthrowing their tables and firmly demonstrating God's will to all those who watched Him. He said to them, "The Scripture says, My house shall be called a house of prayer; but you have made it a den of robbers." (MATTHEW 21:13) Yet in other places, we see Jesus standing falsely accused, without speaking one word in His own defense. So what are we to learn from His communication patterns? He was a lion when He needed to be and yet always a lamb—He never sinned or failed to be excellent in speech. It's a challenge not to defend yourself when someone comes against you. It's difficult to ignore insults and shun retaliation. Isaiah 53:7 says of Jesus, "He was oppressed, [yet when] He was afflicted, He was submissive and He opened not His mouth; like a lamb that is led to the slaughter, and as a sheep before her shearers is dumb, so He opened not His mouth."

Sometimes I find that one of the hardest things God has asked us to do is to be Christlike in our communication with others. When somebody is rude and tells you off, mistreats or insults you, it is hard to just stand there and look at them with godly love and just wait on God. Thank God, He gives us the power to change and to become like Christ. I still feel the reaction of my old nature sometimes, but more and more I am learning self-control. The key to improvement is to learn to confront when God says to confront and to leave an issue alone when God says to leave it alone.

Pray for the Right Friends

Don't link up with those who will pollute you.

—2 CORINTHIANS 6:17 (THE MESSAGE)

True friends don't try to control you—they help you be what God wants you to be. Put your faith in God, and ask Him to give you friends who are truly right for you. Perhaps you never thought of using your faith for right friends, but God offers us a new way to live. He invites us to live by faith. There is no part of your life God is not concerned about, and He wants to be involved in everything you want, need, or do.

I cannot make myself acceptable to all people, and neither can you, but we can believe that God will give us favor with the people He wants us involved with. Sometimes we try to have relationships with people God does not even want us to be associated with. Some of the people I really worked hard to be friends with in the past, often compromising my own conscience in order to gain their acceptance, were the very ones who rejected me the first time I didn't do exactly as they wanted me to. I realize now I wanted their friendship for wrong reasons. I was insecure and wanted to be friends with the "popular" people, thinking my association with important people would make me important.

We should put our faith in the Lord to help us choose right friends, as well as everything else that concerns us.

A Merry Heart

A merry heart does good, like medicine, but a broken spirit dries the bones.

—PROVERBS 17:22 (NKJV)

I've found that listening to good, uplifting, godly music is an excellent way to keep a merry heart. When we listen to it, we tend to find ourselves humming or singing along, even when we are not aware of it. When we have a merry heart, we can have joy in our heart even while going about our work. We can also have more energy and vitality because the Bible tells us that the joy of the Lord is our strength. We have a choice. We can grumble our way through our troubles, or we can sing our way through our troubles. Either way, we have to go through troubles, so we may as well go through them happily.

Doubt Has to Go!

And Moses said to the Lord, O Lord, I am not eloquent or a man of words, neither before nor since You have spoken to Your servant; for I am slow of speech and have a heavy and awkward tongue.

—EXODUS 4:10

When God called Moses to be His spokesman to Pharaoh and the Israelites, Moses claimed that he wasn't eloquent enough to do what God wanted done because he had a "mouth problem." God's response was, "Who has made man's mouth? . . . Is it not I, the Lord?" (EXODUS 4:11). We think sometimes that God does not know about all of our weaknesses—but He does.

When I began to realize that God was calling me to minister His Word on a large scale, I reminded Him that I was a woman. I doubt that He had ever forgotten that fact. I did not have a problem with it myself, but I knew others who did, and it created a certain amount of doubt in me. That doubt had to go before I could go.

In verse 12 God told Moses, "Now therefore go, and I will be with your mouth and will teach you what you shall say." The next time God tells you to speak for Him and fear rises up within you, remember: if He has sent you, He will be with your mouth and will teach you what to say.

The Importance of Keeping Your Word

When you vow a vow or make a pledge to God, do not put off paying it; for God has no pleasure in fools (those who witlessly mock Him). Pay what you vow. It is better that you should not vow than that you should vow and not pay.

—ECCLESIASTES 5:4-5

I was recently involved in an event that required people to sign up ahead of time, indicating whether or not they would be attending. We had nine hundred people say they were coming, and only seven hundred showed up. Very few of them made any effort to cancel or even communicate that they were not coming. The problem was twofold: first, they did not keep their word, and second, we had purchased and cooked meat for nine hundred, and since seven hundred showed up, we obviously had lots of meat left over.

This is a widespread problem today in our society. Most people don't think anything at all about saying they will do a thing and then changing their minds without any good reason, except they did not feel like doing what they said they would do. Our words are a verbal contract.

Don't make commitments rashly without giving thought to whether or not you are prepared to follow through. I am sure that some of the two hundred people who failed to show up had good reasons for not doing so, but I am equally sure that most of them just plain didn't see the need to keep their word. When we keep our word, even if it is inconvenient for us to do so, it shows good character. We should be concerned about our example because the world is watching those of us who claim to be Christians. They want to see if we are all talk or if we are living what we are saying we believe.

One Step at a Time

I press on to lay hold of (grasp) and make my own, that for which Christ Jesus (the Messiah) has laid hold of me and made me His own.

—PHILIPPIANS 3:12

Following God is like climbing a mountain. If God showed us how high the mountain really is that He wants us to climb, we might be afraid to take the first step. We might argue that we're not ready, that we're not at all prepared to go all the way to the top. So He covers the top of the summit with a cloud, and all we can see is the step before us. That first step looks manageable, so we take it. And then we take another step, and another, and another, until one day we find ourselves at the top of the mountain without even realizing where we were headed when we began. Then we are very glad we took the journey.

I recall a woman who came to me complaining that she could not hear from God, that He was not speaking to her even though she was seeking Him about some things. Then the Lord told me that there was no point in speaking to her about doing something else until she had done the last thing He had told her, which she had not done yet.

In God's plan for us, we cannot skip steps that we don't like and move on to other ones. We cannot skip the hard steps or the ones that require sacrifice. I repeat: following God's plan for our lives requires investment. We must sacrifice *self-will* to have *God's will*. We must sacrifice *our way* to find *His way*. Don't be afraid of sacrifice—it eventually sets us free to be all we desire to be.

Looking Nice Is Not a Sin

Let not yours be the [merely] external adorning with [elaborate] interweaving and knotting of the hair, the wearing of jewelry, or changes of clothes; But let it be the inward adorning and beauty of the hidden person of the heart, with the incorruptible and unfading charm of a gentle and peaceful spirit, which [is not anxious or wrought up, but] is very precious in the sight of God.

—1 PETER 3:3-4

Does God really care what I look like? Do I have to be thin?" More than one person has asked themselves some variation of this question. The answer is that God doesn't judge us based on our looks. Thankfully, He sees our hearts. But He does want us to look the best we can for His glory and honor. We represent Him and should always live with excellence in every area. Excellence simply means to take what you have and do the most you can with it. God does care what you feel like inside, and, ultimately, looking your best is simply a reflection of a healthy, happy, spirited internal state. I'm not talking *Cosmopolitan* cover-model good looks; the layers of touch-ups and fakery on those covers would astonish you. I'm talking the kind of normal, healthy appearance that makes people respond positively to you and that helps you feel the best you can about yourself.

What Peter means is that you shouldn't confuse outer beauty for what is most important, which is a gentle and peaceful spirit.

God cares most that you go forth clothed in righteousness. But righteousness *plus* a nice outfit never hurt anyone. If people see that you respect yourself, they'll respect you too. Like everything else in life, it is a question of balance. Keep the big picture in mind. Ask yourself, "What is the work that God has put me on earth to do?" Then decide what amount of attention you should pay to how you look and feel to get the maximum energy, health, and charisma you need to do that work as successfully as possible.

Learn to Receive

*I will bless you [with abundant increase of favors] . . . and you
will be a blessing [dispensing good to others].*

—GENESIS 12:2

Nothing frustrates me more than people who don't know how to accept gifts. It's a joy to express my love or appreciation to someone by giving them a gift I know they'll like. But if the response is, "No, no, I can't accept that," or "Really, you shouldn't have," or "No, take it back," then that drains all the joy out of it. It becomes downright embarrassing if you have to force a gift on someone. You may even wonder if you should have offered the gift at all. Receiving a gift graciously stems from inner security. Those who are uncomfortable getting gifts usually have some deep-seated insecurity that prevents them from accepting others' kindness. They feel so low that they can't imagine they deserve anything. Or they worry that the gift burdens them with reciprocation. They would rather reject the gesture than have to engage in a relationship.

In my life and work I have opportunities to give many gifts, and I also get some. When I do, I genuinely appreciate it and tell people so. Be a giver and expect God to bless you through others. When they do, say thank you and graciously receive their offers. The greatest gift that can be given is offered to each of us every day, yet few of us have the faith and self-esteem to accept it. God offers us His love. All we have to do is open our hearts and make the decision to receive it. Then we in turn get to pass it on to others. Receiving God's love is an important step because we can't love others without it. We cannot give away what we do not have.

Overcome Evil with Good

Do not let yourself be overcome by evil, but overcome (master) evil with good.

—ROMANS 12:21

We overcome evil with good. I believe this truth is one of the most powerful weapons we possess, and the best-kept secret. God wants everyone to know it, but Satan keeps us so entrenched in our problems and personal pain that few of us ever understand the dynamics of it. We can get Satan back for the painful things he has brought into our lives by being good to others. We overcome him (evil) by being good to other people. Actually, it is God who overcomes Satan as we allow Him to work His good through us. Satan wants to use our pain to destroy us, but we destroy his plan by doing the opposite of what he expects.

Being good to someone else not only defeats Satan, it also releases joy in our own lives. Historically, people who have been hurt by someone frequently experience depression. I believe this is partially due to the fact that their attention is on their own pain instead of on what they can do to relieve someone else's pain. God has not called us to "in-reach"; He has called us to "out-reach." When we reach out to others, God reaches into our souls and heals us. He is the only One Who can heal the brokenhearted and make the wounded better than new.

The Camels Are Coming!

When they saw the star, they were thrilled with ecstatic joy. And on going into the house, they saw the Child with Mary His mother, and they fell down and worshiped Him. Then opening their treasure bags, they presented to Him gifts—gold and frankincense and myrrh.

—MATTHEW 2:10-11

We all remember the Christmas story: how Jesus was born of Mary in a stable and laid in a manger, how the Wise Men came from the east following a star that led them to the Holy Child, how they came in and worshiped Him, laying before Him precious gifts of gold, frankincense, and myrrh.

In this story we see that Mary and Joseph didn't go out seeking gifts. Although they were forced to spend the night in a cold, dark stable, they didn't send out messages asking for gifts. But because they were in the middle of God's will, He sent them Wise Men from the east mounted on camels loaded down with provisions.

I once heard a sermon preached on this subject in a church in Minnesota. It was titled, "The Camels Are Coming." The basic message was that if we are in the will of God, He will always bring our provision to us. We don't have to try to chase it down; it will seek us out. We don't have to try to make things happen; God will bring them to us.

I believe the camels will come for each of us if we will stay in the will of God. The only way we can expect this kind of provision is by being faithful to stay where God has placed us and do the work He has given us to do for His kingdom's sake. When we begin to believe this, we are free to cast our care upon Him. We don't have to stay up all night fretting and worrying, trying to figure out what to do to take care of ourselves. We can simply deposit ourselves with God.

I'm Okay and I'm on My Way

But the path of the [uncompromisingly] just and righteous is like the light of dawn, that shines more and more (brighter and clearer) until [it reaches its full strength and glory in] the perfect day [to be prepared].

—PROVERBS 4:18

I have not arrived, and neither has anyone else. We are all in the process of becoming. For much of my life I felt that I would never be okay until I arrived, but I have learned that is not the truth. My heart desires to be all God wants me to be, and I want to be like Jesus. My flesh does not always cooperate with me. In Romans 7, Paul says the good things he wants to do, he cannot do and the evil things he does not want to do, he always finds himself doing. He says he feels wretched. I can relate to that—how about you? In verse 24 he cries out, "Who will release and deliver me from [the shackles of] this body of death?" Then in the following verse, as if he had received an answer that was a revelation to him, he says, "O thank God! [He will!] through Jesus Christ (the Anointed One) our Lord!"

Yes, we all have a way to go. I was distraught about how far I had to go, and it seemed Satan reminded me of it daily, sometimes even hourly. I carried a constant sense of failure, a feeling that I just was not what I needed to be, that I was not doing good enough, that I should try harder—and yet when I did try harder, I only failed more. I have now adopted a new attitude: "I am not where I need to be, but thank God I am not where I used to be. I'm okay, and I'm on my way!"

I now know with all my heart that God is not angry with me because I have not arrived. He is pleased that I am pressing on, that I am staying on the path. If you and I will just "keep on keeping on," God will be pleased with our progress. Keep walking the walk. A walk is something taken one step at a time. This is an important thing to remember.

Powerful Prayer

The effective, fervent prayer of a righteous man avails much.

—JAMES 5:16 (NKJV)

The earnest (heartfelt, continued) prayer of a righteous man makes tremendous power available [dynamic in its working].

—JAMES 5:16

For prayer to be effective it must be fervent. However, if we misunderstand the word *fervent,* we may feel that we have to "work up" some strong emotion before we pray; otherwise, our prayers will not be effective. At times I experience a great deal of emotion while at prayer, sometimes I even cry. But there are plenty of times when I don't feel emotional and don't cry. I am sincere in my praying, but I don't *feel* anything out of the ordinary. We can't base the value of our prayers on feelings. I remember enjoying so much those prayer times when I could *feel* God's presence, and then wondering what was wrong during the times when I didn't *feel* anything. I learned after a while that faith is not based on *feelings* in the emotions, but on knowledge in the heart.

Also, James 5:16 states that the fervent prayer of a "righteous" man is powerful. This means a man who is not under condemnation—one who has confidence in God and in the power of prayer. It does not mean a man without any imperfection in his life.

The fact that James instructs us to pray powerful, effective prayers like the righteous men and women of God—and then gives a discourse on Elijah and how he was a human being just like us, and yet prayed powerful prayers—should give us enough "scriptural power" to defeat condemnation when it rises up to tell us we cannot pray powerfully because of our weaknesses and faults.

Be Yourself

Now you [collectively] are Christ's body and [individually] you are members of it, each part severally and distinct [each with his own place and function].

—1 CORINTHIANS 12:27

Being satisfied and happy with yourself is a very important key to enjoying your life. Because of my background, I had many weaknesses in the area of accepting myself and being me. I was always comparing myself with others, jealous of them and their possessions and abilities. I wasn't being myself; I was trying to keep up with everyone else.

I often felt pressured and frustrated because I was operating outside my gifts and calling. When I finally realized I could not do anything unless God had ordained it and anointed me to do it, I started relaxing and saying, "I am what I am. I cannot be anything unless God helps me. I am just going to concentrate on being the best me I can be."

God has made every one of us unique. He personally made you and gave you gifts, talents, and abilities. Just think about it: Nobody else in the world is exactly like you. That means what is best for someone else may not be best for you. So, when you are tempted to say to God, "I wish I looked like somebody else," or "I wish I could do this or that like them," don't say it. Be satisfied with whom God made you to be. Remember that He made you exactly the way He wants you to be. If you try to be like someone else, you will miss the beautiful life God has planned specially for you.

With God, Nothing Is Wasted

Gather up now the fragments (the broken pieces that are left over),
so that nothing may be lost and wasted.

—JOHN 6:12

No experience in your life is ever wasted or in vain if you give all your cares to the Lord. Even if your fragmented life looks like an abandoned battlefield, Jesus can reshape all the pieces of your past into something beautiful.

After Jesus had fed five thousand people with just a few loaves of bread and two small fish, He told His disciples, "Gather up now the fragments (the broken pieces that are left over), so that nothing may be lost and wasted." (JOHN 6:12) The disciples gathered up twelve baskets of food from the leftovers, still much more than the small offering of loaves and fishes that was made to Jesus in the first place.

God set me free from fear, insecurity, emotional addictions, and the bondage of a deep-rooted sense of rejection. Then He reshaped my fragmented life and gave me the glorious privilege of teaching His people how they can be whole; how they can have fruitful, happy lives and ministries; and how they can enjoy healthy, loving relationships.

We need inner strength to keep from being overwhelmed by outward circumstances. We must allow God to gather up our fragmented dreams and remold us into the image of Christ. To do that, He may have to crush the few pieces we have left into fine clay, water us with His Word, reshape our lumpy mass of leftovers, and put us back on His potter's wheel. But He is more than capable of designing something miraculous from whatever we have left to give Him.

Go to the Throne Before the Phone!

If you seek [Wisdom] as for silver and search for skillful and godly Wisdom as for hidden treasures, then you will understand the reverent and worshipful fear of the Lord and find the knowledge of [our omniscient] God. For the Lord gives skillful and godly Wisdom; from His mouth come knowledge and understanding.

—PROVERBS 2:4-6

Don't run around seeking counsel from just anyone. Pray first, asking the Lord whether it is His will that you go to another human being for counsel or whether He desires to counsel you Himself. In my own life I have had many, many problems, yet I never went to anyone else for counsel with the exception of one time. On this occasion I visited a lady in ministry who had been abused herself. I do not mean to discredit her, but she really was not able to help me. It was not her fault; she simply was not anointed by the Lord to do so.

God is not obligated to anoint what He does not initiate. So often people run to others without following the guidance and leadership of the Holy Spirit, and it never bears good, lasting fruit. *When you are in trouble, go to the throne before you go to the phone.* I do not mean to suggest that it is wrong to seek counsel. I am just suggesting that you pray and allow the Lord to lead and guide you through the Holy Spirit. Let Him choose the right counselor for you. Just because a person has been through what you are going through, or is a close personal friend, does not mean that individual is the right counselor for you. So I repeat, pray!

Peace to You

> *Peace I leave with you; My [own] peace I now give and bequeath to you.*
> *Not as the world gives do I give to you. Do not let your hearts be troubled,*
> *neither let them be afraid. [Stop allowing yourselves to be agitated and*
> *disturbed; and do not permit yourselves to be fearful and intimidated and*
> *cowardly and unsettled.]*
>
> —JOHN 14:27

Just before He was to go to the cross, Jesus told His disciples He was leaving them a gift—His peace. After His resurrection, He appeared to them again, and the first thing He said to them was, "Peace to you!" (JOHN 20:19). To prove to them who He was, He showed them His hands and His side and then said to them once more, "Peace to you!" (v. 21). Eight days later, He again appeared to them, and again His first words to them were, "Peace to you!" (v. 26).

Obviously Jesus intends for His followers to live in peace despite what may be going on around them at the time. What He was saying to His disciples—and to us—is simply, "Stop allowing yourselves to be anxious, worried, and upset."

In Psalm 42:5, the psalmist asks, "Why are you cast down, O my inner self? And why should you moan over me and be disquieted within me? Hope in God and wait expectantly for Him, for I shall yet praise Him, my help and my God."

When we begin to become worried, upset, cast down, or disquieted within, we need to hope in God and wait expectantly for Him, Who is our Help and our God.

List of Joyce Meyer Books
Used in *New Day, New You*

A Leader in the Making
Approval Addiction
Battlefield of the Mind
Be Anxious for Nothing
Beauty for Ashes
Do It Afraid
Enjoying Where You Are on the Way to Where You're Going
How to Hear from God
How to Succeed at Being Yourself
If Not for the Grace of God
In Pursuit of Peace
Look Great, Feel Great
Making Marriage Work
Managing Your Emotions
Me and My Big Mouth
Reduce Me to Love
Seven Things That Steal Your Joy
Straight Talk
The Battle Belongs to the Lord

About the Author

JOYCE MEYER is one of the world's leading practical Bible teachers. A #1 *New York Times* bestselling author, she has written more than eighty inspirational books, including *100 Ways to Simplify Your Life, Never Give Up!*, the entire Battlefield of the Mind family of books, and two novels, *The Penny* and *Any Minute*, as well as many others. She has also released thousands of audio teachings, as well as a complete video library. Joyce's *Enjoying Everyday Life*® radio and television programs are broadcast around the world, and she travels extensively conducting conferences. Joyce and her husband, Dave, are the parents of four grown children and make their home in St. Louis, Missouri.

TO CONTACT THE AUTHOR,
PLEASE WRITE:

Joyce Meyer Ministries
P.O. Box 655
Fenton, MO 63026
USA
(636) 349-0303
www.joycemeyer.org

Joyce Meyer Ministries—Canada
Lambeth Box 1300
London, ON N6P 1T5
Canada
1-800-727-9673

Joyce Meyer Ministries—Australia
Locked Bag 77
Mansfield Delivery Centre
Queensland 4122
Australia
(07) 3349 1200

Joyce Meyer Ministries—England
P.O. Box 1549
Windsor SL4 1GT
United Kingdom
01753 831102
Joyce Meyer Ministries—South Africa
P.O. Box 5
Cape Town 8000
South Africa
(27) 21-701-1056

OTHER BOOKS BY
JOYCE MEYER

New Day, New You Devotional

I Dare You

The Penny

The Power of Simple Prayer

The Everyday Life Bible

The Confident Woman

Look Great, Feel Great

Battlefield of the Mind*

Battlefield of the Mind Devotional

Battlefield of the Mind for Teens

Battlefield of the Mind for Kids

Approval Addiction

Ending Your Day Right

21 Ways to Finding Peace and Happiness

The Secret Power of Speaking God's Word

Seven Things That Steal Your Joy

Starting Your Day Right

Beauty for Ashes (revised edition)

*Study Guide available for this title.

The Value of Partnership

The partners of Joyce Meyer Ministries play an enormous part in reaching out in love to a hurting world. Because of the ongoing help of our partners, we are using TV, radio, the Internet, and the printed page to reach millions with the truth of God's Word. The support of our partners also allows us to reach out to the poor and hungry, prisoners and orphans, and thousands of others through our humanitarian efforts worldwide. Joyce Meyer Ministries desires to reach the world with the good news of the gospel and help as many people as we can, and our goal to help the hurting is increasingly being expressed through our many outreaches among the nations. In everything we do, it is the faithful support of our ministry partners that makes it possible.

If you are not a partner and are interested in becoming a monthly partner with Joyce Meyer Ministries, please call (636) 349-0303, or visit our website at www.joycemeyer.org.